The Globalisation of Mod

The Globalisation of Modern Architecture: The Impact of Politics, Economics and Social Change on Architecture and Urban Design since 1990

By

Robert Adam

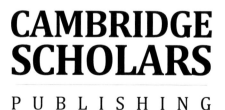

The Globalisation of Modern Architecture:
The Impact of Politics, Economics and Social Change on Architecture
and Urban Design since 1990,
by Robert Adam

This book first published 2012. The present binding first published 2013.

Cambridge Scholars Publishing

12 Back Chapman Street, Newcastle upon Tyne, NE6 2XX, UK

British Library Cataloguing in Publication Data
A catalogue record for this book is available from the British Library

ISBN (10): 1-4438-4824-7, ISBN (13): 978-1-4438-4824-4

Sarah

TABLE OF CONTENTS

Conclusion: The End of the Era, What Now?

LIST OF ILLUSTRATIONS

Colour Illustrations

Charts

PREFACE

This project began with the idea that any study of architecture and urban design today must begin with an understanding of how these activities sit in the modern world. This much is so obvious that it barely needs to be said. So, what is it that characterises the modern world? Today, most discussions of architecture in particular start with an arts-based, technological or philosophical view of the modern world. These are, of course, legitimate in their own terms but these things are not the way that most people conduct their lives in the modern world—the people who occupy the buildings, the people who commission the architects and urban designers, the people who see the buildings and occupy the new places. Beyond individual experience the modern world is primarily navigated through social interaction, the way society is ordered and the struggle of everyday life—the social, political and economic structure of society. In design terms, this is what society demands of buildings and places, how society demands it and how society provides the resources to make it. These things lie at the core of all activity in the built environment. And yet, very little contemporary architectural description and theory is presented in these terms at any level of detail. I decided that this would be a legitimate framework for a description of recent architecture, at least as relevant as a description of architecture and urban design as an artistic, technological or philosophical pursuit, if not so intellectually attractive.

Examining recent history, I had to ask what it was in the social, political and economic condition that was unique to modern life—"modern" meaning the last few decades. The fashionable word "globalisation" kept emerging in descriptions of the late twentieth century and, indeed, it became clear that there was something about the way the world had become more connected in this period that seemed to be particular. This led me to a study of some of the huge body of work on globalisation produced in recent decades. I came to see the current phase of globalisation as an aspect of the modern political and economic condition that had a clear beginning and, as my studies stretched to the end of the first decade of the twenty first century, seemed to develop some sort of end. Global interconnectedness was not all that was going on during this period but it was unusually significant. I have, therefore, used globalisation as a summary term and core concept for the recent modern condition.

Exploring sociology and economics in particular led me into both unfamiliar and familiar territory: unfamiliar as areas of academic study but familiar as the stuff of newspapers and current affairs. No field of interest seemed to be excluded and quite soon I came to see architecture and urban design in a different light. Stripped of the primacy they held when seen from the professional perspective, architecture and urban design took their proper place as secondary or more probably tertiary activities in the broader structure of society. This led to me see every design debate as a minor facet of larger forces and, if anything had any significance at all in architecture and urban design, it would have its place in the wider picture. If this was the case, as surely it must be, change in society would be reflected by change in architecture and vice versa. Everything that was happening was therefore in some way relevant and, although I may have disapproved of something that was happening in my own professional field, my approval or disapproval was much less important than the fact that it pointed to the social, political and economic forces that lay behind it. This illuminated architecture and urban design in often surprising ways.

This seemed to me to be a fruitful area for study but dauntingly wide. Everything I have written here is just a point in my studies when I felt I had to put it down in some coherent form. There is always another book to be read, another fact to be discovered and another area to be explored—as so many of my friends and colleagues tell me all the time.

The width of the subject is such that I have so many people to thank for all manner of information and advice that I am almost bound to miss some of them. I can start at the beginning with my father, once a general practitioner, who stimulated in me a restless curiosity, an interest in the role of current affairs in all aspects of life and a reluctance to take anything at face value. I have the privilege of continuing these discussions with my father in his mid-nineties and he was able to correct some of my twentieth century history. Remaining at a general level, throughout my research and while writing this book I have been running a large architectural and urban design practice. My fellow directors have given me passive support and many of my staff have taken an interest and given me active encouragement. Staff in the urban design course at the University of Strathclyde, where I have a visiting professorship, have been an invaluable source of information, debate and encouragement in what has been an otherwise academically lonely pursuit. Fellow members of the international charity, INTBAU, that I helped to set up, have been both friends and valuable informants on events and attitudes around the world. Through them and associated organisations I have been able to travel to Brazil, Russia, India, China, the USA (where I have many friends), Iran, Libya, Israel and most of the European countries. My work and academic activities have also taken me to Canada, Qatar, Dubai and Japan.

Many others have helped me in one aspect or another of a very broad subject area. Tony Chapman of the Royal Institute of British Architects organised a RIBA conference in Barcelona based, or so he told me, on my suggested subject of identity. Paul Finch, an old friend and sometime ideological sparring partner, gave me great encouragement by publishing my first paper on globalisation in the Architectural Review and then asked me to speak on the subject at the World Architecture Conference, also in Barcelona. My attendance at these events and the talks given by major global architectural figures gave me invaluable first-hand information on attitudes in the architectural profession. Individuals have helped me in a number of certain subject areas. Ben Bolgar identified useful sources on urbanism and Hank Ditmar used his personal experience to check the history of New Urbanism. My colleague Mark Hoare checked my account of the sustainability movement. My nephew Jasper Chalcraft and his partner Monica Sassatelli, both sociologists, have guided me on source material from time to time. Calder Loth, formerly the Senior Architectural Historian of the Commonwealth of Virginia, helped me with the history of the conservation movement in the USA. Peter Oborn of Aedas gave me his valuable time to discuss global architectural practice. John Hare, Professor Paul Richens of Bath University and Robin Partington gave me a great deal of information on the development of digital drafting.

The right photographs were important to illustrate the text and provide a parallel narrative. They come from mixed sources— private, professional and archive. Many friends and colleagues took or provided me with photographs of buildings and places around the world. Many architectural practices were generous in their donation of illustrations. I am very grateful but I will not list them here individually as they are credited in the List of Illustrations.

As with any book drawing on a very wide range of sources, I have relied on many authors, papers, articles, events, broadcasts, observations and conversations. The book is synthesis of these sources structured to tell a particular story. I hope that all those whom I quote are content with the context of their material and that readers will refer to the footnotes to identify the many authorities who have unknowingly assisted me.

Robert Adam, March 2012

WHERE WE ARE TODAY

Architecture, Urban Design, Politics and Economics

As I look at the world at the moment of writing, momentous events are unfolding around us. The greatest economic recession since the Great Depression has not yet run its course, the fragility of the European Union has been exposed, and the underpinning of the North Atlantic economies has been shaken to the core, their economic and political systems all undergoing radical reform as they attempt to extricate themselves from a legacy of crippling debt. In the east, the two great emerging economies have grown stronger. India, its growth largely self-generated, has been virtually untouched by the economic crisis. China, which had funded much of the borrowing frenzy that brought down the United States and Europe, experienced a decline in exports but its economy has continued to grow steadily and it has emerged as the world's second-largest economy. At the same time, the USA, from the confidence of its position as the only world superpower after the collapse of the Soviet Union, is seeing its global influence decline as it tries to extricate itself from decline and two inconclusive foreign wars. Meanwhile, the largely Muslim south Mediterranean states are at various stages in a revolution that has swept across the region, toppling dictators and creating the uncertainties of democracy in nations with no democratic history. At such times, we know from experience that cultural and artistic change will follow these major economic and political changes, locked together as they are in an inescapable embrace.

Architects and urban designers are commissioned by commercial and political clients who have no choice but to respond to these economic and social conditions. Although they are significant participants in cultural and artistic developments, architects and urban designers are first and foremost service industries and minor players in the broad sweep of social and political developments. No major social changes can be traced back to architecture. Even though urban design can change lives it, too, follows political and economic directions. It must be clear that any assessment of architecture and urban design would be inadequate without a full account of how wider changes in society have driven them.

****

However, when I look at *my* world of architecture and urban design, I see no seismic change to equal the momentous political and economic shifts that the press reveals daily. High Modernism still dominates architectural practice; globally famous architects are still the heroes of the profession and in demand by status-seeking cities; glass tower blocks are still under construction; and great networks of boulevards are planned around iconic buildings and mega-blocks in new developments around the world.

Looking back at other major political and economic revolutions, we can see the direct effect on architectural and urban theory and practice. The end of the Second World War sealed the victory of Modernism; the breakdown of the post-war consensus in the late 1960s and the oil crisis of the 1970s opened the way for the simultaneous—and apparently contradictory—rise of the baroque Modernism of high-tech and the ironic historicism of Postmodernism; and the recession of the early 1990s led to the collapse of Postmodernism and the resurgence of Modernism. This is, of course, hindsight. On the ground, the picture is always more complex. In the 1950s and early 60s much post-war reconstruction was carried out by followers of the classical tradition, while old-school modernists were still practicing in the 1980s and 90s (Oscar Niemeyer is still designing at the time of writing aged 103), and Postmodernism has survived well into the new century.

It is a common observation that the broad patterns of historic change are only clearly observed by looking back. The effects and outcome of even the most dramatic historic events often do not manifest themselves for some time. Our perception of current change is hampered by the fact that, while all aspects of society are linked, all historical events and ideological shifts do not occur in an identical time frame: in particular the inertia of social and cultural change is not matched by the drama of catastrophe, revolution and invention. This has been explained by the concept of "cultural lag," a term coined by the sociologist William Ogburn in 1922.[1] He identified a time lag between changes in what he called material invention and non-material culture. While Ogburn limited the concept to rapid advances in technology, technology cannot be isolated from fast-moving events in politics and economics. Ogburn's concept can be expanded with reference to the idea of multi-speed history put forward by the French historian Fernand Braudel, leader of the *Annales* school of historiography.[2] Braudel believed that "past and present mingle inextricably together,"[3] but divided the movement of historical time into three broad categories: *longue durée* [long duration], *moyenne durée* [medium duration] and *evénéments* [events]. While events came and went and soon became, according to Braudel, "dust," they were played out against a slower moving and often cyclical history, which in turn occurred within a framework of gradual and geographic change (in which he included culture). This provides a useful framework for understanding how slow-moving cultural change can coexist quite naturally with more rapidly moving events.

But even without reference to the slow movement of cultural change, there are good reasons why changes in architecture and urban design move relatively slowly. At the most elementary level, the real product takes a long time to come to fruition. A major building, from the time of conception to occupation, will rarely take less than five years, and commonly ten. Urban design is even more slow-moving. A major urban design project may take twenty years or more to complete and, indeed, it is highly likely that the original design will have been overtaken by changing circumstances well before its completion. The complexities, high capital costs and commercial risks in architectural and urban design practice have established the need for a long, informal, post-qualification apprenticeship in the construction-industry design professions. Architects and urban designers rarely reach any position of influence before the age of forty and, indeed, the professional rule-of-thumb definition of a "young architect" is someone below forty years of age. Most designs will, therefore, be under the control of (if not actually designed by) men or women who ended their formal education at least twenty years previously. Add to this the project lead time (noted above) and most practitioners may be well into their fifties before they have a substantial body of work behind them, and major international architects are often beyond formal retirement age.

It has been empirically observed that artists and scientists form their critical creative outlook in their twenties, and recent research by Timothy Salthouse places the peak of cognitive ability at about twenty-seven.[4] This refines the pioneering work undertaken by Harvey C. Lehman in 1953, who charted the creative peak across different sciences and arts between twenty-six and forty, the maximum "age of achievement" being at around forty.[5] This seems to indicate that architects and urban designers, whose full-time education is unusually long, will have established their creative outlook at about the time they complete their formal education and will have reached the peak of their ability before most have established their reputations.

Architects pay lip service to the creativity of youth but, for practical reasons, achievement in the profession is largely for the middle-aged and beyond. Major architects are likely to be acting out creative ideas formed some thirty years previously. This is bound to have a restraining influence on progress and change in architecture and urban design.

The slow pace of architectural and urban design culture makes it hard to detect the influence of major political and economic events on these disciplines. This creates a complex picture where an ideological position that has arisen in response to long-past circumstances is confronted by new conditions as they arise. We also know that social, economic and political developments will affect design, and we know from past observation that, when the appropriate historical distance allows us to see through the confusion, architecture and urban design will change to reflect the new realities on the ground.

****

Many of the social, political and economic events that affect our way of life at present can be traced back to the Black Monday financial crash of 1987 and the recession of the early 1990s. Until 2008, the period from about 1992 to 2008 had been one of unusual stability in the North Atlantic economies and was named by economists the "Great Moderation." This was also the period when China, India, the countries of the former Soviet Union, and many other nations, entered into the free-market system which the North Atlantic countries had established after the Second World War. The Great Moderation in the North Atlantic countries was, consequently, part of a more widespread global political and economic condition usually called "globalisation." Although the world economy had been interdependent for decades, if not centuries, increased communication and political conditions at the end of the twentieth century were quite different from previous periods of partial or total global interaction. The 1992 to 2008 period can therefore be distinguished from these previous versions of globalisation and termed the "New Global Era."

While the dramatic events following 2008—still playing out at the time of writing—will have a profound effect on our future way of life, our response to these events will be seen in the context of the New Global Era for some time. Some of the ideals of architecture and urban design may well pre-date the New Global Era, but the last two decades will have had a significant impact. To understand what is happening now in society and in architecture and urban design, we must examine the New Global Era in detail and try to understand how the disciplines of architecture and urban design have responded, and how this will influence their future response.

References

1. William F. Ogburn. *Social Change with Respect to Culture and Original Nature*. New York: B.W. Huebsch, 1922.
2. Fernand Braudel. *La Méditerranée et Le Monde Méditerranéen à l'Epoque de Philippe II*. Paris: A. Colin, 1949.
3. Fernand Braudel. "Personal Testimony." *Journal of Modern History* 44 (4) (1972): 467.
4. Timothy Salthouse. "When Does Age-Related Cognitive Decline Begin?" *Neurobiology of Aging* 30 (4) (2009): 507–14.
5 Harvey C. Lehman. *Age and Achievement*. Princeton: Princeton University Press, 1953.

PART I:

SETTING THE SCENE

A: A Short History of Globalisation and Architecture from 500 BCE to 1939 CE

The New Global Era is only the latest manifestation of a process of global interconnection that has been developing since the dawn of mankind. As with every period of global interaction, there is something very particular about this last stage of globalisation, but some of the underlying forces behind it have their origins in the eighteenth and nineteenth centuries. To understand the present condition, and to see how it differs from previous periods, we must take a brief overview of the history of globalisation.

Empires and Birth of Faith-Based Styles

The process of connecting different parts of the world to one another began 70,000 years ago when *Homo sapiens*, gifted with an intellect that allowed for adaptation to an alien environment, walked out of Africa. The process of connecting the disparate communities created by this first human migration would have to wait more than 60,000 years, until the Neolithic revolution established levels of organisation and a concentration of power that facilitated the creation of empires.

Figure 1. (left) Roman Doric Column, York, Northern England
Figure 2. (right) Roman Doric Column, Leptis Magna, Libya

Ancient empires standardised architecture across continents.

The ancient empires were never global in the strict sense of the word but, between the fifth century BCE and the fifth century CE, the Persian, Roman and Han empires created connections of power and culture over great distances. The Greek historian Polybius, writing in the second century BCE, understood the significance of the emerging Roman Empire: "Formerly the things which happened in the world had no connection among themselves … But since then all events are united in a common bundle."[1] By the second century CE, the Greek philosopher Diogenes of Oenoanda could propose the concept of a global humanity: "In relation to each segment of the earth, different people have different native lands. But in relation to the whole circuit of this world, the entire earth is a single native land for everyone, and the world a single home."[2]

While empires were based on conquest and power, trading routes created cultural connections over thousands of miles: Indian sculptures were imported to ancient Rome; from the Han Empire onwards, the Silk Road traded luxury goods over 6,500 kilometres; and in the fifth century BCE, Aramaic was being spoken along the Middle-Eastern trading routes from the Nile to the Indus.

The ancient world saw the establishment of two major globalising forces that are active to this day: the great monotheistic religions of Christianity and Islam. In the first century CE, Saul of Tarsus opened up a Middle-Eastern tribal sect to a universal membership that eventually led to its adoption as the official religion of the Roman Empire around three centuries later. In the seventh century CE a merchant from Mecca, Abu al-Qasim Muhammad, following a mountain-top revelation, transcribed the Quran as the word of God and proclaimed that there was no god but Allah for all mankind.[3] As the Prophet Muhammad, he and his followers set in motion a wave of conquest and conversion that, a century after his death, spanned from Spain to India.

With power and religion came culture. One expression of that culture was architecture. The Roman Empire spread classical architecture and the temple form from North Africa to England. Christianity spread the use of the Roman hall or basilica for religious assembly, and reproduced more or less literal copies of major centres of worship throughout Europe in the succeeding centuries. Muslim Mughal rulers introduced a Persian architectural style throughout the Indian subcontinent in the sixteenth century CE. The architectural styles of the two monotheistic religions are derived from the types already prevalent at the time and place of their first wave of expansion. The symbolic association of religion with its architecture has spread geographically specific styles around the globe as Christianity and Islam, to this day, continue their expansion.

European Discovery and the Enlightenment

It was the European voyages of discovery from the fifteenth to the seventeenth centuries that finally connected all human settlements across the world, creating a condition that can properly be called "global." The discovery of the Americas and Australia by Europeans from 1492 to 1606 created for the first time a condition whereby all humans on earth could, in principle at least, know of one another.

As European exploration, occupation and trade expanded, the two major powers in the East, China and Japan, were entering long periods of self-imposed trading isolation. The Japanese policy of isolation, or *kaikin*, was unbroken from 1641 to 1853. The Chinese policy of *hai jin*, or "sea ban," was first instituted by the Ming dynasty, and trading restrictions continued intermittently during the Qing dynasty from the seventeenth century onwards. In 1793 the Emperor Qianlong rebuffed a British trading overture by King George III, pointing out that "we possess all things. I set no value on objects strange or ingenious, and have no use for your country's manufactures."[4] The advanced civilisations of the Indian subcontinent had never constituted a nation, and their continuous power struggles left them open to organised and competing European campaigns for trading dominance backed by force. The newly discovered continents of America and Australia, on the other hand, were at a significantly lower level of material development and their populations quickly succumbed to European diseases, conquest and colonisation.

These conditions favoured European domination of world trade and, by the end of the eighteenth century, as Immanuel Wallerstein pointed out, "successive expansions have transformed the capitalist world-economy from a system located primarily in Europe to one that covers the entire globe."[5] By this time, European knowledge of the geography and varied peoples of the world had a profound influence on the predominantly science-based and rationalist philosophical movement, the Enlightenment. From the Enlightenment arose principles that have echoed down the following centuries to the present, and lie at the foundation of current globalising institutions and ideals.

****

The seventeenth century European Wars of Religion and the English republican revolution, or Civil War, initiated a radical reconsideration of the concept of government.

The rights of groups or individuals to religious and personal freedom in the face of long-accepted autocratic monarchies or states were examined in England, most notably by the English philosopher John Locke. Locke wrote in 1689, in the *Second Treatise on Civil Government,* that "every man has a property in his own person: this no-body has any right but to himself."[6] The search for religious freedom initiated the increased colonisation of North America, where Locke had a part in the drafting of the Fundamental Constitutions of Carolina, which declared that "civil peace may be maintained amidst diversity of opinions, and our agreement and compact with all men may be duly and faithfully observed." These ideas found their way into the American Declaration of Independence in 1776 as "unalienable rights" of the individual to "life, liberty and the pursuit of happiness."

In practice, the relationship of these rights to those of the state was independently defined in 1648 by the Treaties of Westphalia, which ended thirty years of European religious wars. This gave religious groups some rights of worship, but otherwise gave states absolute rights over their citizens. Although European dominance in the succeeding centuries exported the Westphalian concept of the autonomous nation state to the rest of the world, the dilemma of how to reconcile unalienable and universal rights of the individual with the rights of the state over the lives of its citizens was not resolved until the twentieth century.

In his Carolina Constitution, Locke specifically recognised the rights of "natives of that place" and Enlightenment philosophers could, as Christopher Martin Wieland wrote in 1788, "regard all the peoples of the earth as so many branches of a single family, and the universe as a state, of which they, with innumerable other rational beings, are citizens, promoting together under the general laws of nature the perfection of the whole." [7] This view of mankind was not based on any kind of global equality but a belief, expressed by Immanuel Kant towards the end of the eighteenth century, that "the history of mankind viewed as a whole, can be regarded as the realisation of a hidden plan of nature," so that "all the capacities implanted by her [nature] in mankind can be fully developed." [8] This plan was to be led by Europeans. In 1800, Johann Gottlieb Fichte pointed out that "the most civilized nations of modern times are the descendants of savages," and so present-day primitive peoples will in future become civilised in turn: "It is the vocation of our race to unite itself into one single body, all possessed of a similar culture." [9] A. R. J. Turgot had already explained in the mid-eighteenth century that this would lead to state where "the human mind [is] enlightened ... and isolated nations are brought closer to one together. Finally commercial and political ties unite all parts of the globe; and the whole human race ... advances, ever slowly, towards greater perfection ... What perfection of human reason!" [10] Distinct traces of these ideas can be found today in American foreign policy [11] and the founding principles of the United Nations.

In the Enlightenment, the idea emerged for the first time that, as Fontenelle put it in 1688, "unreasonable admiration for the ancients is one of the chief obstacles to progress." [12] In 1796 Nicolas de Condorcet predicted that after "successive changes in human society," the sun will shine "on an earth of none but free men, with no master save reason; for tyrants and slaves, priests and their stupid or hypocritical tools, will have disappeared."[13] By 1814, the Comte de Saint-Simon could, with confidence, reverse the long-standing idea that antiquity represented an ideal for the modern world, declaring that "the golden age is not behind us, but in front of us."[14] In the eighteenth century, rapid industrial change, republican revolution and a greater awareness of the peoples around the world who did not share these "advances" led to a widespread belief in "the total mass of the human race moving slowly forward." [15] The state of affairs that pointed most directly to this future state of grace was modernity. This progress would, apparently inevitably, be driven by the European (and now North American) societies that had pioneered this industrial and social change. The idea of a moral duty of enlightened Europeans and North Americans to deliver their version of progress and modernity to other nations around the globe has survived into twentieth and twenty-first century political thought in the North Atlantic countries. As John Gray tells us: "We live today amid the dim ruins of the Enlightenment project, which was the ruling project of the modern period."[16]

Colonisation and the Spread of European Culture

Armed with advanced technology and industrial power combined with a belief in superiority in progress, modernity and religion, the European states traded, conquered and colonised their way around the world in the nineteenth century. In 1854, the English Cardinal Newman expressed a view common among his contemporaries, that European civilisation was "so distinctive and luminous in its character, so imperial in its extent, so imposing in its duration, and so utterly without rival upon the face of the earth" that it could justifiably "assume to itself the title of 'human society,' and its civilization the abstract term 'civilization'."[17] Global culture therefore became European.

Figure 3. (left) Convento de S Francisco, Olinda, Brazil, 1585.
Figure 4. (right) Drayton Hall, South Carolina, 1742.

When colonisers destroyed native culture, the home architecture
of the colonists became the architecture of the colony.

The Americas had already become the cultural outposts of
Spain, Portugal, France and Britain, their indigenous populations
decimated by disease and genocide or banished to the margins. In
the nineteenth century, Australia and New Zealand followed the
same pattern under British colonisation. Language, government,
urban design and architecture were direct models or developments
of their European originals. By this time, European Russia had
already taken over vast and sparsely populated areas to the north and
east, and moved south into the small, mineral-rich Transcaucasian
countries, and east to the islands bordering Japan. This created a
huge uniform European administrative, urbanised and linguistic zone
stretching from the Baltic to the Pacific under Russian control.

The Indian subcontinent and much of the Asian Pacific rim were
colonised by Britain, France and Holland, but here, as with the
predominantly French colonisation of the African southern
Mediterranean nations, well-established and ancient cultures vied
with European cultural imports. Directly imported classicism and
gothic revival competed with established architecture, not only

between native and colonial architects but also among the colonial architects themselves, some of who became enthusiastic orientalists, moving from half-understood hybrids to full-blown local styles.

Sub-Saharan Africa became the victim of a frantic European land-grab right through to the mid-twentieth century as latecomers to European nationhood sought status with the few remaining colonial opportunities. As tribal boundaries and cultures were subsumed by arbitrary borders, colonial languages were imposed, complete European administrative systems introduced and, without traditions of monumental architecture, colonial styles established.

Figure 5. Gateway of India, Mumbai; George Wittet; 1924. Indo-Saracenic architecture by a British Architect.

When colonisers encountered societies with a developed tradition of monumental architecture, on occasion hybrid styles emerged.

Not even the isolated Asian states were immune. The American navy forced Japan to open its markets to international trade in 1858. In the Opium Wars from 1839 to 1860, Britain forced the Chinese Qing dynasty to lift trade and tariff limitations and, with other European powers, took trading outposts under colonial control.

Although these important ancient cultures retained their political systems and national identity, Japan in particular enthusiastically adopted European institutional structures, uniforms, male dress and, in major cities and trading areas in China and Japan, buildings appeared in European styles.

The First Great Globalisation

By the final decades of the nineteenth century, under the stabilising influence of the *Pax Britannica*, the world entered its first modern global era. In 1848 Karl Marx observed that "in place of the old local and national seclusion and self-sufficiency, we have intercourse in every direction, universal interdependence of nations."[18]

Facilitated by the development of ocean-going steamships and few restrictions on travel, the largest movement of peoples the world had ever seen took place. Without accounting for internal migration within the great nation states and the travels of colonisers and traders, by the end of the nineteenth century three million people were migrating each year: some twenty million Europeans migrated to the United States; it has been estimated that more than twenty million Chinese emigrated to the Americas and Southeast Asia; the British Empire enabled and encouraged the emigration of Indians to Africa and the West Indies; convict transportation declined and the British government provided financial incentives to Australian immigrants from the 1840s, much assisted by the 1851 gold rush.

International capital could move freely around the world. The first trans-Atlantic telegraph was laid in 1861. 1840 saw the creation of the first human rights organisation with a global agenda: the British and Foreign Anti-Slavery Society. A number of global agreements, such as the Paris Convention for the Protection of Industrial Property in 1883 and the Berne Convention for the Protection of Literary and Artistic Works in 1886, regulated trade between nations. Between 1873 and 1912 the major Eastern powers adopted the Gregorian calendar, and in 1884 the meridian was almost universally agreed to

be in Greenwich, England (France held out for a Paris meridian for
another twenty years).

In 1919, John Maynard Keynes described the peak of this first
modern global era with a caricature of a London capitalist in 1914:

> The inhabitant of London could order by telephone, sipping his
> morning tea in bed, the various products of the whole earth, in such
> quantity as he might see fit, and reasonably expect their early
> delivery upon his doorstep; he could at the same moment and by
> the same means adventure his wealth in the natural resources and
> new enterprises of any quarter of the world, and share, without
> exertion or even trouble, in their prospective fruits and advantages.
> ... The projects and politics of militarism and imperialism, of racial
> and cultural rivalries, of monopolies, restrictions, and exclusion ...
> were little more than the amusements of his daily newspaper, and
> appeared to exercise almost no influence at all on the ordinary
> course of social and economic life, the internationalisation of which
> was nearly complete in practice.[19]

As industrialisation became more widespread in the later nineteenth
century, it became clear that the key to success in the international
arena was the garnering of capital, the advancement of heavy
industry, and the creation of well-equipped, substantial and loyal
armed forces. All this required size and political and economic
control, as well as a clearly defined nation with a large and patriotic
population. Existing nations developed national myths to galvanise
their citizens, and new nations such as Germany, Italy and Greece
were forged out of shared ethnic identities. National competition
started to limit the prevailing laissez-faire conditions: the movement
of people started to be controlled, nations and empires became
protected trading zones, and national unity created an identity (often
a fictionalised history) set in opposition to similarly devised identities
created by rival nations.

In architecture, nationalist sentiment found an outlet in various
manifestations of national romanticism. In Britain, the Arts and
Crafts movement, and later the baroque revival, set out to re-create

a national style first from the vernacular and then the English baroque. A newly unified Germany also adopted the baroque revival, looking to the great baroque and rococo architecture of early eighteenth century German ascendancy for inspiration. Italy, in turn, looked to its illustrious renaissance past to guide the architecture of urban expansion following unification. Greece turned to a Beaux Arts version of neo-classicism to tie the new state to its long-lost ancient civilisation. Russia revived its distinctive Russo-Byzantine style. In the United States, Frank Lloyd Wright developed the Prairie Style which, as the name suggests, was seen as a unique expression of American national character. The Shingle Style and Greene and Greene's American Arts and Crafts buildings also self-consciously created "a new and native architecture"[20] for the United States.

The rise of nationalism, as the nineteenth century turned into the twentieth, created a dangerous mixture of industrial power, jingoism, militarism and economic competition. The first modern global era was destroyed in an orgy of industrialised warfare with the start of the First World War in 1914, ending what was for many privileged Europeans a golden era.

Nationalism, Internationalism and the Birth of Modernism

From the start of the First World War in 1914 to the fall of the USSR in 1989 nationalism and internationalism were uneasy companions.

Dramatic and highly visible technological advances were linked to an optimistic idea of modernity that seemed to float free of old national boundaries. Henry Ford, possibly the most symbolically significant figure of the new industrial and consumer modernity, summed it up in 1929:

> Machinery is accomplishing in the world what man has failed to do by preaching, propaganda, or the written word. The aeroplane and wireless know no boundary. They pass over the dotted lines on the

map without heed or hindrance. They are binding the world together in a way no other system can. The motion picture with its universal language, the aeroplane with its speed, and the wireless with its coming international programme—these will soon bring the world to a complete understanding.[21]

At the other end of the spectrum, the German dictator Adolf Hitler, now the most potent symbol of the dangers of nationalism, said in his election campaign of 1932: "There's so much internationalism, so much world conscience, so many international contracts; there's the League of Nations, the Disarmament Conference, Moscow, the Second International, the Third International—and what did all that produce for Germany?"[22]

The tensions inherent in the combination of internationalism and nationalism can be seen in the attempts to create the first supranational political organisation. The devastation and the international impact of World War I inspired the thirty-one signatories of the Treaty of Versailles and thirteen others to sign the Covenant of the League of Nations in 1919, so creating the first permanent international security organization. The primary aim of the League of Nations was "to promote international co-operation and to achieve international peace and security."[23] However, as the Italian dictator Benito Mussolini memorably put it, "The League is very well when sparrows shout, but no good at all when eagles fall out,"[24] and it failed in its primary objective. Although the US President, Woodrow Wilson, was one of the principal exponents of the League of Nations, the US Senate blocked American membership. Signatories with extreme nationalist governments left one by one: Japan and Germany in 1933, Italy in 1937, Spain and Russia in 1939. The period between the two world wars were, in fact, marked by a series of nationalist conflicts that included the Greco-Turkish war, the Italian colonisation of Ethiopia, the Japanese invasion of Manchuria, and the Spanish Civil War. Although the League of Nations would not formally disband until 1946, to all intents and purposes it ceased to operate at the outbreak of the Second World War.

Internationalism and nationalism both found their own expression in contemporary art and architecture. Internationalism, combined with a belief in the revolutionary and transformative power of new technology, found expression though the various movements that came to be gathered under the title of "Modernism." In 1919, Erich Mendelsohn, lecturing at the Berlin *Arbeitsrat für Kunst*, or Art Soviet, said:

> What today is the vision and faith of a single individual, will one day become a law for all. Therefore all trends seem necessary to achieving the goal, and hence to solving the problem of a new architecture … just as every epoch that was decisive for the evolution of human history united the whole known globe under its spiritual will, so what we long for will have to bring happiness beyond our own country, beyond Europe, to all peoples.[25]

Much as the League of Nations was influenced by the Enlightenment ideals of a universal humanity—and in particular the philosophy of Immanuel Kant—Modernism was influenced by the Enlightenment idea of modernity and the inevitable and universal progress of mankind. This was coupled with the nineteenth-century romantic concept of the avant-garde, where "modernity is the transient, the fleeting, the contingent," and the artist must look "in the deep unknown to find the new."[26]

In the fast-moving world of painting and sculpture, Modernism in its various guises—such as Cubism, Expressionism, Fauvism and Vorticism—made a significant impact with sophisticated collectors. Its revolutionary ambitions did not, however, make it so attractive to the slower-moving world of architecture where work was largely commissioned by establishment organisations or wealthy individuals, and national identity was still a potent force. Early Soviet Russia, however, did at first find the radical philosophy and international ambitions of Modernism a perfect fit for its Marxist ideals of international revolution. There was a brief flowering of Modernist Constructivism until the USSR turned to Russian nationalism under the dictatorship of Joseph Stalin. In the unstable German Weimar

Republic the Bauhaus School was established in 1919, and taught a revolutionary design philosophy linked to socialist thinking and a commitment to the modernity of machine production. This was closed down when the National Socialists came to power. In other European countries Modernism was largely a minority choice for a few rich patrons with an interest in the arts, but by 1932 there was a sufficient body of work and unity of style for a highly influential exhibition of modernist architecture to be mounted at the Museum of Modern Art in New York and published as the "International Style."

The "International Style" title stuck for about thirty years until the style did, indeed, become international, although it was, in reality, a European or Western style. It was claimed that it was a "contemporary style, which exists throughout the world",[27] but for the American architect John Gaw Meem in 1934 it was clear that it "reflects contemporary Western civilisation, especially our devotion to the ideal of scientific truth."[28] As with the Enlightenment philosophers, early Modernism coupled Western culture with an evangelical superiority towards other cultures.

Also in accordance with Enlightenment thinking, Modernism was explicitly opposed to the continuation of tradition, including national traditions; as Kasimir Malevich said in 1924: "Life must be purified of the clutter of the past."[29] The ferociousness of modernist opposition to traditional architecture was however matched by the persistent predominance of the traditional.

Under National Socialism in Germany, the vernacular *Völkisch* Movement from the early twentieth century took on a new lease of life alongside a stripped classical style that expressed the imperial ambitions of the government. Although the Fascist state in Italy was not averse to the progressive symbolism of Modernism, its pretentions for the recreation of Imperial Rome were promoted with grandiose simplified classicism. In Russia, Stalin too favoured an elemental classicism, but with rich applied decoration, often with explicit Soviet symbolism, that gave it a distinctly Russian character.

Among the democratic countries, Britain transformed its Arts and Crafts architecture into a mock-Tudor nationalism that appealed to its burgeoning house-buying public. Alongside this, classicism was promoted both as a revival of the simple architecture of the early-nineteenth-century Regency as well as a more high-blown style appropriate for the world's largest Imperial power. In the United States, owing to the coincidence of independence with the high point of imported British classicism, the national style continued to be resolutely classical. This manifested itself either in the Colonial Revival or in a high-style Beaux Arts classicism (inherited from a French system of architectural education) that was applicable to neo-classical public monuments as well as the development of the great American invention, the skyscraper. American Beaux Arts teaching was exported to a newly republican China where it proved adaptable to the creation of a modern and monumental version of Chinese traditional architecture.

In spite of widely different political ideologies and nationalist sentiments, in inter-war Western architecture a stripped-down form of classicism was almost universal. Across the various architectural expressions of ethnic origins, national identity, empire, or the aspiration to empire lay powerful influence of an inventive and modern traditional architecture with origins in Sweden and France.

At the 1923 World Exhibition to celebrate the tercentenary of the southern Swedish port of Gothenburg, a new and imaginative classicism particular to Sweden and the other Scandinavian countries impressed international visitors. The new Swedish architecture, later called "Swedish Grace," combined a spare Nordic vernacular with a revival of early-nineteenth-century neo-classical Biedermeier. It was both simple and highly original, and part of a wider flourishing of the decorative and applied arts in Scandinavia. New Swedish design was widely admired and highly influential throughout Europe. Two years later, at the important Paris *Exposition Internationale des Arts Décoratifs et Industriels Modernes*, Swedish design took thirty-five Grands Prix and forty-six Gold Medals.

Although the new Swedish design was, for all its originality, clearly based on classical traditions, in the sentiment of the time it conformed to the rule of the 1925 Paris *Exposition*, in that it was only open to anyone "whose production presents ... clearly modern tendencies. That is to say, any copying or counterfeiting of ancient styles is strictly forbidden." Indeed, while the *Exposition* included a modernist *Pavillon de l'Esprit Nouveau* by Le Corbusier and a Constructivist pavilion for the USSR by Konstantin Melnikov, it was most notable for the introduction of the new *Style Moderne* (much later called "Art Deco" in abbreviation of the exhibition title). The *Style Moderne*, like new Swedish design, was a liberal interpretation of classical traditions, by turn stripped down, re-ordered and heavily decorated with novel patterns. The style was primarily decorative and could absorb Egyptian, Aztec, Cubist, Expressionist and other influences. Its freedom, modernity, *joie de vivre* and adaptability gave it widespread appeal, and *Style Moderne* buildings were designed throughout Europe, the Americas and Asia.

In spite of later art-historical attempts at categorisation, the boundaries between stripped-down nationalist classicism, designs influenced by the new Swedish Classicism, *Style Moderne*, and even the fringes of more doctrinaire Modernism were not at all clear cut. Some architects would remain dogmatically attached to the traditional or the modernist, whereas others would switch from one style to the other at will.[30] In spite of an undoubted atmosphere of aggressive or defensive nationalism where even resolutely internationalist Modernism could be attacked as a German import,[31] a predilection for formal simplicity (even if it sometimes had lavish surface decoration) was shared by most architectural styles and nations.

Figure 6 (top left). Technical College Building; Leningrad, Gegello and Krichevsky; 1932. Revolutionary Modernism, known as "Constructivism" in Russia.

Figure 7 (top right). Musee d'Art Moderne de la Ville de Paris; Dondel, Aubert, Viard and Dastugue; 1937. French Style Moderne.

Figure 8 (bottom).   Luftgaukommando, Dresden; Wilhelm Kreis; 1938. Fascist architecture.

Architecture in the 1920s and 30s took different directions expressing nationalism, internationalism and more, but the distinctions between styles were not always clear.

In the dark days of the Great Depression, in the years before the outbreak of the Second World War, Modernism had been outlawed in the totalitarian states and, although very few buildings were constructed, had become the radical choice for younger architects in the European democracies. Modernists, expelled by the Nazis from the influential Bauhaus School, left Germany and became established in Britain and the United States. Following the 1930 Stockholm Exhibition, Swedish architecture began a seamless shift towards Modernism. By the time the global social, political and economic order came to be re-written at the cessation of hostilities, these cultural shifts would transform the art and architecture of the post-war world.

References

1. Polybius, *Universal History*, mid-second century BCE.
2. Diogenes of Oenoanda, from an inscription on a portico wall in the ancient city of Oenoanda, Lycia (in modern Turkey) on the third and fourth century BCE Greek philosopher Epicurus, inscribed late second century CE.
3. Quran 7:158.
4. E. Backhouse and J. O. P. Bland. *Annals and Memoirs of the Court of Peking* Boston, Houghton Mifflin, 1914, 322–331.
5. Immanuel M. Wallerstein, *Geopolitics and Geoculture: Essays on the Changing World-System*. Cambridge: Cambridge University Press, 1991, 163.
6. John Locke, *Second Treatise on Civil Government*, 1689, Chapter 5, Section 27.
7. Kwame Anthony Appiah, *Cosmopolitanism: Ethics in a World of Strangers*. New York: Norton, 2007, xv.
8. Immanuel Kant. "Perpetual Peace." 1795, Eighth Thesis. From Ted Humphrey, trans., *Perpetual Peace and Other Essays on Politics, History, and Morals: A Philosophical Essay*. Hackett Publishing Co., 1983, 163.
9. Arthur Herman. *The Idea of Decline in Western History*. New York: The Free Press, 1997, 25.
10. Ibid., 26.

11. For example, from the Council on Foreign Relations, Washington D.C. September 8, 2010, "A Conversation with U.S. Secretary of State Hillary Rodham Clinton.": "the world is counting on us today, as it has in the past. When old adversaries need an honest broker or fundamental freedoms need a champion, people turn to us."

12. Bernard le Bovier de Fontenelle. *Le Progrès des Chose.* 1688

13. Nicolas de Condorcet. *10th Epoch: Future Progress of Man.* 1796

14. Comte de Saint-Simon. *Réorganisation de la Société Européenne.* 1814

15. Jaques Turgot. *Plan d'un Ouvrage sur la Géographie Politique.* 1751

16. John Gray. *Enlightenment's Wake: Politics and Culture at the Close of the Modern Age.* London: Routledge, 1995, 145.

17. John Henry Cardinal Newman. *The Idea of a University.* New York: Holt, Rinehart and Winston, 1960, 189.

18. Karl Marx and Friedrich Engels. *Manifesto of the Communist Party,* Chapter 1, 1848.

19. John Maynard Keynes. *The Economic Consequences of the Peace.* New York: Harcourt, Brace, and Howe, 1920, 8.

20. Special Citation by the American Institute of Architects, 1952.

21. Henry Ford. *My Philosophy of Industry.* London, Harrap, 1929, 11–12 .

22. Quoted by Nayan Chanda. *Bound Together: How Traders, Preachers, Adventurers, and Warriors Shaped Globalisation.* New Haven: Yale University Press, 2007, 279.

23. Covenant of the League of Nations, 1919.

24. Benito Mussolini's response to the League of Nations' condemnation of the conduct of Italy's war in Ethiopia in 1936.

25. Erich Medndelsohn. "The Problem of a New Architecture," lecture to members of Arbeitsrat für Kunst, 1919, quoted by Ulrich Conrads. *Programmes and Manifestos on 20th-century Architecture.* London: Lund Humphries, 1970, 55.

26. Charles Baudelaire. "The Painter of Modern Life," (1859). In *Selected Writings on Art and Artists,* edited by P.E. Charvet, 402. Cambridge: Cambridge University Press, 1981, 402.

27. Henry-Russell Hitchcock & Philip Johnson. *The International Style.* New York: Norton, 1995, 35.

28. John Gaw Meem. "Old Forms for New Buildings." *American Architect* 145 (1934): 10–20.

29. Kasimir Malevich. "Suprematist Manifesto Unovis," 1924, quoted by Ulrich Conrads in *Programmes and Manifestos on 20th-century Architecture*. London: Lund Humphries, 1970, 87.
30. For example, the British Architect Oliver Hill. His work included the modernist Midland Hotel in Morecombe, England, the Arts and Crafts Court House in Argyll and Sutherland, Scotland, and the Queen Anne style Long Newnton Priory, Tetbury, England.
31. In particular, the publication by the leading British architect Sir Reginald Blomfield, in which he asks: "Are we to accept this Modernism as a step forward, or are we to regard it as a step downhill which, if unchecked, will end in the bankruptcy of Literature and the Arts?" Sir Reginald Blomfield. *Modernismus: A Study*. London: MacMillan and Co., 1934, v.

PART I:

SETTING THE SCENE

B: The New World Order 1945–1992: Global Commerce, Politics and the Triumph of Modernism

Establishing Global Institutions

The world order re-formed after the Second World War to a framework of power, economics and culture that would last for more than half a century. The United States took up its position as a major international power and came out of the political and economic isolation of the preceding inter-war period.

In 1904, the Harvard-based German psychologist, Hugo Munsterberg, drily proclaimed, "the duty of America is to extend its political system to every quarter of the globe: other nations will thus be rated according to their ripeness for this system, and the history of the world appear one long and happy education of the human race up to the plane of American conception."[1] When Congress rejected United States membership of the League of Nations, however, it reflected a contradictory, inward-looking national mentality borne of a legacy of refugee immigration, continental proportions and two benign land borders. This same isolationism lay behind the Smoot–Hawley Tariff Act of 1930, which sought to protect United States farming and industry from foreign competition after the Wall Street Crash of the previous year. International retaliation deepened the crisis and prolonged the Great Depression such that it was only lifted by industrial mobilisation on the United States' entry to the Second World War.

Not only did the war draw the United States, somewhat reluctantly, into the international arena, it heightened its long-established sense of moral ascendancy and provided popular recognition of the political power of its huge economy. Alongside a new international role came an understanding that earlier isolation had exposed rather than protected the United States from conflict and the risks of global trade. Even before the attack on Pearl Harbour forced the United States into the war (economic and moral support for Britain had been in place for some time), the first moves were made to define the post-war world.

In August 1941, Britain and the United States issued a joint statement, later called "The Atlantic Charter," which defined Allied objectives in the Second World War. This included a popular right to self-determination, the lowering of trade barriers, global economic cooperation and advancement of social welfare. By September, the ten governments at war with the Axis powers agreed to the principles of the Charter. At the end of the year, when the United States became one of the Allied combatants, President Roosevelt devised the name "United Nations" for the Allies. In 1942, the United States, the USSR, Great Britain, the Republic of China and forty-five other nations signed the *United Nations Declaration*, based on the Atlantic Charter, in which the signatories, in a clear reference to the United States Declaration of Independence, agreed to "defend life, liberty, independence and religious freedom, and to preserve human rights and justice." At the end of the war, after a United Nations Conference on International Organization in San Francisco, the "Charter of the United Nations" was drawn up, founded on, but greatly expanding, the "United Nations Declaration." This had to be legitimised, first by the agreement of the four signatories of the "United Nations Declaration," plus France, and then by the majority of the other participants. In October 1945, the United Nations was created to "maintain international peace and security" and harmonise "the actions of nations." A new supra-national political order was thus created to replace the discredited League of Nations, with the United States as a major sponsor, and according to a charter based on the political ideals of the North Atlantic liberal democracies.

During the war, the framework was also established for international monetary control. In 1944, a conference of the forty-four Allied powers at Bretton Woods in New Hampshire, USA, agreed that in a post-war world there would be global open markets and the free movement of capital. The Bretton Woods Conference established a system for regulating exchange rates based on the US dollar and set up the International Monetary Fund (IMF) and the World Bank. Although, the system could not come into full force until 1959 (when all European currencies became convertible) and collapsed in 1971 (see below), economic internationalism, the principles of global free trade and the core international economic institutions are still effective today.

In the final stages of the Second World War the full horror of Nazi atrocities became apparent, and the Human Rights Commission of the United Nations, chaired by Eleanor Roosevelt (wife of the recently deceased President), felt that the "Charter of the United Nations" did not provide sufficient protection of the individual against oppressive states. In 1948, the "Universal Declaration of Human Rights" was adopted by the United Nations. This gave the individual rights over and above his or her state. These rights included those of property ownership, religious freedom, participation in government and even paid holidays. They also included entitlement "to a social and international order" (Article 28) and the provision that no "State, group or person" could do anything to destroy these rights (Article 30). Today we see the Declaration as something close to a universal truth, but at the time it was unprecedented, and its adoption was not universally supported. It is not surprising that in 1948 the Soviet Bloc countries, South Africa and Saudi Arabia abstained (the last for religious reasons), but it was also opposed at the time by the American Anthropological Association as expressing only "the values prevalent in the countries of Western Europe and America."[2] Its principal drafters were, indeed, either from Western Europe or North America, or had been

educated in American institutions. Even now, objection remains
outside the sway of North Atlantic culture; as Ziauddin Sardar said in
1998: "since an autonomous, isolated individual does not exist in
non-Western cultures and traditions, it does not make sense to talk
of his or her rights."[3]

By 1950 the framework for international trade and political
interaction that remains in place to this day had been established.
This included the promulgation of the same European Enlightenment
principles that had guided the creation of the United States and the
central role of the US dollar in the world economy. The centre of
power shifted from one English-speaking nation to another; Britain
had been bankrupted by the war and would soon be driven to
dismantle its formerly pre-eminent empire. The United States
remained as one of the few combatants in the Second World War
with very little territorial damage and, unlike the other principal
combatants, had an economy stimulated rather than wrecked by the
war. From its newly dominant position the United States advanced
its political and trading position by providing financial support to the
ravaged economies of Europe, encouraged Britain to break up its
empire, and ensured that its own power was accompanied by
military alliance and advantageous conditions for American products.

The only check on the universal spread of American-led trade and
political ideology was the formation of the Soviet Bloc, the
communist victory in China and the Cold War. The USSR, although
a United States wartime ally and with its economy crippled by
invasion, was dominated by a fiercely nationalist Russia and espoused
a communist political system explicitly hostile to the capitalism and
libertarianism by which the United States defined itself. The defeat of
Germany allowed the USSR to consolidate its power and add to the
boundaries of the pre-Soviet empire the newly "liberated" nations of
Eastern Europe. As the USSR exercised more coercive power over
the Eastern European countries now under its sway and closed their
borders, the new political landscape came to be known as the "Cold
War"—an expression coined by the British author and journalist
George Orwell in 1945[4] and taken up by the US journalist, Walter

Lippmann, with his 1947 book of the same name. By 1949, a civil war in China had established another communist regime in Asia, which was at first allied with its Russian neighbour. The growing power and influence of the United States and its possession of the nuclear bomb created an arms race and increasing hostility and paranoia within both the USA and the USSR.

The Cold War would not only define world politics for the next forty-four years, it would also be instrumental in setting the scene for major cultural changes in the post-war world.

The Cold War and Victory of Modernism

In the United States, the war had accelerated the economy out of the Great Depression. Wartime technological advances in electronics and aviation created new industries, and military automobile construction turned into a huge expansion in private motoring. The growth of service industries and favourable international trading conditions created a vigorous consumer economy. Car ownership and low-interest mortgages for private housing led to the massive urban sprawl that continues to distinguish American life. The new consumer economy was more than an economic success story for the United States: the US came to be seen by many countries as the fount of modernity and progress. Economic growth and a rising standard of living were politically linked with liberty, personal freedom and modernity, and defined as the essential ingredients of the American way of life. This was deliberately contrasted with the struggling economies and the repressive regimes of the Soviet Bloc, which had rejected the European Recovery Progam, or Marshall Plan, owing to its non-negotiable trading conditions with the USA. This excluded the USSR from the Organisation for European Economic Co-operation, formed to administer the Marshall Plan, which later became the Organisation for Economic Co-operation and Development (OECD)—the free trade system based on the leadership of the United States. Free trade, modernity, prosperity

and the way of life of the United States became weapons in the Cold
War, weapons that would include art and architecture.

The association of modernity and progress with new directions in
the arts had already been grasped by revolutionary European
modernists in the pre-war years. Although it had its adherents and its
own brand of artistic and architectural modernity, the United States
received a major influx of pioneering German modernists when they
fled from Nazi persecution in the 1930s. The Bauhaus founder
Walter Gropius moved first to Britain and then to the United States
and, from 1938 to 1952, was Chairman of the Harvard Graduate
School of Design, teaching with his Bauhaus colleague Marcel
Breuer. In 1938 the Armour Institute of Technology (later the
Illinois Institute of Technology) asked the pioneering German
modernist, Mies van der Rohe, to be the Director of its Department
of Architecture. These influential figures joined home-grown
modernists such as Louis Kahn (Dean of the Yale School of
Architecture from 1947 to 1957), Eero Saarinen and Charles Eames
to transform American architecture. The relocation of the early
pioneers, their obligation to their new homeland and their interaction
with United States commercial architectural firms brought about an
important reorientation of Modernism away from its original
association with socialism, to the service of the free market and
commerce. Although the rapid suburban expansion of private
housing was generally traditional in form, wealthy sophisticates
commissioned fashionable modernists for trophy houses. Public
housing and high-status institutional buildings turned increasingly to
the new style, drawing on the incongruent benefits of economy and
ostentatious novelty.

Speaking from his adopted United States, in the same year as the
publication of the "Universal Declaration of Human Rights," the
architect Walter Gropius, seemed to echo the ideals of the United
Nations:

> I would like to suggest that in a period when the leading spirits of
> mankind try to see human problems on earth as an interdependent

entity, any chauvinistic sentimental national prejudice regarding the development of architecture must result in narrowing limitations. The emphasis should be on, "Let us do it together," with each nation, each individual giving his share without giving up regional expression, the emphasis being on teams rather than on individuals. I dare say that we are today much more influenced by each other than in former centuries, because of the rapid development of interchange and intercommunication. This must be welcome, as it enriches us and promotes a common denominator of understanding, so badly needed.[5]

Although these sentiments in isolation seem laudable, they must be seen in the context of the views of Dean Acheson, one of the architects of the Marshall Plan and US Secretary of State from 1949 to 1953, who said that, "in the final analysis the United States [is] the locomotive at the head of mankind, and the rest of the world is the caboose."[6]

The Soviet Bloc understood this very well. They described the "International Style," promoted by Gropius, as "cosmopolitan" in a wholly negative sense: "As in other capitalist countries, building in predominantly formalist and subordinated to the cosmopolitan ideology of American imperialism. This is why buildings look alike whatever their location ... shapeless boxes are an expression of the profit hunger of monopoly capitalism under American dominance."[7] While in the early years after the war there was a brief flirtation with Modernism in the Eastern European states, Russian influence and the promotion of Modernism as propaganda for American modernity persuaded even pre-war pioneers to recant. In 1949 at the *Congrès Internationaux d'Architecture Moderne* (CIAM) in Bergamo, Italy, the Polish architect Helena Syrkus, a prominent pre-war modernist, told an audience including Le Corbusier, Josep Sert and Ernesto Rogers[8] that "the countries of the east have come to the conclusion that we should have a greater respect for the past." The Soviet Union took great care to train architects from their new client states, some of which had responded most positively to Modernism in the pre-war years (such as Czechoslovakia and Hungary), with architectural education

Figure 9. Crown Hall, Illinois Institute of Technology, Chicago; Ludwig Mies van der Rohe; 1956.

Figure 10. Opera House, Leipzig; Kunz Nierade; 1960.

**After the Second World War architecture divides
between East and West.**

in Moscow or organised tours for professionals in Moscow and Leningrad (St Petersburg). Literal versions of Russian classicism, such as the Palace of Culture and Science in Warsaw, were rare. Soviet-trained architects were instead encouraged to adapt architecture from approved historical periods.[9]

On the other side of the Iron Curtain, the United States government used agencies such as the CIA and the United States Information Agency (USIA)—an organisation created by the Department of State to promote United States culture abroad—to actively promote modernist art and architecture as an expression of free thinking and liberty alongside more seductive consumer items, all representing the American way of life. As Raymond Loewy put it in a speech to the Harvard Business School in 1950: "The citizens of Lower Slobovia may not give a hoot for freedom of speech but how they fall for a gleaming Frigidaire, a stream-lined bus or a coffee percolator."[10] Travelling exhibitions were organised, such as the 1955 "50 Years of American Art" curated by the Museum of Modern Art, showcasing modern industrial design alongside modernist architecture, which went to Paris, Zurich, Barcelona, Frankfurt, London, The Hague, Vienna and Belgrade. Architects, planners and engineers were taken on study tours to the USA in the late 1940s and early 1950s, and met luminaries such as Lewis Mumford and European émigrés including Walter Gropius and Mies van der Rohe. Germany was a special case for attention, and an exhibition called We're Building a Better Life [*Wir bauen ein besseres Leben*] was staged in West Berlin, Stuttgart and Hanover before going to Paris and Milan in 1952. This included an ideal dwelling built in the appropriately named George-Marshall-Haus pavilion and featured technically advanced American consumer products with, as its curator Edgar Kaufmann said, an "emphasis to be placed upon [the] fortunate outcome of American economic philosophy."[11]

Embassy building had always been an exercise in national propaganda and, as an anonymous article in *Arts and Architecture* declared in 1954: "the United States Government is making modern American architecture one of its most convincing demonstrations of

the vitality of American culture."[12] Embassy designs went to
modernists such as Walter Gropius (Athens), Josep Luis Sert
(Baghdad) and Edward Durrell Stone (Delhi). Pietro Belluschi,
leading American modernist and chair of the selection board, rather
patronisingly "felt great elation to think of the possible influences of
that such design many have on local architects."[13] This attitude was
not limited to state institutions. In a close parallel to Stalin's gift of a
building to Warsaw, the Benjamin Franklin Foundation, founded by
Eleanor Dulles (sister of the head of the CIA), gifted Berlin the
Kongresshalle, a cultural centre designed by the American modernist
architect Hugh Stubbins Jnr., complete with a quotation on "the love
of liberty" by Benjamin Franklin in the entrance. Even the
construction of luxury hotel chains were harnessed to carry the
American message abroad. In 1957 Conrad Hilton wrote in his
autobiography that each of his foreign hotels was a "laboratory"
where the peoples of the world could "inspect America and its ways
at their leisure" as "bulwarks against the communist threat."[14]

As the original home of Modernism, Western Europe was fertile
ground for this propaganda, and young architects who had been
radical promoters of Modernism in the pre-war years returned from
military service to a continent ready for the construction of a new
and better world. Modernism offered freedom from the nationalism
that had led to conflict, a synergy with technological advances
accelerated in the war, but now directed to the peacetime economy,
an industrial attitude to construction that would speed up
reconstruction, a clean modernity that looked to an optimistic future
rather than a discredited past, and a radicalism that was required to
reform out-dated social structures. In addition, it was highly
commended by its earlier Nazi proscription. In the context of the
time it was irresistible but, as left-of-centre governments came into
power and social reform was seen to be more urgent than the spread
of consumer durables, it did not have quite the flavour of the capitalist
evangelism promoted by the continent's American paymasters.

Many devastated cities in continental Europe sought to forget
their recent ordeal and rebuilt their pre-war fabric. Britain, destitute

Figure 11. (left) US Embassy, Athens; Walter Gropius; 1961. Modernist embassy designs were used by the USA as built propaganda to convey a modern and free society.
Figure 12. (right) Conrad Hilton in front of model of Istanbul Hilton. Hilton Hotels were designed as microcosms of the American way of life and were promoted by Conrad Hilton as cultural ammunition in the Cold War.

The United States made modern architecture into a cultural weapon in the Cold War.

but with the optimism of the victor, gradually re-built and re-ordered its bomb-damaged cities in the latest modern style. Germany, in a monumental national struggle for recovery, often kept to original but improved city plans, but built in an economic elementary Modernism. Where new towns were constructed or new areas laid out, the memory and survival of the dirty and cramped conditions that the industrialised countries had inherited from the nineteenth century led to a drive for rationality, cleanliness and open space. Socially conscious planning had been proposed by modernist urban reformers in the 1930s. New developments, such as the growth of car ownership and the opportunity for tall buildings, were combined with a "rational" segregation of different use functions and methods of transport, changing space between buildings into space around buildings and a paternalistic attitude to the population. Orderly ranks of monolithic modernist structures set in urban parks and crossed by elevated roads were published as the way for the future in Europe and the USA. After the war, the destruction resulting from the conflict was combined with the deliberate destruction of historic areas, designated as slums, and pre-war urban planning theories could at last be realised by governments energised to control and intervene to create a better society.

The frivolity of the *Style Moderne* was dismissed as inappropriate for the serious business of creating a new society and it quickly became little more than a period piece. Simplified classicism, however, survived along with its pre-war practitioners but, as architecture schools around the world gradually abandoned their classical teaching and it was all but banned by reform-minded trade journals, it passed into obscurity. A few solitary practices soldiered on supported by loyal private and wealthy clients or building restoration.

Within a decade, the architecture of the post-war era in the non-communist countries was almost universally modernist. In 1948, Henry Russell-Hitchcock, who had mounted the *International Style* exhibition in 1932, could confidently assert that "we could now consider International Style to be synonymous with the phrase 'Modern Architecture'."[15] In 1952, Jawaharlal Nehru, the first Prime Minister of the newly independent India, commissioned Le Corbusier and a team of European modernists to design Chandigarh, a new capital for the Punjab State that would be "symbolic of the freedom of India, unfettered by the traditions of the past, an expression of the nation's faith in the future."[16] In 1955, the American architect Pietro Belluschi could return from his travels abroad and report that "throughout the Eastern countries we visited, architecture is a superficial imitation of the more obvious western forms ... And this is happening not only in Baghdad or in Agra or in Karachi but in Italy, in France, and even in Finland, wherever reconstruction of bombed-out areas has taken place."[17] In 1956 President Juscelino Kubitschek of Brazil launched a competition for a new capital as "the dawn of a new day for Brazil."[18] Lúcio Costa won the contest for the urban plan, working with the leading Brazilian modernist, Oscar Niemeyer. In Iraq in 1957, in the final days of the Hashemite kingdom, Walter Gropius was commissioned to design the new University City. In these projects and many more, in nations free from Soviet influence, the attraction of novelty and the association of Modernism with modernity and progress had a particular appeal.

In 1956, events in the Soviet Union signalled a change of direction. Stalin had died in 1953 and, after a power struggle inside the communist party, one of Stalin's inner circle, Nikita Khrushchev, came to power. In the so-called "Secret Speech" to the Twentieth Party Congress he denounced Stalin's oppressive policies and adopted a policy for the improvement of living standards with the objective of catching up with Western standards. This included liberalisation of the arts and a more open dialogue with the United States, which led to the 1958 "US-USSR Agreement on Cultural Exchange." Arising out of this agreement, in 1959 the USIA took a version of its German We're Building a Better Life exhibition to the American National Exhibition in Moscow. A lavish display of consumer goods and imagined lifestyle of an "average" American family in a typical prefabricated "dream home" was explicitly designed to attract the envy of Russian visitors. As one of the advisers to the exhibition made quite clear, this was intended as a third front in the Cold War: "By spurring the Russians to increase production of consumer goods we may be helping ourselves more than we are helping them"[19] A tour of the exhibition by Vice President Richard Nixon and Nikita Khrushchev embarrassed the latter into making the famous and manifestly false defence[20]: "You think the Russian people will be dumbfounded to see these things but the fact is that newly built Russian houses have all this equipment right now."

Khrushchev had already signalled the end of Stalinist traditional architecture in a speech to the Soviet All-Union Conference for Builders and Architects in Moscow in 1954. He told architects that they "must know the new progressive materials, reinforced concrete sections and parts and, most of all, must have an excellent understanding of construction economy."[21] This gave a licence for architects to join with industrial designers in the new project to catch up with the United States by taking on the role of technocrats and, in the interests of efficiency and economy, explore new forms under the politically acceptable banner of "experiment." It also allowed Soviet designers to give additional legitimacy to their work by re-connecting with their own revolutionary Constructivist past. In 1957 a revived competition for the un-built Palace of the Soviets in Moscow was particularly significant: the original 1931 competition had included entries from many leading modernists but the choice of a monumental classical design signalled the start of two decades of obligatory traditional architecture approved by Stalin. The 1957 competition could again include proposals for unambiguously modernist designs, with a reasonable anticipation of success (the project was in fact abandoned). In the 1960s a utopian housing scheme was planned for a new district of Moscow by Mosproject 3, also known as the Institute of Standard and Experimental Projects, which was not only clearly modernist but included the Soviet ideals of communal living pioneered by early Constructivists. Modernism was re-established in the Soviet Union and became the style of the "Khrushchev's modernisation."

By 1960, with the Soviet Union finally converted, Modernism could legitimately claim to be the International Style. The success of this North Atlantic architectural movement was complete. Throughout the world, in the name of liberty, capitalism, socialism, reform or efficiency but, above all, modernity and progress, there was a new architecture based on an aesthetic break with the past, expressive geometry and the explicit use of new materials.

Figure 13. Legislative Assembly Building, Chandigarh, India; le Corbusier; 1962. States could use North Atlantic Modernism to mark out their modernity and claim their place in the new world order.

Figure 14. Apartment Buildings, Ulitsa Zhukovskogo, St Petersburg, Russia; 1960s. After Stalin's death, the USSR used industrialised Modernism to accelerate its building programme and express its progressive ambitions.

By the end of the 1960s Modernism had become a global style.

The Golden Age of Capitalism and Heroic Modernism

The 1950s and 1960s were the "Golden Age of Capitalism" in the OECD. This was the American Post-War Economic Boom, the German *Wirtschaftswunde*, the Italian *Miracolo Economico* or Economic Miracle, the Japanese *Izanami* period (a mythological allusion), and the French *Trente Glorieuses* or the Glorious Thirty years (in fact it was twenty-three, but the allusion to the *Les Trois Glorieuses* days of the 1830 revolution was irresistible). The British Prime Minister, Harold MacMillan, told his political party in 1957 that "most of our people have never had it so good," although a sclerotic industrial system and the dismantling of the British Empire had in fact by now reduced the former world power to a second-league nation. Nonetheless, in the 1960s, the coming-of-age of the post-war generation fuelled a remarkable outburst of creativity that briefly put Britain at centre-stage in a new popular youth-based consumer culture.

The communist countries did not fare so well. In the Soviet Union, Khrushchev's "Secret Speech" was not secret for long and the apparent relaxation of Russian tyranny led to unrest in Poland and full-scale revolution in Hungary, which was brutally suppressed. A persistent exodus of skilled workers from East Germany through the jointly controlled city of Berlin led to the construction of the Berlin Wall, a highly visible symbol of popular communist failure. The United States faced down the Soviet Union in the 1962 Cuban Missile Crisis and the USSR suffered an exceptionally poor harvest in 1963, threatening starvation and leading to a major depletion of gold and foreign currency reserves. In 1964 Khrushchev was deposed by Leonid Brezhnev who led the Soviet Union until his death in 1982. For the first decade of his rule, Brezhnev presided over a conservative period of moderate growth, but with a forty per cent increase in military expenditure. He also restored the powers of the KGB, put dissident writers on trial and overturned Khrushchev's cultural reforms. Now reduced to a pared-down Modernism and without any latitude for new thinking, architecture in the Soviet Union under Brezhnev was largely represented by utilitarian pre-cast concrete apartment blocks or a pale shadow of more dynamic developments in the West.

Communist China, at first allied to Russia and then at loggerheads, was crippled first by The Great Leap Forward, a hugely disruptive programme to transform China from an agricultural to an industrial economy, and then, in 1966, the culturally and economically devastating Cultural Revolution. As China turned in on itself in an orgy of economic and cultural self-destruction and factionalism it would have no significant part to play in international economic and political affairs until the death of Mao Zedong in 1976. There was little enthusiasm or economy to support anything more than sparse and impoverished construction. Official architecture was influenced by post-war Russia and its Beaux Arts inheritance, creating an up-scaled reinterpretation of Chinese traditional architecture.

The combination of a capitalist system, liberal-democratic government and Keynsian economics (of state intervention in a market system) in the OECD countries now appeared to be so successful that a permanent equilibrium seemed to have occurred. In 1960, the American sociologist, Daniel Bell, called this "the End of Ideology," arguing that all ideological debate of the past had become irrelevant in the face of the superiority of the capitalist and liberal-democratic system, and society would only now be subject to technocratic refinement.[22] In architecture too, the great style debates of the past seemed to be over forever. There was a professional consensus that Modernism was the only legitimate direction for the future. To suggest otherwise would be a regression to a discredited past, a denial of the historical process itself, and did not warrant recognition, let alone debate. While in the United States and Britain in particular traditionally designed housing was still the predominant product constructed for open-market sale, this was simply ignored or regarded as a temporary aberration, soon to be corrected. Operating in a condition of complete self-confidence, modernist architecture entered into a heroic age.

For a decade there was an extraordinary period of architectural creativity. Unified behind a moral belief in the pursuit of a new future, building design branched out in a number of different directions that would set the aesthetic agenda for modernist architecture to this day. Carried along by the same sense of destiny and reassured by their technocratic conviction, cities, governments and corporations gave the architectural profession full rein.

Pre-war pioneers continued to practice. Mies van der Rohe perfected geometrically refined glass-walled structures. With his influence on architects such as Gio Ponti and Minoru Yamasaki and commercial firms such as Skidmore, Owings and Merrill, the sheer-façade corporate office tower achieved a definitive form. Le Corbusier's work entered a new phase that turned from rational rectilinear structure to expressive sculptural form. The rather eccentric late-period work of the great American nationalist architect, Frank Lloyd Wright, occasionally took a similar direction. These free forms were developed into dramatic structural expressionism in the designs of architects such as Eero Saarinen, Pier Luigi Nervi and Frei Otto. Walter Gropius, while contributing to the definitive office block with his PanAm Building in New York, occasionally turned to elemental historical forms (figure 15). Heavily abstracted allusions to the past, often reduced to little more than proportions, were also employed by Wallace Harrison at the Lincoln Center in New York and by Leslie Martin in Britain, but most powerfully by Louis Khan.

Above all, the architecture that has remained emblematic of the period is the large concrete-clad structure that owes its origins to the most influential building of the post-war era, Le Corbusier's 1947 Unité d'Habitation in Marseilles. Massive and domineering buildings such as Kallmann, McKinnell and Knowles's Boston City Hall in the US (figure 16), more delicate concrete structures such as Ernö Goldfinger's Trellick Tower in London or Kenzo Tange's geometric concrete in Kurshiki City Hall in Japan were built in cities around the world. In 1966 the British architecture critic, Reyner Banham, gave the type its own name with his book *The New Brutalism: Ethic or Aesthetic*. The term was originally coined by the British architect-couple Peter and Alison Smithson in 1953 from the French *béton brut*, raw concrete, but the translation to the more aggressive English expression seemed to better express its uncompromising assertiveness.

Among the variety of modernist experiments of the period were the beginnings of the architecture that would emerge in the following decades. Alvar Aalto, a Finnish architect whose work went back to the Swedish classicism of the 1920s, and Aldo van Eyck from Holland looked for a way to make Modernism more sympathetic to human scale and local conditions (figure 17). The sculptural forms of Sydney Opera House by Jorn Utzon and the projects of Arata Isosaki, on the other hand, renounced the core functionalist ethos of Modernism for buildings that advertised their presence by simply being extraordinary. Archigram, a small group of young architects in 1960s London, also published fantastic projects proposing a technologically driven future with huge structures and mechanical imagery. In 1963, a young American architect, Robert Venturi, after a scholarship at the American Academy at Rome, a two-year European tour and nine years of teaching, built a house for his mother in Philadelphia and three years later published *Complexity and Contradiction in Architecture*. The house and the book, in their different media, questioned the central modernist tenets of aesthetic authenticity and the rejection of historic style. It would take a major shift in the social, political and economic condition to bring each of these isolated experiments to centre stage.

Figure 15. PanAm building, (now the MetLife Building), New York; Emery Roth &
Sons with Walter Gropius and Pietro Belluschi; 1963.   European modernists
abandoned their socialist ideals and adapted their architecture to the commercial
demands of the expanding capitalist economy of the USA.

Figure 16.   Boston City Hall, Boston; Kallmann McKinnell & Knowles; 1969.
Concrete became a major expressive medium with Brutalism, named after the French
for "raw concrete", béton brut.

Figure 17.   Childrens' Home and Tripolis Office Complex, Amsterdam; Aldo van Eyck; 1960 and 1990. A number of architects set out to humanise the mechanical and industrial legacy of Modernism.

The 1960s, the heroic decade of Modernism.

The Breakdown of the Post-War Consensus and a Crisis of Confidence in Architecture

A wide range of social and political developments came together in and around 1968, signalling the breakdown of the post-war consensus and launching a decade of economic crisis and political instability.

Cold War paranoia had drawn the United States into a disastrous war in Vietnam. By 1965 there were American troops on the ground, and by 1968 they were fighting an increasingly savage conflict in ever-increasing numbers. The growing United States army was made up of conscripts from a post-war generation raised on a heady mixture of American libertarianism and consumerism. The combination of the "Alternative Culture" that had gathered in the "Summer of Love" in San Francisco the year before and the massacre of civilians at My Lai by their conscripted contemporaries were toxic. Student protests became increasingly violent, leading to a generational confrontation and the shooting of students at Kent State University two years later. Social unrest in the US was not restricted to war protest. The "Long Hot Summer" of race riots in Detroit left forty dead in 1967, and in 1968, the civil rights activist, Martin Luther King, was assassinated by a white supremacist.

Unrest spread to European cities and took on its own dynamic as young people combined anti-war protest with deep-rooted resentment of the complacency of their ruling classes. In May 1968, Paris and eventually the whole of France erupted as students, anarchists and trade unions joined together to shut down the country. President de Gaulle, wartime leader and national hero, went into hiding. In Germany, Andreas Baader and other left-wing revolutionaries bombed department stores in Frankfurt-am-Maine and killed three members of the public in a protest against right-wing oppression and the Vietnam War. This would lead to the establishment of the Red Army Faction or Baader-Meinhof Gang that would intermittently terrorise Germany over the next thirty years.

The Soviet Bloc, China and India had their problems. Reform of industry to a more capitalist profit-based system in the USSR in 1965 was adopted by the Eastern European client states. This led to demands for more widespread reform and, in January 1968, Czechoslovakia liberalised its political system. In March, students in Poland rioted and occupied their university buildings. The Polish students were expelled and a period of repression followed. In August, the Soviet Union and other Soviet Bloc countries invaded Czechoslovakia and deposed Alexander Dubček, its reformist leader. In the same year, China had entered into its latest phase of cultural self-destruction and Mao Zedong initiated the "Down to the Countryside" movement that exiled young intellectuals to rural areas. Many died from malnutrition, disease and overwork. India, suffering from withdrawal of international aid following war with Pakistan, devalued the rupee in 1966 and, in 1969, the Congress

Party, which had ruled India since independence, split following a poor showing in the 1967 election.

It was, however, the creation of Israel—one troubled outcome of the Second World War—that finally brought down the post-war economy. The establishment of a Jewish state where none had existed for two millennia and the expulsion of the predominantly Muslim Palestinian population created instability in the Middle East that persists to this day. Moral, financial and military support from the United States and guilt-ridden Europe linked the North Atlantic nations to the aggressive actions of the new state. The oil, which had fuelled the Western economies, came largely from Muslim countries that were appalled by the Israeli treatment of Palestinians. When Israel annexed land from Egypt, Syria and Jordan and occupied the whole of Jerusalem—the second-most holy Muslim city—after the Six Day War in 1967, Arab members of the Organisation of Petroleum Exporting Countries (OPEC) wanted the organisation to take retaliatory action on the US and its allies. Frustrated by inaction, in 1968 three Arab nations created a sub-group of OPEC, the Organisation of Arab Petroleum Exporting Countries. In 1973, when the Israelis again defeated their Arab neighbours in the Yom Kippur War, the Arab world was outraged and the new organisation embargoed oil exports to Western Europe and the USA. As the fuel that had driven post-war growth dried up, the Western economies faltered, leading to a sharp drop in world trade, high unemployment and record levels of inflation.

The economic crisis was compounded by political scandal and, in the United States and Britain, political instability. In 1973 the Watergate scandal broke and by the following year, after proof of his complicity in crime and deception, United States President Nixon was forced to resign in favour of his undistinguished Vice President. The term of his successor, Jimmy Carter, was dogged by the economic crisis and ended with the national humiliation of the kidnapping of American embassy staff following the 1979 Islamic revolution in Iran. In Germany, Willy Brandt, the figurehead of the German post-war recovery, first as mayor of Berlin and then as

Chancellor, resigned in 1977 when one of his advisers was found to be an East German spy. In 1974 the British Labour government came to power without a majority, and an election the following year gave them a majority of just three. Weak government, unemployment, inflation and poor industrial relations in Britain led to the enforcement of a three-day working week and the rationing of power.

As the confidence of the Golden Age waned, attitudes to the natural and built environment changed. The wreck of an oil tanker off the British coast in 1967 and an oil and chemical fire in Ohio, USA in 1969 drew public attention to the damaging effects of post-war industrial expansion and established popular support for a burgeoning environmental movement. Greenpeace was founded in Canada two years later. On the other hand, the destructive effects of new development on historic places were evident every day. In Britain and the United States there had been organisations and laws to protect historic buildings and places for some years, but these had limited effect. In 1968, Britain passed laws to prevent the demolition of historic buildings and commissioned studies of major historic cities. In 1969, in an address to the European Conference of Ministers responsible for the Immovable Cultural Heritage, Prince Albert of Belgium stated that "we are beginning to realize that the preservation and enhancement of historic sites must ... be understood and recognized by the public at large, not as a nostalgic rear-guard action by a select few, but as a modern concept." In 1972, the United Nations Education, Scientific and Cultural Organisation (UNESCO) published the *World Heritage Convention*, which linked built and natural heritage and declared 1975 as the European Architectural Year. In the same year, a National Neighbourhood Conservation Conference was held in New York, which launched a series of city-based conservation organisations. In the US in 1978 the Federal Government created the Heritage Conservation and Recreation Service to strengthen the operation of the National Register of Historic Places.

The growth of the Heritage Movement was a direct response to widespread disillusion with the destruction of historic cities and the intrusion of deliberately incongruous buildings. Familiar places—receptacles of memory and symbols of communal identity—had become strange and uniform. By the end of the 1960s, the thrill of novelty had worn off the modernist re-building programme. Ten-to-fifteen-year-old buildings were no longer new, and some were already beginning to show alarming signs of deterioration. Gratitude for spacious living and good plumbing felt by the first inhabitants of the vast new public housing projects had passed, and there came a nostalgia for the streets that had been lost to the non-places between modernist blocks. Theories of a better life with streets in the sky, free from the soot of industry and recreation in sunlit parks had in reality created social isolation, fragmented lives and urban deserts.

Two events drew these tendencies into sharp focus. In Britain in 1968, a gas explosion in one apartment in a twenty-two storey block killed four residents living below. The block, Ronan Point in East London, had been completed only two months previously and was built in one of the rapid construction systems used by cities to speed up the delivery of their new housing targets. The media coverage of this event created a widespread crisis of confidence and drew attention to the wider failings of the architectural type. In 1972, in St Louis, Missouri, the city authorities blew up the first part of a housing project built in 1954 to provide 2,870 apartments in accordance with the latest modernist planning theories. Although the failure of the development had a political as well as architectural background, the destruction of such a large high-profile complex became emblematic of the failure of all such schemes and was later held up by the critic, Charles Jencks, as "the day Modern architecture died."[23]

The architectural profession responded to this seismic shift in attitudes to their work by turning both inwards, and outwards.

Figure 18. Pacific Design Center, West Hollywood, California; Cesar Pelli; 1975. Modernist materials were used to create buildings that were more sculpture than an expression of their function.

Figure 19. House VI, Cornwall, Connecticut; Peter Eisenman; 1975. Eisenman pioneered an architecture that went beyond function and introduced deliberate complexity inspired by the landscape and the architect's own ideas.

In the 1970s Modernism began to move away from the principles of functional and structural expression.

Brutal concrete structures were abandoned, but many architects simply shifted to glossier or lighter materials. With the justification of Modernism through the logic of function discredited, the field was open to pursue other philosophies for inspiration. Function could be contradicted, form could be arbitrary and Modernism could enter into a new level of self-indulgent invention. The American architect Peter Eisenman, with his House IV in Connecticut built between 1973 and 1975, deliberately contorted the rational grid and use of space to create a record more of the architect's design process than the function of the house—a process he called "postfunctionalism." Cesar Pelli designed the Pacific Design Centre in Los Angles in 1975 as a huge blue-glass sculptural form little related to the internal function, as much a self-advertisement as a building (figure 18). The ubiquitous tower block followed suit, becoming less a subject for rational form than a sculptural opportunity, slick curved and cubic forms vying with complex exteriors such as Arata Isozaki's 1974 Gunma Museum in Japan. Engineering and the 1930s ideal of modular components could be exaggerated to create aesthetic drama. Richard Rogers and Renzo Piano won the competition to build a new cultural centre in Paris in 1971. The design exposed the structure and mechanical engineering on the outside in a deliberate reference to the fantasies of the Archigram group creating a Baroque form of Modernism.

In a contrary move to engage the disaffected public, and following in the theoretical slipstream of Robert Venturi's book, a number of architects re-engaged with the traditions that had been expunged from architecture by Modernism. The most direct attempt to assuage public disquiet with the stylised strangeness of Modernism was to return to a mythical past when tradition rather than style dictated architectural form—the vernacular. This had the double advantage of drawing on local materials and types and minimal impact. In Britain, where it was called the "neo-vernacular," it had a profound influence on the private housing market, which persists to this day, but in its heyday was inflated for use on almost all building types. In the USA it was represented most distinctly by the indigenous Shingle Style.

Figure 20. Place de la République, Troyes, France; 1970s. New Vernacular. Concern with the preservation of the character of towns led to a new popular architecture loosely based on local historic precedent.

Figure 21. Center for Theological Inquiry, Princeton, New Jersey, USA; John Blatteau at Ewing Cole Cherry Parsky Architects; 1982. Traditional and classical architects emerged from the shadows in the wake of a crisis of confidence in Modernism.

Figure 22.   Portland Building, Portland, Oregon; Michael Graves; 1980. The building that launched postmodern classicism, an architecture that would define the next decade.

As confidence in Modernism faltered, traditional architecture reappeared in the mainstream.

Populism also took the form of direct engagement with the public in both town planning and architecture in the form of "community architecture." This could be either a planning process where architecture took second place or, as with the Swedish architect Ralph Erskine, a process where public participation influenced the design of buildings. A more direct attack on modernist planning was made by the Krier brothers, Rob and Léon, from Luxembourg.

Once the crack appeared in the modernist monolith, architects who had already been practicing in a very literal classical style, such as John Blatteau in the US and Quinlan Terry in Britain, came out of the shadows. Even established architects turned to recognisable but deliberately different historical forms, such as Ricardo Bofill in Spain, Robert Stern and even the old modernist crusader Philip Johnson in the United States, and James Stirling in Britain. The wider move

away from the certainties of Modernism was recorded by the critic
Charles Jencks in 1975 under the term "Postmodernism," taken from
recent French literary theory.[24] In literature, Postmodernism was a
populist reaction to Modernism and became a philosophical term
when Jean-François Lyotard used it to describe the end of the "big
idea" of modernity and the advent of uncertainty and diversity ("I
define postmodern as incredulity toward metanarratives"[25]).
Postmodernity in architecture could also be broadly defined as the
breakdown of the orthodox beliefs of post-war modernity but, when
expressed visually, it would unavoidably take on a particular and
recognisable form.

Western Recovery and the Fragmentation of Architecture

Financial and political instability instigated a series of shifts in world
affairs. The cost of the Vietnam War, high inflation and the first
American balance-of-payments and trade deficit in the twentieth
century led President Nixon to take the US dollar off the gold
standard in 1971. This ended the currency equilibrium set up by the
Bretton Woods System in 1944. Cooperation over world trading
relationships were, however, too important to abandon and, in
1974, the United States created the "Library Group" made up of
financial officials of the United States, the UK, West Germany,
France and Japan. This became the Group of Five, or G5 (the G6
when Italy joined in 1975, and the G7 when Canada joined in 1976)
which together with the World Bank and the International Monetary
Fund, which had survived the collapse of the Bretton Woods System,
monitored and controlled the free-market international economic
system. Ironically, uncontrolled exchange rates promoted the
movement of capital internationally as it stimulated speculation on
exchange rates. At the same time, increased revenues from higher oil
prices in the Middle East were too great to be absorbed by the sparse
populations of the Arab countries and, paradoxically, were invested
in the same countries that had suffered from the 1973 embargo

(demonstrating the futility of future embargos). As the Middle Eastern states suddenly found they had among the highest Gross Domestic Product (GDP) per capita in the world, they imported foreign expertise to set up governmental institutions and develop their cities. Architects and urban designers from Britain in particular (many states had been British protectorates until 1971) and from the United States found employment in the Middle East when work was scarce at home.

The word "globalisation" began to enter common usage, and the Apollo XI moon landing in 1969 gave popular momentum to the concept of one earth and global interdependency. Although the word had existed in economic literature since the 1960s, its more general use has been traced to American Express advertising in the mid-1970s.[26] In 1979 it had appeared in an EEC document and its use accelerated in official documentation into the 1980s.[27] In 1972 at the United Nations Conference on the Human Environment, it is claimed that René Dubois first used the catch phrase "Think Globally, Act Locally." This has been disputed, but by 1980 the phrase had become sufficiently well-established to be the title of a conference on future trends in Canada and remains a catchphrase to this day. While a new global perspective was emerging, the first signs of identity politics emerged on both sides of the Atlantic. In 1973, Finland gave the Sami, the nomadic peoples who ranged across the north of the Nordic countries, a legal right to their own parliament within the Finnish State. Other Nordic countries eventually followed. In 1977 the Canadian government gave the province of Quebec unique language rights, the first of a series of acts that eventually led to the recognition of Quebec as a "nation" within the state of Canada.

Fragile economic conditions were changing the industrial base in the North Atlantic economies. The assembly-line process and worker protection of the Fordist manufacturing system faltered as markets declined and the consumer economy stimulated a demand for product variety. While the North Atlantic economies began to move away from heavy manufacturing to service industries, the electronics industry had begun to accelerate, facilitating automation and "just-in-time" manufacture. The first electronic data-communication network was established by the US Department of Defense in 1969, and the first e-mail was sent three years later. Microsoft was founded in 1977 and the first mobile phones were tested in 1979.

A revolution in Iran in 1979, deposing the Shah in favour of a fundamentalist Muslim state, was followed the next year by an opportunist attack on Iran by Iraq. A sudden drop in oil exports from these major producers triggered an energy crisis. Saudi Arabia increased supplies to compensate, but the effect was to drag the world economy into another recession. Ronald Reagan was elected president of the USA in 1981 as the recession was coming to an end and, working closely with the new right-wing UK Prime Minister, Margaret Thatcher, transformed the free-market economic system and the world balance of power. Together, the two politicians embarked on a mission to cut back state intervention and spending in their countries, rejecting the Kenysian economic policies of the post-war years. Margaret Thatcher brought down the once-powerful British trades unions and set in motion the privatisation of state-owned industries. The UK also deregulated the international banking system, placing London at the centre of the growing international banking economy. Reagan lowered state spending and decreased taxation to liberalise the economy while increasing defence spending to contain the Soviet Union, which he called "the Evil Empire." Privatisation and the liberalisation of markets were pursued to some extent by many of the North Atlantic economies and were the foundation of the "Washington Consensus," a liberal economic policy named and promoted by the Institute for International Economics in 1969—the "consensus" being the agreement of the IMF and the World Bank, also based in Washington, DC. This policy was best known for its imposition on failed economies as a condition of rescue plans by the IMF. While the economies of the UK, the United States and Western Europe expanded in the 1980s, many developing economies did not fare so well.

The building boom that followed the economic boom was defined by the growth of Postmodernism. When Charles Jencks identified and named the style in 1975[28] there were few projects to illustrate it. The term was, however, the subject of debate among architects in 1980 when several projects established Postmodernism as a major new architectural direction.

Jencks was on the committee chaired by the Italian architect Paolo Portoghesi for the first architecture pavilion at the Venice Biennale in 1980. This was entitled "The Presence of the Past" and featured the *Strada Novissima* (the Newest Street) with a series of facades all in a free interpretation of classical architecture. Chosen participants included Robert Venturi, Charles Moore and Thomas Gordon-Smith from the USA; Paolo Portoghesi and Aldo Rossi from Italy; Hans Hollein from Austria; Ricardo Bofill from Spain; and Léon Krier from Luxembourg. Versions of the display were sent to Paris and San Francisco and it was widely published, to the dismay of modernist architecture critics. Jencks later regretted that this exhibition focused the wider postmodern phenomenon into, what he called, "Postmodern Classicism,"[28] but the association stuck as more classical projects appeared.

That year, the established US modernist architect Michael Graves won a competition for the Portland Building in Oregon, which Graves described as "making classical classifications," and which the local press described as "the Temple."[30] It was a revolutionary design at the time, and was to become one the defining buildings of Postmodernism (figure 22). Equally revolutionary was the maverick US architect Philip Johnson's design for the AT&T headquarters building in New York, under construction at the time and well-published in illustration. This stone-clad tower had a full width broken pediment at roof level, and a neo-classical entrance hall. In France, Ricardo Bofill was also planning a huge new development in Montpellier as a formal monumental classical composition. In London, Terry Farrell had just designed a small and temporary pavilion as a capricious interpretation of a classical temple and established himself as the leading postmodernist in Britain. As

Western economies grew, developers, corporations and academics would demand versions of the new and fashionable Postmodernism which fitted so well with the prevailing climate of wealth, ostentation and excess.

In 1980, Robert Davis employed two married Miami architects, Andrés Duany and Elizabeth Plater-Zyberk, to plan a new town on the south Florida coast called Seaside. The new town would be a test-bed for New Urbanism, an American planning theory based on a return to "the urban conventions which were normal in the United States from colonial times until the 1940s"[31]—in other words, before Modernism and the American post-war suburban explosion.

The Prince of Wales, heir to the UK throne, made a dramatic entry into the modernist-postmodernist architectural debate in 1984 at the 150th anniversary of the Royal Institute of British Architects. In a controversial speech he asked, "why can't we have those curves and arches that express feeling in design? ... Why has everything got to be ... functional?" and hoped "that the next 151 years will see a new harmony ... in the relationship between architects and the people of this country." In 1988 he engaged Leon Krier to plan the new town of Poundbury in the county of Dorset. The status and influence of the Prince of Wales, not just in Britain but worldwide, gave a major boost not only to the more literal practitioners of Postmodernism (his speech resulted in a major project for Robert Venturi in London), but also for a small but growing group of classical revivalists.

Many members of the architectural establishment were unhappy, not just in Britain, and not just with the intervention of a highly influential non-expert in their field, but with the new direction that architecture seemed to be taking. By 1980, any architect under the age of 50 in the Western nations would have been trained exclusively in modernist schools where the inclusion of any literal elements from the pre-Modernist past would have been an anathema. Richard Meier, a disciple of Corbusier, reflected the view of many architects when he said that he saw Postmodernism "as a stylizing of architecture as mere decoration," was "very much against it," and did not think that it had "any enduring quality or value."[32]

One response was a short paper, "Towards a Critical Regionalism, Six Points for Architecture of Renaissance" published in *The Anti-Aesthetic, Essays on Post-Modern Culture* in 1983. The American-based British architectural critic Kenneth Frampton set up a theoretical position that he called "Critical Regionalism" (a term originally used by Alexander Tzonis and Liane Lefaivre in 1981 for a localising strand of Modernism) defending Modernism and attacking Postmodernism. The essay offered "a contemporary architecture of resistance … free from fashionable stylistic conventions, an architecture of place rather than space, and a way of building sensitive to the vicissitudes of time and climate."[33] In practice, this popular idea led to conventional modernist buildings that used local instead of industrial materials, and had some site-specific features or a highly abstracted or symbolic reference to something local.

There were also successful architects whose work seemed to follow the core principles of Modernism who were raised to the level of heroes by their profession. By the late 1970s, the work of architects such as Richard Rogers, Norman Foster, Nicholas Grimshaw and Michael Hopkins in Britain, Renzo Piano in Italy, Gunter Behnisch in Germany, some of the work of Skidmore Owings and Merrill in the USA, and others, had been identified as a type and given the name "High Tech." Although the designs were based on an assembly of engineering and servicing components—what Rogers called "the rich potential of modern industrial society"[34]—in practice the parts were often individually designed, highly engineered and expensive. Equally, the principles behind the designs implied that there should be flexibility in the application of the components, but this too proved to be elusive. Famous High Tech buildings such as the Pompidou Centre and the Sainsbury Centre by Norman Foster needed extensive reconstruction or servicing soon after construction. This architecture did, however, project a strong image of innovation, efficiency and modernity which was attractive both to the architectural profession and those organisations that wished to project a similar image.

Figure 23.   Lloyds Building, London; Richard Rogers; 1986. High-Tech: the mechanical tradition of Modernism turned into decoration.

Figure 24. Parc la Villette, Paris; Bernard Tschumi; 1987. Deconstruction: an architectural style that used philosophical ideas to put sculptural effect before function.

New directions in Modernism were established in the 1980s.

While the High Tech architects claimed justification for their work according to the established modernist principles of efficiency and function, other architects were developing theories that found their innovation and modernity by going beyond anything so prosaic. Some architects were inspired by the literary and linguistic theories of "Deconstruction" of the French philosopher Jacques Derrida, theories that Derrida himself admitted were complicated and difficult to explain. His theories were based on the principle that ideas and texts have no one fixed meaning but are built up of layers of interpretation that can be deconstructed and reinterpreted to provide new, complex and even arbitrary possibilities for understanding. Derrida could not understand why architects would be interested in his ideas of "anti-form, anti-hierarchy, anti-structure—the opposite of all that architecture stands for."[35] But Peter Eisenman and Bernard

Tschumi were not only interested in, but actively engaged with Derrida.

Eisenman had pioneered "this new theoretical base"[36] in the 1970s with postfunctionalism (see above). In the 1980s a new generation of architects in their forties were attracted by the intellectual challenge and opportunities for originality offered by Deconstruction. Bernard Tschumi, a Swiss-French architect, won a competition for the design of Parc de la Villette in Paris in 1982 and filled it with seemingly arbitrary collections of pavilions and landscape where "the culture of architecture is endlessly deconstructed and rules are transgressed,"[37] so that there is no simple or single interpretation of the design (figure 24). Tschumi was fortunate to be able to build, and so bring Deconstruction to the attention of the profession. The Polish architect Daniel Libeskind found it hard to persuade clients that his theory of "moving layers of construction enables one to recover modes of awareness quite removed from the initial hypothesis of rationality,"[38] would make a satisfactory building, but finally won the competition for the Jewish Museum in Berlin in 1989 with a dramatic sculptural design. Libeskind and his near contemporary Zaha Hadid earned their living and developed their ideas through teaching throughout the 1980s. They were, nonetheless, popular with the architectural profession, because they saw themselves, as Hadid said in 1983, as "reinvestigating Modernity" to "go forward along the path paved by the experiments of the early Modernists."[39] They provided the radical alternative to Postmodernism that the profession craved and, in time, this would bring them fame and success. Their future would, however, be determined by international events.

Setting the Stage for the Global Economy

In May 1983, the American economist Theodore Levitt published an influential paper, "The Globalization of Markets," in the *Harvard Business Review*, where he stated that "The world's needs and desires have been irrevocably homogenized" and that "the global corporation operates with resolute constancy—at low relative cost—as if the entire world (or major regions of it) were a single entity; it sells the same things in the same way everywhere ... Ancient differences in national tastes or modes of doing business disappear." He predicted that "only companies that adopt a global approach to markets will achieve long-term success." Levitt had understood the impact of a dramatic expansion of international communication and trade. Air passenger numbers would double in a decade, multinational news corporations began to take over national media, Direct-to-Home (DTH) satellite television was launched, and fax machine ownership multiplied by a factor of eighty. The United States' share of world GDP reached an all-time high in 1985, by 1983 McDonalds had restaurants in thirty-two countries, and MTV was launched in 1981 with MTV Europe broadcast from 1987. The expansion of international affairs went beyond trade and culture. The World Commission on Environment and Development (WCED), known by the name of its Chair Gro Harlem Brundtland, was convened by the United Nations in 1983 to address growing concern "about the accelerating deterioration of the human environment and natural resources and the consequences of that deterioration for economic and social development." This led to the 1987 Stockholm Conference and the publication of *Our Common Future*, the first attempt to bring environmental sustainability into the international political arena, and which introduced the definition of sustainable development that is still in use today.

The Russian economy and those of its Eastern European satellites, unlike the OECD countries, stagnated. Brezhnev died in office aged seventy-five in 1982, and was followed by two leaders in their late 60s or 70s, neither of whom survived for more than eighteen months. This gerontocracy was mirrored across the eastern European states. Throughout the Soviet Bloc there was a lack of political initiative but an urgent need to reform a failing industrial and agricultural system. When a much younger Mikhail Gorbachev came to power in 1985, he attempted to restore Soviet finances. One of Brezhnev's final acts had been to order the invasion of Afghanistan and launch a futile and expensive war. President

Reagan's policy of increased defence spending and confrontation also led to a commensurate increase in Soviet defence expenditure, which it could ill afford. Gorbachev improved relations with the United States and reached an agreement on a reduction in defence spending. In 1988, Soviet forces withdrew from Afghanistan. At home, he introduced *perestroika* [restructuring] of the Soviet industrial system, and accompanied this with *glasnost* [openness], giving greater freedom of speech to encourage participation in his reforms from a cowed and unmotivated population. Although some private ownership was permitted, the intention was to allow the Soviet system to recover and modernise rather than bring about a root-and-branch transformation. The system was, however, too entrenched to deliver significant results, and poor export performance and two bad harvests created consumer shortages among populations now able to openly criticize the system. When the people of the Eastern European states became restive, Gorbachev made it clear there would be no more intervention from the Soviet Union. Hungary quickly established a multi-party system and freedom of travel, setting up a chain reaction that led in 1989 to the breaching of the Berlin Wall separating East and West Germany and the opening up of European borders. The liberalisation of Eastern Europe raised expectations among many of the constituent nations of the Soviet Union, and one-by-one they began to demand more autonomy. The political situation rapidly spiralled out of control and there was a failed reactionary *coup d'état*. Gorbachev recovered power, but by the end of 1991, the Soviet Union was formally disbanded and fragmented into fifteen republics. Russia became a democratic nation and the first elected President, Boris Yeltsin, banned the Communist Party and called in the IMF, the World Bank and the US Treasury Department to establish a free-market economy. The Cold War had come to an end in Europe.

In China, Mao Zedong died in in 1976. After a two-year power struggle with Mao's wife and three associates—the "Gang of Four"— a reforming leader, Deng Xiaoping, took control. This put an end to twenty-five years of botched attempts to modernise through forced restructuring, misguided social and political initiatives and, according to recent research,[40] the death of forty-five million people. Deng Xiaoping took a different path, reminding the Communist Party in 1978 that "Engels never flew on an aeroplane; Stalin never wore Dacron," and declaring that "Socialism and the market are not incompatible." China would achieve the "Four Modernisations," first proposed in 1963, of agriculture, industry, science and technology, and defence by whatever means possible—as Deng Xiaopeng put it: "It doesn't matter if the cat is black or white provided it catches mice." In 1979, Deng negotiated diplomatic recognition from the United States and visited in the same year, going to the Boeing and Coca Cola factories, and signing cooperation agreements on science, technology, education, commerce and space. In the following years, agricultural marketing and pricing were liberalised, private enterprise was permitted and the state was decentralised. In 1980, the first Special Economic Zone was created with the objective of attracting foreign investment, promoting exports and setting up a localised market-driven economy. It was followed by twelve others. In 1984, fourteen coastal cities were opened up to foreign economic investment, and controls on residence were lifted so that underemployed farmers could move from the countryside to provide labour for expanding industries. After decades of stagnation, Chinese GDP had doubled in just ten years.

Although the transformation of China was remarkable, all did not go smoothly. One step in economic liberalisation was the lifting of price controls in 1988, but this led to galloping inflation and in a few months prices rose by ninety-five per cent. Panic buying led to a shortage of durables and consumer products, and in Shanghai the authorities had to distribute food and fuel. Construction came to a halt, and workers lost their jobs. When they returned to their villages things were no better and, desperate for work and without a social security system, they came back to the cities. At the end of the year, the government admitted that the precipitate removal of price controls had been a failure but, by this time, the trust of the people had been lost. In 1989 it became worse, unemployment continued to rise, economic growth fell to its lowest level since 1978, and money stopped circulating. Discontent and opposition grew rapidly, fuelled by the new climate of free speech and protest in the academic community. The death (from natural causes) of a disgraced liberal reformer, Hu Yaobang, was the spark that ignited outbursts of protest throughout the country cumulating in a mass demonstration in Tiananmen Square in Beijing.[41] Ten years of carefully managed reform were on the brink of collapse. With memories of the devastation of the Cultural Revolution fresh in the minds of the leaders, and with an eye to the chaos then engulfing the Soviet Union, the leadership savagely suppressed the demonstrators, rounded up protestors nationwide and purged public institutions of political liberals.

As one of the critical factors in the protest had been financial hardship, the government realised that the only way to maintain stability without the risk of political unrest was to ensure that the economy continued to grow and deliver individual prosperity. As Deng Xiaoping said three years later: "We should persist in taking on two tasks: one is to carry out reform and opening up, the other is to clamp down on various criminal activities. And we must attach equal importance to both,"[42]—criminal activities being, of course, political opposition. Although the government moved to the left—and even the scriptwriter of a popular but critical television programme, River Elegy, was driven into exile—industrial modernisation and economic liberalisation continued unabated. In 1990, the Shanghai stock exchange reopened forty years after Mao Zedong had closed it down, and a new financial district, Pudong, was founded on the opposite bank of the Yangtze River. China unambiguously confirmed its place in the international free-market economy.

What became known outside China as the "Tiananmen Square Massacre" was the first such protest to have been fully exposed to the world media. The resulting suspension of World Bank loans and the withdrawal of foreign direct investment in China demonstrated that it was no longer possible to combine political isolation with open international trade. In addition, the 1989 protests made it clear that entry into the global trading system also meant entry into the established supra-national political order. Immediately after the suppression of the protest, non-governmental organisations (NGOs) such as Amnesty International and Human Rights Watch, founded in Britain and the United States respectively, began to focus on Chinese abuses of the 1948 Universal Declaration of Human Rights, and new organisations such as Human Rights in China were established in New York. In spite of a claim that "Asian values" put the welfare of the collective over that of the individual, political leaders from the North Atlantic states in particular persisted in criticism of the Chinese state on its human rights record.

China and Russia opened up their economies to the free movement of capital in the 1980s and early 1990s, and in 1992 they were joined by India, the last major protectionist economy. The world economy could now claim to be genuinely global. As China and Russia discovered, however, membership of the World Bank and IMF system was not without conditions. The supra-national political and economic system had at its core the New World Order, the institutions and methodology established under the leadership of the United States after the Second World War. This included not only financial regulation based on United States and UK law, but also a political and ethical framework that was based on Enlightenment and North Atlantic ideals. This would have a profound effect on social, political and cultural development as the world entered the New Global Era that defines the world today.

References

1. Hugo Munsterberg. *The Americans*. New York: McClure, Philips, 1904, 6.

2. Ronald Nitzen. *A World Beyond Difference: Cultural Identity In The Age of Globalisation*. Oxford: Blackwell, 2004, 92–3.

3. Joost Smier. *Arts Under Pressure: Promoting Cultural Diversity in the Age of Globalisation*. London: Zed books, 2003, 172–3.

4. George Orwell. "You and the Atomic Bomb." *Tribune*, October 19, 1945.

5. "What is Happening to Modern Architecture?" New York, Bulletin of the Museum of Modern Art XV 3, Spring 1948. Symposium in MOMA, February 11, 1948.

6. Said to McGeorge Bundy, quoted by Douglas Brinkley & Dean Acheson. *The Cold War Years, 1953–71*. New Haven: Yale University Press, 1993, 133.

7. *Handbuch für Architekten*. Berlin: Verlag Technik, 1954. Quoted by David Crowley in "Europe Reconstructed, Europe Divided." In *Cold War Modern: Design 1945-1970*, edited by David Crowley & Jane Pavitt. London: V&A Publishing, 2008, 45.

8. Helena Syrkus. "Art Belongs to the People." In *Architecture Culture 1943-1968*, edited by Joan Ochman. Rizzoli, New York, 1993, 120.

9. David Crowley, ibid.

10. Raymond Loewy. *Never Leave Well Enough Alone*. Baltimore: The John Hopkins University Press, 2002, xxiv.

11. Edgar Kaufmann Jnr (curator). "What is Modern Design?" Museum of Modern Art, New York, Distrib. Simon Schuster, 1950, 8

12. Quoted by Liane Lefaivre in, "Critical Regionalism: A Facet of Modern Architecture since 1945." In *Critical Regionalism: Architecture and Identity in a Globalized World*, edited by Liane Lefaivre & Alexander Tzonis. New York: Prestel Verlag, 2003, 31.

13. Pietro Belluschi. "Regionalism in Architecture." New York: Architectural Record, December 1955, 132–9.

14. Annabel Jane Wharton. *Building the Cold War: Hilton International Hotels and Modern Architecture*. Chicago: University of Chicago Press, 2001, 35.

15. "What is Happening to Modern Architecture?" op. cit., 298.

16. Jawaharlal Nehru, from a speech on visit to the project on April 2, 1952. Official Website of the Chandigarh Administration: http://chandigarh.gov.in (accessed September 2011).

17. Pietro Belluschi. *The meaning of Regionalism in Architecture*. New York: Architectural Record, December 1955, 131–9, 325.

18. From a speech by President Juscelino Kubitschek on October 2, 1956, on his first visit to the site of Brasília Brazília with Oscar Niemeyer and the war minister, General Henrique Teixeira Lott. The phrase was repeated frequently and the Presidential Palace, also designed by

Niemeyer, was named the Palácio da Alvorada, the Palace of the Dawn. www.mimoa.eu (accessed September 2011).

19. Norman K Winston as told to Leonard Gross in "Six Things Mikoyan Envied Most in America." New York: This Week Magazine, March 29, 1959.

20. Richard H. Shepard. "Debate Goes on TV over Soviet Protest." *New York Times*, July 26, 1959.

21. Pravda and Izvestia, December 20, 1954, reproduced in Joan Ochman, ed. *Architecture Culture 1943-1968*. New York: Rizzoli International Publications, 1993, 184.

22. Daniel Bell. *The End of Ideology: On the Exhaustion of Political Ideas in the Fifties*. New York: Free Press, 1960.

23. Charles Jencks. *The Language of Post-Modern Architecture*. New York: Rizzoli, 1984, 9.

24. John Barth. "The Literature of Exhaustion." Washington DC: Atlantic Monthly, August 1967.

25. Jean-Francois Lyotard. *The Postmodern Condition: A Report on Knowledge. 1979*. Minneapolis: University of Minnesota Press, 1984, xxiv.

26. Nitzen, op. cit., 47.

27. Nayan Chanda. Bound Together: How Traders, Preachers, Adventurers and Warriors Shaped Globalization. New Haven: Yale University Press, 2007, 246.

28. Charles Jencks. "The Rise of Post Modern Architecture." *Architectural Association Quarterly* 7 (4) October/December 1975.

29. Charles Jencks. *The New Paradigm in Architecture*. London: Academy Editions, 2002, 115.

30. Barbarelle Diamonstein. *American Architecture Now*. New York: Rizzoli, 1980, 57.

31. Leon Krier. "The Poundbury Master Plan." Prince Charles and the Architectural Debate, London, Architectural Design 59 5/6, 1989.

32. Diamonstein, op. cit., 113.

33. Hal Foster, ed. *The Anti-Aesthetic, Essays on Post-Modern Culture*. Seattle: Bay Press, 1983.

34. Frank Russell, ed. *Architectural Monographs: Richard Rogers + Architects*. London: Academy Editions, 1985, 12.

35. Bernard Tschumi. "Six Concepts." Lecture, Columbia University, February 1991. In *Architecture and Disjunction*, edited by Bernard Tschumi. Cambridge, MA: The MIT Press, 1996, 250.

36. Peter Eisenman. "Post Functionalism." In *Oppositions 6*. Cambridge, MA: MIT Press, Fall 1976. Reprinted in Charles Jencks & Karl Kropf, eds. *Theories and Manifestos of Contemporary Architecture*. Chichester: Academy Editions, 1997, 267.

37. Bernard Tschumi, "The Pleasure of Architecture." London, Architectural Design 47 (2) 1977, 216.

38. Daniel Libeskind. *Between Zero and Infinity*. New York: Rizzoli, 198. Reprinted in Charles Jencks & Karl Kropf, op. cit.

39. Zaha Hadid. *Planetary Architecture Two*. London: Architectural Association, 1983.

40. Frank Dikötter. *Mao's Great Famine, The History of China's Most Devastating Catastrophe, 1958–1962*. New York: Walker & Company, 2010.

41. John Naisbitt & Doris Naisbitt. *China's Megatrends: The 8 Pillars of a New Society*. London: Harper Collins, 2010, 58–9.

42. Records of Comrade Deng Xiaoping's Shenzhen Tour, People's Daily Online, January 18, 2002:
http://english.people.com.cn/200201/18/eng20020118_88932.shtml

PART II:

THE NEW GLOBAL ERA AND THE GLOBAL ELITE

The End of the Cold War and the Dawn of the New Global Era

In the years between the fall of the Berlin Wall in 1989 and the retirement of the Chinese leader Deng Xiaoping in 1992, the economic and political world system was transformed. A series of events and technological changes came together to create the period referred to here as the "New Global Era." This was quite unlike the last great global era at the turn of the twentieth century either in its extent or effect, its international and local impact making it the defining characteristic of the age. It has had a major effect on the way of life of almost everyone on the planet, and it drives our political, social and economic system today. It was inevitable that a seismic shift in world affairs of this scale would also transform contemporary cultural and artistic practice.

As the economist Joseph Stiglitz said: "With the fall of the Berlin Wall in late 1989, one of the most important economic transitions of all time began."[1] The breaching of the Wall was a deeply symbolic event; it was the precursor of the collapse of the Soviet Union in 1991, and the end of the Cold War. But this was only one of a number of critical events that took place during these four years.

Although the communist economic system was discredited by its contribution to the failure of the Soviet Union, at this time the rival free-market system, represented by the OECD, did not seem to be in good health either. On October 19, 1987 the US stock market in one day fell further than the worst day of the crash that launched the

Great Depression in 1929. This was named "Black Monday" with deliberate reference to the "Black Tuesday" of October 1929. The causes of this crash are not universally agreed. A simultaneous announcement of a new law restricting take-overs, a United States trade deficit and a housing loan crash may have conspired to create a classic share-selling panic, exacerbated by automated selling. The market quickly recovered but the economic fundamentals did not and, in 1990, the United States economy entered a nine-month recession. In the UK, high inflation driven by rapid economic expansion and attempts to harmonise with the continental European economy led to punitive interest rates and a savage three-year recession from 1990 to 1992. These two economic failures marked the end of the Reagan and Thatcher booms of the 1980s, and brought down the latter in a Conservative Party coup d'état in 1990 and Reagan's Republican successor, president George H. W. Bush, in the 1992 election.

Germany, the engine of the continental European economy, survived the crises of Anglo-Saxon economies, partly supported by a sudden growth in population after re-unification with recently-liberated East Germany. In 1992, however, Germany also entered into a recession, bringing down its economic partners: France, Italy, Spain, Portugal, Denmark and the Benelux countries. In 1991 an asset-price bubble crippled the Japanese economy, and the country entered the "lost decade" of zero economic expansion.

Outside the OECD countries, however, major changes were taking place that would transform the free-market system. In 1990, as part of its staged entry into the world economy, China reopened the Shanghai stock market. In 1991, a financial crisis and near bankruptcy drove India to reform its restrictive economic controls and open up the economy to attract foreign investment. In 1992, Yegor Gaidar, deputy Prime Minister of Russia and an economist, following advice from the IMF, the World Bank and the United States, liberalised foreign trade, prices and the currency in a socially devastating "shock therapy" to propel the moribund Russian economy into the free-market.

As the United States and European countries emerged from their recessions in the 1991 to 1994 period, they operated in an entirely new international economic climate. Three major nations and some of their former satellites, previously closed to free trade and with about fifty per cent of the world's population, had not only opened for business, but had done so by joining the trading system that had been established by OECD countries in the years after the Second World War. Furthermore, financial trading itself was just entering a new period of internet transactions, as in 1991 the World Wide Web was launched and E-trading began. The development of advanced information technology (IT) was an essential ingredient in the new economy. As Manuel Castells says, "if there were no computers and no global telecommunications … there would be no global economy and world-scale communication."[2]

The development of this new open international trading climate was called "globalisation" which, as we have seen above, was a term that had come into common usage in the 1980s. In the coming years its impact would far outreach the international exchange of capital, but the idea of globalisation is still frequently defined in accordance with its economic foundations. In 1987, in the *American Banker*, globalisation was defined as "a short-hand term for the various forces transforming capital markets and the financial service industries on a world-wide basis."[3] In 2002, Anne Krueger, the first deputy managing director of the International Monetary Fund, defined globalisation as: "a phenomenon by which economic agents in any given part of the world are much more affected by events elsewhere in the world."[4] Or more simply put by the French sociologist, Alain Turraine, it is "the triumph of capitalism practically, politically and intellectually."[5]

Capital markets do not, of course, exist in isolation, and the operation of a free market in financial transactions will have a widespread economic impact. This is described by American economist, Jagdish Bhagwati, as the "integration of national economies into the international economy through trade, direct foreign investment (by corporations and multinationals), short-term capital flows, international flows of workers and humanity generally, and flows of technology"[6] (chart 1).

Once it becomes possible, as the Nobel Prize-winning economist Milton Friedman famously said, "to produce a product anywhere, using resources from anywhere, by a company located anywhere, to be sold anywhere,"[7] the consequences will not stop with investment and industry. Martin Wolf, Chief Economics Commentator of the *Financial Times*, makes it clear that "the economics of globalisation are … the driving force for almost everything else."[8] The political economist Andrew Sobel provides a comprehensive list of "almost everything else":

Globalization consists of multiple processes by which people in one society become culturally, economically, politically, socially, informationally, strategically, epidemiologically, and ecologically closer to peoples in geographically distant societies. These processes include the expansion of cross-border trade, production of goods and services via the multinational corporation, outsourcing of work across borders, movement of peoples, exchange of ideas and popular culture, flow of environmental effects and disease from one state to another, and routine transfer of billions of dollars across borders in an nanosecond. They connect communities, cultures, national markets for goods and services, and national markets for labor and capital. The food we consume, clothes we wear, jobs we perform, air we breathe, water we drink, cars we drive, transport that delivers our goods, information we access, capital that powers our economies, services we use, computers we use, places we travel, education we seek, diseases we contract, drugs and therapies we employ to combat illness, and just about every aspect of day-to-day life have some global component. The world is figuratively shrinking as activities in one nation increasingly spill over to influence activities in other nations.[9]

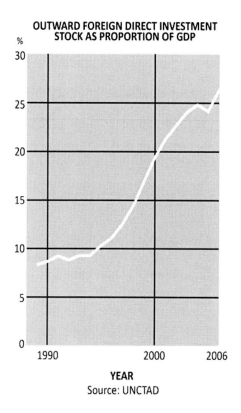

Chart 1. Outward Foreign Direct Investment 1990–2006

The impact of the New Global Era was clear to most observers. Speaking to a meeting of the World Bank and the International Monetary Fund (IMF) in 1995, President Clinton saw the emerging condition as "the most intensive period of economic change since the industrial revolution."[10] On an individual level, Friedrich Schorlemmer describes (from 1993) how the collapse of an orderly communist society could lead to a personal crisis:

> The joy of freedom is at the same time a falling into a void. Now let everyone look after himself. What are the rules? Who's in charge? ... the West's caravan moves on, calling to us: "Come with us. We know the way. We know the goal. We don't know any way. We

don't know any goal. What is certain? That everything's uncertain, precarious. Enjoy our lack of ties as freedom."[11]

We also have the unique testimony of Nelson Mandela, released from twenty-seven years in prison in 1990: "What struck me so forcefully was how small the planet had become during my decades in prison; it was amazing to me that a teenage Inuit living at the roof of the world could watch the release of a political prisoner on the southern tip of Africa."[12]

The Social and Cultural Impacts of Globalisation

The political drama that ushered in the New Global Era also gave it particular public and academic prominence. According to historian Richard Crockatt, globalisation became "the most discussed paradigm for the post-cold war international order." The advantage for the historian and commentator was that it "could be shown to have had a history and to that extent it could be employed to link the period of cold war with what preceded it and followed it."[13] There have been more cautious and revisionist views of the supposed economic and social dominance of global finance and institutions, most notably from Pankaj Ghemawat in his recent book, *World 3.0*,[14] but despite frequent exaggeration and simplification we are, even according to Ghemawat, at the very least in a semi-global era. In recognition of the importance of the phenomenon, sociologists in particular have struggled to find a satisfactory definition of globalisation.

Looking for a more fundamental and society-based definition of globalisation, many sociologists go beyond simply recording well-recognised changes in economics, capitalism, information technology and travel.

A commonly observed outcome of extended social and economic contact through travel, communication and commerce is the homogenisation of culture and place. The Swedish social anthropologist Ulf Hannerz sums this up succinctly: "Humankind has ... bid farewell to that world which could ... be seen as a cultural mosaic, of separate pieces with hard well-defined edges. Cultural connections increasingly reach across the world."[15] This is expressed territorially by the sociologist Anthony McGrew as "a process of deterritorialization: as social, political, and economic activities are increasingly 'stretched' across the globe they become in a significant sense no longer organised solely according to a strictly territorial logic."[16] A more nuanced view is that while some aspects of society may be homogenised, globalisation also fragments others. Martin Albrow considers "that the multiplication and diversification of worlds rather than homogenization or hybridization better express the dominant forms of cultural relations under globalised conditions."[17] The social anthropologist Arjun Appadurai combines this with a discussion of the widely perceived sense that homogenisation is in reality Americanisation or Westernisation: "Globalization does not necessarily or even frequently imply homogenisation or Americanisation, and to the extent that different societies appropriate the materials of Modernity differently, there is still ample room for the deep study of specific geographies, histories, and languages."[18]

The speed of communications and travel which creates the condition for a homogenised or potentially homogenised world will also create a new relationship between time and space. The sociologist Roland Robertson describes globalisation as "a concept [that] refers both to the compression of the world and intensification of consciousness of the world as a whole."[19] Ulrich Beck believes that "from now on nothing which happens on our planet is only a limited local event; all inventions, victories and catastrophes affect the whole world, and we must reorient and reorganize our lives and actions, our organizations and institutions, along a 'local-global' axis."[20]

While the social definitions of homogenisation, fragmentation and space-time compression can be mutually inclusive, there is not the same unanimity as to whether globalisation is modern or Postmodern.

For the sociologists Peter Berger and Anthony Giddens there is no ambiguity. Berger sees globalisation as "*au fond*, a continuation, albeit in an intensified and accelerated form, of the perduring challenge of modernization."[21] Giddens is equally emphatic: "one of the fundamental consequences of modernity ... is globalization."[22] Giddens defines modernity in a number of ways, principal among these is as "a post-traditional order."[23] As increased contact with Western culture (which Giddens believes is post-traditional and modern) has undermined the basis of traditional societies, in accordance with his own definitions, there is some logic to his view. He has little time for the idea of Postmodernism. He is of the opinion that "we have not moved beyond modernity but are living precisely through a phase of its radicalization."[24] But, as according to Giddens this means that "we have entered into a period of high modernity,"[25] we are at least in a phase of modernity that is "post" an earlier "low" or "original" period of modernity, even if we are not in a Postmodern state as defined by Jean-François Lyotard.[26]

If, on the other hand, the definition of modernity is taken roughly in accordance with that of Lyotard, as based on a "metanarrative" such as progress or liberal democracy or Enlightenment rationality, then either globalisation is driving the world to another metanarrative, which would be a homogenised or westernised condition, or it is fragmenting into a complex series of views of the world. Those who adopt the latter view see globalisation as a Postmodern phenomenon. This is the position of Jan Aart Scholte, who says that "global relations have, by eliminating territorial buffers, intensified intercultural contacts and heightened general awareness of cultural diversity and contingency. Many people have thereby come—in line with postmodernist precepts—to regard their knowledge as socially and historically relative."[27] Martin Albrow takes the slightly different view that the "Modern Project" has reached its conclusion in a version of the End of History which is, consequently, the end of modernity: "Globality promotes the recognition of the limits of the earth but is profoundly different from modernity in that there is no presumption of centrality of control. The unification of the world which was the outcome of the Modern Project generates the common recognition that the project has ended."[28] The disturbing outcome of the "new era of postmodernity," as noted by Mike

Featherstone, is "that we are seeing the generation of global conditions in which certain groups of people are becoming involved in situations demanding more flexible classifications, situations in which it is not possible to refer to one set of overriding cultural rules which can arbitrate without ambiguity."[29]

The flexible and indeterminate condition which Featherstone describes, and the lack of overriding rules, combined with the scale and anonymity of the global capital market, can be dangerous and unsettling to existing interests and vulnerable groups. The globalisation of the world economy is, however, largely seen as inevitable. Anne Krueger believes that "globalization is like breathing: it is a not a process one can or should try to stop; of course, if there are obvious ways of breathing easier and better one should certainly do so."[30] The anthropologist Ronald Niezen believes that "no one, however much they may wish to, can isolate themselves to the point of living a simple existence, outside the reach of global institutions."[31]

There are, nonetheless, many who see the global economic system as undemocratic and its many outcomes as, in various ways, damaging. These include important participants in the process such as John Cavanagh, director of the Institute of Policy Studies in Washington and Joseph Stiglitz, Nobel Prize winner and former Chief Economist of the World Bank. Cavanagh wrote in 1996: "globalisation is a paradox: while it is very beneficial to a very few, it leaves out or marginalises two-thirds of the world's population."[32] In 2002, Stiglitz gave his view based on his intimate working knowledge of its economic operation and impact:

> Globalization can be a force for good: the globalization of ideas about democracy and of civil society have changed the way people think, while global political movements have led to debt relief and the treaty on land mines. Globalization has helped hundreds of millions of people attain higher standards of living, beyond what they, or most economists, thought imaginable but a short while ago … But for millions of people globalization has not worked. Many

have actually been made worse off, as they have seen their jobs destroyed and their lives become more insecure. They have felt increasingly powerless against forces beyond their control. They have seen their democracies undermined, their cultures eroded.[33]

But Stiglitz believes that "the problem is not with globalisation, but with how it has been managed."[34] These insiders share a concern, if not an outlook, with anti-globalisation protestors who come together as informal associations, ranging from anti-capitalists to threatened indigenous peoples, to protest at global economic forums such as the World Trade Organisation in Seattle in 1999 or the G8 Conference in Genoa in 2001. These groups are themselves, however, global and organise through global instruments. The social anthropologist, Jeffrey Juris, observes that "global justice activists have made innovative use of global computer networks, informational politics, and network-based organisational forms."[35] Ronald Niezen sees the same principles at work as "the indigenous peoples' movement has made use of human rights and institutions of global governance in order to shelter their collective 'traditional' ways of life."[36]

Many of these protestors represent groups or interests that are frustrated by their powerlessness in the face of the huge force of global capital and corporations. Even for willing entrants to the global free market, the outcome could be devastating. In the years after the creation of the new financial order, the free movement of capital in and out of countries created a series of financial and political crises in south-east Asia, Russia and South America. These led to the fall of governments and financial hardship for millions of the citizens of those countries.

****

In 1997 a number of countries in Eastern Asia had enjoyed three decades of vigorous growth, known as the East Asian Miracle. The economies of Indonesia, South Korea, Thailand and the Philippines, while strong, were protected by government controls on capital and international transactions. Under pressure from the IMF and the United States Treasury, these countries were persuaded to open up and liberalise their economies, so expanding the global investment market. Full membership of the global economy, however, did not just mean openness to investment, it also meant openness to speculation. Indonesia lifted currency controls in July 1997 at a time when it had a high foreign debt. Speculators, predicting devaluation, created a run on the currency. This crippled an otherwise strong economy and the loss of trade in the region dragged the other East Asian countries into their own economic crisis. Fifteen per cent of Thai males lost their jobs, a quarter of the South Korean population fell into poverty, and there were inter-ethnic riots in Indonesia.

The economic slowdown brought about by the East Asian Crisis reduced the global consumption of oil. This tipped the shaky economy of Russia, which relied on natural resources for eighty per cent of its export income, into increasing debt. The "shock therapy" of 1992, recommended by the IMF, the World Bank and the US Treasury, had dramatically reduced the standard of living in Russia while creating a robber-baron economy, where newly-rich oligarchs linked to the government protected their capital by moving it out of the country. With little investment in industry, Russia had become dependent on the minerals in its vast hinterland, and its economy was thus highly vulnerable to commodity-price fluctuations. The drop in oil prices, the cost of a war in Chechnya and the national debt panicked investors: inflation rose to eighty-four per cent, and on August 13, 1998 the Russian stock exchange crashed. Four days later, the government devalued the rouble (which dropped by seventy per cent against the US dollar), defaulted on its domestic debt and declared a moratorium on payment to foreign creditors. By the end of the next year an unwell and exhausted president Boris Yeltsin resigned and Vladimir Putin came to power.

In the summer of 1998 a general widespread loss of confidence in emerging economies led to a run on the Brazilian currency—which then spread to the other South American countries—recovering from a 1980s debt crisis and a period of economic stagnation dubbed their "lost decade."

This series of global financial crises were, according to Joseph Stiglitz in his book *Globalisation and its Discontents*,[37] to a significant extent the outcome of the rationalisation of the new global economy on the North-Atlantic model. This economy was managed by the IMF and the World Bank, organisations set up after the Second World War, and all largely controlled by the United States and its original European allies and operating under the liberal-economic principles of the Washington Consensus. It was to these organisations that troubled economies turned for financial assistance, which was often tied to enforced economic and even political re-structuring. The financial models used, appropriate for the political, legal and fiscal structures long established in the United States and Europe, were unsuitable for less stable emerging economies and often deepened an existing crisis. They were seen less as a bail-out for the countries in trouble than protection for international bankers and the North-Atlantic financial infrastructure. The only major countries to survive this process relatively unscathed, China and India, had maintained some control over their markets and avoided the full economic liberalisation of the Washington Consensus.

In the 2000s, the East Asian countries and Brazil recovered. The North Atlantic countries, however, eventually enjoyed an unprecedented seventeen years of economic stability. Triumphant economists dubbed it the "Great Moderation," and the economics journalist, Gerard Baker (now Managing Editor of the *Wall Street Journal*), wrote on January 19, 2007 in *The Times*: "Economists are debating the causes of the Great Moderation enthusiastically," and put the apparent success at the door of "the liberation of markets," the "creation of the secondary mortgage market" and "the power of creative destruction," concluding with the claim that "the turmoil of free markets is the surest way to economic stability and prosperity."[38] In view of events a year and two days later, these comments would seem ironic. World stock markets plunged, and by September 2008 the fourth-largest US investment bank, Lehman Brothers, filed for bankruptcy, and the United States government bailed out the American International Group (AIG), which had insured against the losses in the complex loan packages that were bringing down the North-Atlantic financial system. The Great Moderation had collapsed dramatically, and the North-Atlantic countries entered a long and deep debt-driven recession, in which they remain at the time of writing. China, India, Brazil and the East Asian countries were virtually unaffected. While the Global Era may continue, 2008 probably marks the end of the North-Atlantic phase.

This is the background to world architecture and urban design between 1992 and 2008. It is expected that these disciplines will change in response to these global events. It is often the secondary and sometimes surprising outcomes of these broad social, political and economic transformations that have the most obvious impact on the practice and aesthetic of architecture and urban design.

The Supremacy of the North-Atlantic Economies

While globalisation may be supra-national in its outreach, economics are unavoidably linked to national politics. As the New Global Era was symbolically launched by the collapse of the bellicose Soviet political system, the opponents of that system would inevitably emerge as the victors. The economic success of free-market capitalism, by which the United States and its allies had aggressively identified themselves since the Second World War, was not only the victor in the Cold War, but was the system which the defeated nations eagerly sought to join.

As the east European political and economic situation changed, the fragile political climate could easily have been reversed. Initially, this restrained the US political hierarchy from any overt triumphalism. President George H. W. Bush merely stated, when asked by a journalist for a response to the fall of the Berlin Wall: "I am pleased."[39] There was no such restraint in American society more generally. The publication in 1989 of the paper "The End of History?" by the American political scientist Francis Fukayama,[40] announced that this marked not just the defeat of a competitor nation or its economic system but the final, irreversible and global triumph of the north-Atlantic liberal democratic system itself. At first only published in an academic journal, the paper made Fukayama famous as it chimed perfectly with the long-standing American view of its moral and political destiny and the mood of the time. Even the American entertainment and news media giants, MTV and CNN, tried to get in on the act. Viacom International chairman Sumner Redstone tried to make an extraordinary connection with a claim that: "We put MTV into East Germany, and the next day the Berlin Wall fell."[41] Ted Turner, founder of CNN and the Goodwill Games and maverick philanthropist, made a personal bid for the credit. "I said, 'Let's try and undo this. Let's get our young people together, and let's get this cycle together and let's try to get some world peace going and let's end the Cold War.' And, by God, we did it."[42]

The United States was now the sole superpower, and the international economic and political order it had established with its allies at the end of the Second World War was now the global system. Once the threat of a return to communism in Eastern Europe had disappeared, the United States was not shy about what it must do. In his 2000 State of the Union Address, President Bill Clinton told Americans that "we must reach beyond our borders, to shape the revolution that is tearing down barriers and building new networks among nations and individuals, and economics and cultures: globalization. It's the central reality of our time."[43] Steven Lamy, professor of International Relations at the University of Southern California, set out the underlying motives in 2001: "US foreign policy since the end of the Cold War has involved a careful use of power to spread an American version of liberal democracy: peace through trade, investment, and commerce."[44] The American political commentator, William Pfaff, describes it more succinctly as, "an activist foreign policy which presumes that nations and international society can be changed into something more acceptable to Americans."[45]

The new global financial order followed the political order. Alan Murray, Deputy Editor of the *Wall Street Journal*, wrote in 1999: "the nation far outstrips its nearest rivals in economic and military power and cultural influence. America's free-market ideology is now the world's ideology."[46] As the key to political and economic success of smaller nations is to take sides with the most powerful nation, it was the world that came to the North Atlantic economic system, and it would follow that this would give a clear advantage to those that had been operating within it for forty years. International trading protocols were founded in Anglo-Saxon law, and the language of business was English. As an executive at the US Public Relations firm Porter Novelli said in 2000, America is "driving globalization for the simple reason that the top global corporations are US-based. The top institutions are US-based and the business schools that are training people to be global executives are US-based. Likewise, ninety per cent of the internet economy is US-based."[47] The dominant position of US corporations engendered a domineering frame of mind. American brokers, Merrill Lynch, believed that if they were dissatisfied they could "go to the London Stock Exchange and say if you guys don't fix it, we're going to take our 25 per cent a year volume elsewhere. If we do, the London Stock Exchange could die."[48] In 1999 Wal-Mart (as it then was) could announce that as "The United States has only 4.5 per cent of the world's population … that leaves most of the world as potential Wal-Mart customers."[49] As the sociologist Jan Nederveen Pieterse said in 1994, globalisation is, "in effect … a theory of westernisation by another name … it should be called westernisation and not globalisation."[50]

Architectural Practice and the Response to Global Opportunities

The structure of architectural practice followed the same pattern as other business organisations. As with any service industry, architectural firms followed their clients or, if they were particularly enterprising, opened offices where they thought the work might be.

Figure 25. Canary Wharf, London; commenced 1987. The liberalisation of the London Stock Exchange in the 1980s encouraged large commercial American architectural firms to open offices in London to service American financial institutions, creating a North American urban environment in Europe.

The liberalisation of financial trading led to the expansion of international architectural practice.

American and, in particular, British firms had already opened offices in the fast-developing and newly-wealthy Middle Eastern oil states in the 1970s, when work was scarce in their own countries. The deregulation of the London financial markets in 1986, and the allocation of large areas of the old docklands (made redundant by the containerisation of shipping cargo) to tax-exempt development four years earlier, created a building boom and brought in American real estate investors—and with them, their architects. The well-established commercial Chicago firm, Skidmore Owings and Merrill (SOM), opened its first foreign branch in London in 1986. The St Louis based architectural and engineering practice, Hellmuth, Obata and Kassabaum (HOK) opened its first foreign office in Hong Kong in 1984, and then in London in 1988. The New York architects, Kohn Pedersen Fox Associates (KPF) designed some of the major buildings in London's docklands, and opened its first office outside the United States in London in 1989. In 1990 the Baltimore firm RTKL opened offices in London and Tokyo. These architectural practices were large, well funded and had wide experience in the delivery of large commercial buildings. As American banks and real estate investors moved into the rapidly expanding financial centres of London, American architectural firms provided an efficient, familiar and tested service for their compatriots. Their range of services, experience and pragmatic commercial outlook also made them attractive to domestic developers capitalising on the growing global commercial market.

SOM was the world's leading modernist practice, and had been responsible for establishing the glass-walled office block as the standard commercial type. It was also the first to develop a corporate public persona, its buildings being identified by the firm rather than the individual designer. When it opened its London office it had a total of 1,400 employees, far larger than any European practices. HOK eventually expanded to ten offices outside the US, but also established a European network of partner firms to respond to the demands of globally operative clients to match their presence in European capitals.[51]

Robert Cioppa, partner at Kohn Pedersen Fox, explained the thinking behind the practice's expansion to the urban geographer Donald McNeill: "The strategy at the time [was based on] a universal notion that London would become a financial centre, as it was bridging the time zones between Asia and the United States, and that there would be a significant shift in financial institutions to London. So we serviced financial clients, but there were also the developers coming here under the same premise, so it became a service-oriented move."[52]

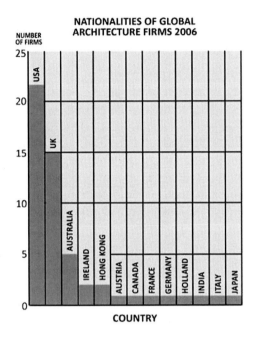

Chart 2. Nationalities of Global Architectural Firms 2006

For these large firms, the boom years of the 1980s gave them their first opportunities to expand outside the United States. As the financial and corporate sector grew beyond the established centres of New York, London, Toyko and Hong Kong in the 1990s, these practices and others opened new offices to respond to the market. The example set by the American firms of size and range of services was followed by British and Australian architects in particular, taking advantage of the global English-speaking business culture. Indeed, by 2006, of the fifty-nine major international firms (with functioning offices in more than one global region), fifty-one have their head offices in Anglophone countries, and two were founded during the British colonial period in Hong Kong (chart 2). The United States hosted thirty-seven per cent of these firms. While British gross domestic product is only fifteen per cent of that of the US, twenty-five per cent of the global practices have head offices in Britain (perhaps a combination of the legacy of Empire and an historic association with the United States). Australia is next with eight per cent, or five practices. The cumulative growth of these firms from 1989, as they established branch offices in other global regions, follows closely other global indicators such as cross-border capital flows and the growth of internet hosts[53] (chart 3, see also charts 1, 4 and 5).

Two practices, with confusingly similar names, Aedas and AECOM, illustrate two different commercial responses to the new global business climate. The expansion of both firms has followed the pattern of international corporate mergers and acquisitions (M&A) which enable firms to rapidly widen their geographic outreach and create economies by pooling expertise, facilitated by the free movement of capital. The years from 1992 to 2000 are known as the "fifth merger wave," notable against previous "waves" for its cross-border mergers. In November 2006, *The Sunday Times* of London reported that the "M&A boom is a truly global phenomenon." In that year, up to that month, there were US $289 billion of deals in the United States, and Britain had reached US $80 billion. Piers de Montfort of Credit Suisse, said: "The common denominator is cheap money … alongside the perennial need for public companies to deliver growth in earnings to achieve premium ratings."[54] This was the high point of the "sixth merger wave" that ended in 2008.

It has always been a dilemma for professional firms that, once they reach a certain scale and become publicly quoted to attract outside investment, they have to continue to grow to maintain investor confidence. Structural limitations in their market can drive them to acquire new firms solely for this purpose and can lead to failure. This tends to limit the range of firms in the sector. Aedas and AECOM by, respectively, matching changes in the emerging global corporate profile and buying high quality firms on a broad front, seem to have avoided this danger.

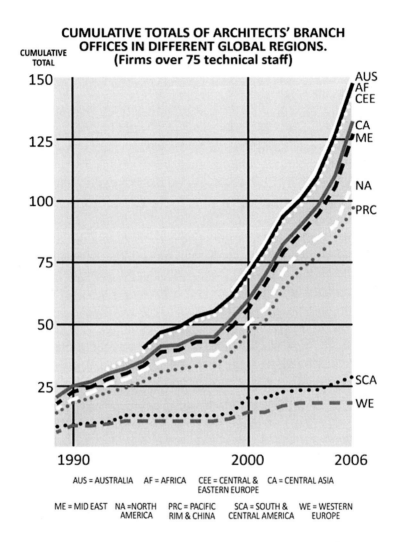

Chart 3. Cumulative Totals of Architectural Branch Offices in Different Global Regions 1990–2006

Aedas was created in 2002 from a merger between the British firm Abbey Holford Rowe and the Australian Hong Kong-based architects LPT. The name "Aedas" was developed with a branding firm to be unique, easy to pronounce, legible in multiple languages, have good *feng shui* and, not least, be at the start of the Roman alphabet. It was given a feeling of maturity and status, at least to speakers of European languages, by being loosely derived from the Latin for "build," *aedificare*. It took over another British firm in 2003 and then abandoned all individual references to the origin of its associates and used only the Aedas brand.[55] In 2006 it merged with east coast and west coast American architects, and in 2009 with a Pakistani and Italian firm. It now has four offices in the Middle East, twelve in Asia, sixteen in Europe, two in the US and one in Brazil. In their 2006–7 Annual Review, the practice asked the rhetorical question, "How do 1,900 creative team members in 26 offices working in 11 key sectors spread across four continents work successfully together?" and answered, "By sharing knowledge, expertise and cultures … we apply our global resources through the Aedas network to deliver progressive local solutions."[56] The company has no headquarters: in 2004 the Chairman, Keith Griffiths, said that: "in the electronic age you don't need to have a physical home base," but could operate with "a network/necklace of offices right across the world."[57] They do, nonetheless, operate from three principal regional bases—Europe, the Americas and Asia—which they see as culturally differentiated: the Asian offices, for example, have largely indigenous staff.[58] The concept of a major global architectural firm operating under a single brand but with regionally autonomous identities is possibly unique, but is a perceptive response to the growth of similarly nationally-disengaged global corporations.

While Aedas is primarily an architectural firm, with naturally associated services such as urban design, interior design and landscape, architecture is only one aspect of the procurement of buildings. Client companies often have little interest in the conventional sub-divisions in consultant teams, which in any event differ from country to country. SOM started as a structural engineering as well as an architectural firm (the engineer John Merrill was one of the founders) and HOK services included engineering. The United States did not have the British tradition of an independent cost consultant or quantity surveyor. Large corporations are attracted by the prospect of one point of contact for the procurement of large and often remote building projects, seen less as architecture than investments. The last decade has seen the rise of consultant conglomerates to answer this demand. As the architectural theorist Neil Leach says: "In the highly digitised age of the 21st century, architecture has become so thoroughly enmeshed within a network of other disciplines that what we are witnessing are new hybrid, mutant forms of practice that serve to reinvent the discourse of architecture as we know it."[59]

The name AECOM is an acronym of "Architecture, Engineering, Consulting, Operations and Management." It was founded in Los Angeles in 1990 after a management buyout of a petroleum industry engineering firm, which was already associated with two US architectural practices: DMJM and Frederick R Harris. Unlike Aedas, it has retained its headquarters in the United States, and is listed in the Forbes 500 largest US firms with 45,000 employees. It also retains its original engineering profile, offering services such as energy and transportation consultation, and mining and geotechnical services. Like Aedas, however, it has expanded through a series of mergers and acquisitions, bringing in thirty companies which have given it ready-made access to Eastern Asia by buying the Chinese architects Citymark in 2007, to Europe and Australasia by bringing in the British architects DEGW, and to the Middle East with the purchase of the British project managers Davis Langdon, the last two in 2010. In 2009 it bought in landscape and masterplanning expertise with the well-established San Francisco firm EDAW, which already had a strong global profile. In that year, its associated firms, which had retained their original names with the AECOM suffix, were subsumed under the single brand title of AECOM. The management philosophy is different from that of Aedas, and is more centralised. As the Virginia-based senior vice president, Jon Miller, said in 2010: "If you're going to be global, your expertise is not going to exist in every location … If you have a project in Kuwait, but not the right people for it on the spot, you can draw from other regions and establish the right talent in the right location. The global market is changing."[60]

Through an aggressive policy of mergers and takeovers, by offering a wide range of services and by concentrating on well-established and successful firms, AECOM has secured a number of major projects, from the construction management of the World Trade Center in New York to the planning of the Olympic site in London.

As firms such as Aedas and AECOM have grown and widened their geographical operations by agglomeration to provide coordinated services to their global client base, they have established offices in cities around the world which are themselves agglomerations of global service industries.

Architects and the Transnational Capitalist Class

The major global cities, identified by Saskia Sassen in her book *Global Cities*, function with "a complex of industries, such as advertising, accounting, legal services, business services, certain types of banking, engineering, and architectural services, etc., which assist, facilitate, complement, and in many cases make possible, the work of large and small firms and of governments."[61] These industries include concentrations of "producer services," such as architecture, and "production of these services benefits from proximity to other services, particularly when there is a wide array of specialized firms. Such firms obtain agglomeration economies when they locate close to others that are sellers of key inputs or are necessary for joint production of certain service offerings."[62] These "agglomeration economies" are found in the centres where architects open their branch offices, not just in the obvious locations such as New York, London and Tokyo, but also in cities such as Abu Dhabi, Shanghai and Mumbai. This agglomeration of migrant businessmen, traders and professionals create their own supra-national community. Sassen notes their effect on urban life: "The high-level professional workforce in global cities is characterised by work and lifestyles that distinguish it from early forms of a small elite of urban rich or the broader middle class. Their numbers are large enough in many of these cities and their preference for urban living is high enough that they have, as a stratum, re-inscribed a good part of the urban landscape."[63]

The existence of what Sassen calls a "transnational elite" has been noticed by a number of sociologists and commentators. They are called by different names, and are given slightly different profiles, but the existence of such a distinct group is widely acknowledged. The Spanish sociologist Manuel Castells calls them "managerial elites"; the sociologist of international law Yves Dezalay refers to them as "global functionaries" or "international elites"; the theological sociologist James Hunter calls them "parochial cosmopolitans"; the urban studies theorist Richard Florida has coined the term "creative class"; and the architectural theorist Keller Easterling uses the term "orgmen." The sociologist Mike Featherstone, in recognition of their group identity, calls them a "third culture." Featherstone also cautions that only 1.5 per cent of the entire global labour force works outside its own country, making this elite only a tiny proportion of even this small group (which highlights their disproportionate power).[64] Recognising their growing social and economic significance, in the last fifteen years some sociologists have made a particular study of the group.

Peter L. Berger, drawing on the work of Benjamin Barber, Samuel Huntingdon, James Hunter and David Martin, has divided globalising groups into four cultures: *Davos culture*, or international business culture (named after the annual World Economic Summit in Davos); *Faculty Club culture*, or the culture of academics, foundations, non-governmental organisations (NGOs) and multinational agencies; *McWorld culture*, or the international purveyors of (largely western) popular culture; and *Evangelical Protestantism*, a powerful, expanding but often ignored instrument in the spread of American culture.[65] He does not specifically locate architecture or other professions in these categories although *Davos culture*, "the culture of the elite and ... of those aspiring to join the elite," is as close as his short paper will allow.

The British sociologist Leslie Sklair has, however, made an exhaustive study not only of this group, which he calls the "Transnational Capitalist Class," or TCC, but also of the position of architects within it. Sklair too has identified four globalising cultures or, as he calls them, "fractions":

(1) owners and controllers of TNCs (transnational corporations) and their local affiliates
(2) globalising bureaucrats and politicians
(3) globalising professionals
(4) consumerist elites (merchants and media).[66]

He identifies four ways in which "the TCC is transnational (or globalising):"

(a) The economic interests of its members are increasingly globally linked rather than exclusively local and national in origin
(b) The TCC seeks to exert economic control in the workplace, political control in domestic, international and global politics, and culture-ideology control in every-day life through specific forms of global competitive and consumerist rhetoric and practice
(c) Finally, members of the TCC seek to project images of themselves as citizens of the world as well as of their places and/or countries of birth
(d) Members of the TCC tend to share similar life-styles, particularly patterns of higher education, and consumption of luxury goods and services.[67]

It is very clear that architects would fit into his third fraction of "globalising professions." Sklair has, however, undertaken a study of the "Transnational Capitalist Class and the Contemporary Architecture in Globalizing Cities"[68] and, rather than limit himself to his fraction of globalising professionals (point 3 above), Sklair has found a place in each of his fractions for the architects.

His first group, the owners of TNCs (point 1 above), are the "corporate fraction," and he allocates two kinds of architectural firm to this group: "strong-delivery firms," of which he lists the top thirty fee earners (twenty-two of which are from the United States); and "strong ideas firms," which he categorises as the designers of iconic buildings and the winners of professional awards.

The globalising bureaucrats and professionals (point 2 above) that commission architects are the "state fraction," and he divides these into two groups: "globalizing states' bureaucrats and politicians and/or their nominees in official agencies," and "interstate and transnational bureaucrats and politicians" such as UNESCO officials.

Sklair's third and most obvious category, globalising professionals (point 3 above), seems to mop up the rest of the architectural profession. He describes these as a "mixed bunch," and includes owners of major architectural firms (presumably excluding those he has already listed in his "corporate fraction"), architectural educators, architectural historians and "designers in general." For Sklair, "what unites them all is their globalising agenda within, more or less, the confines of capitalist globalisation."

Finally, in his "consumerist fraction," he includes "those who use their control of and/or access to the commercial sector and the media to promote the idea of architecture as a transnational practice in the realm of culture-ideology." Sklair links this to the central interest of his paper in iconic buildings. His paper seems to imply that, for architects, globalisation is a primary consideration. Numerically, however, by far the largest sector of architectural practice everywhere is small-scale and local. His reference to the media and its promotion of transnational practice is, however, important (although he does not make this point) as it is this media that promotes global practices and their high-status international projects as a standard to which ambitious architects should aspire.

Cities and the Global Elite

Sklair makes a specific observation that "Members of the TCC tend to share similar life-styles, particularly patterns of higher education, and consumption of luxury goods and services."[69] This phenomenon is also noted by other commentators.

Manuel Castells gives a complete catalogue of "an increasingly homogeneous lifestyle among the information elite that transcends the cultural borders of all societies." This includes:

> … jogging; the mandatory diet of grilled salmon and green salad, with udon and sashimi providing a Japanese functional equivalent; the "pale chamois" wall colour intended to create the cozy atmosphere of the inner space; the ubiquitous laptop computer, and Internet access; the combination of business suits and sportswear; the unisex dressing style, and so on. All these are symbols of an international culture whose identity is not linked to any specific society but to membership of the managerial circles of the informational economy across a global cultural spectrum.[70]

Richard Florida describes the urban environment that attracts the group he calls the "creative class": "they want to work in progressive environments, frequent upscale shops and cafes, enjoy museums and fine arts and outdoor activities, send their children to superior schools, and run into people, at all these places, from other advanced research labs and cutting-edge companies in their neighborhood."[71]

Sklair's Transnational Capitalist Class "seek to project images of themselves as citizens of the world," and their international mobility is one of their defining characteristics. The Hungarian philosopher Agnes Heller described the lifestyle of an imaginary member of this mobile elite in 1995: "Let's accompany her on her constant trips from Singapore to Hong Kong, London, Stockholm, New Hampshire, Tokyo, Prague and so on. She stays in the same Hilton hotel, eats the same tuna sandwich for lunch, or, if she wishes, eats Chinese food in Paris and French food in Hong Kong. She uses the same type of fax, and telephones, and computers, watches the same films, and discusses the same kind of problems with the same kind of people."[72]

A similar lifestyle is reported by the principals of international architectural practices. Norman Foster, in a telephone interview with the journalist Martin Spring in 2007, says: "I've just come from Madrid; it will be Milan tomorrow, Beijing on Thursday and Friday

and then St Petersburg. I thrive on all this travel: I love it."[73] *Index*
magazine, trying to interview Rem Koolhaas, notes that:

> He might be in Los Angeles planning the new Universal Studios
> Headquarters; in China, Rome, or Lagos, Nigeria, conducting
> research with his students from the Harvard Graduate School of
> Design; in Basel, fine-tuning Ian Schrager's upcoming New York
> hotel with Herzog & de Meuron; in Seattle collaborating with
> Microsoft on the new public library; in New York, San Francisco, or
> Milan meeting with Prada; in Las Vegas with the Guggenheim; or,
> more likely than not, on an airplane.

Koolhaas tells the journalist Jennifer Sigler with pride, "Do you
know that in the past week I've been swimming in Lagos, in Milan, in
Switzerland, in Rotterdam, in London, in L.A., and in Las Vegas?"[74]

In 1994, the anthropologist Jonathan Friedman identified this
international elite as a distinct cultural group with shared properties
and a common outlook.[75] Norman Foster talks about his own office
in these terms: "Today in our London studio you can hear perhaps 35
languages spoken. It is so cosmopolitan that I sometimes joke that it
is another country."[76] A South African executive describes how this
has affected the sense of identity of his generation: "The
multinational company is replacing the country as a concept of what
"home" is. [Young] people in my field ... are more company citizens
than they are South Africans, English, Americans, Australians or
whatever ... Citizenship of a multinational for them is much more
important than national citizenship—it gives them more sense of security and identity, more material reward and less pain ... In the
modern age ... there is much less reason to identify with a particular
country, especially in IT, finance and marketing."[77] Mike Featherstone
sees in this outlook a loss of identity with particular or local places:
"These are the groups which develop cosmopolitan dispositions and
have weaker attachment to localities. They value mobility, creativity,
syncretism, change and innovation."[78]

  The economic significance of the international elite as key
workers in the new global economy makes them a target group for

cities wishing to attract the business activity which they represent. As Ian Angell, leading commentator on the impact of information systems, says, "knowledge workers are the real generators of wealth. The income of these owners of intellectual and financial wealth will increase substantially, and they will be made welcome anywhere in the world."[79] John Griffith-Jones, chairman of the international accountants KPMG, in a report to the mayor on maintaining London as a global financial centre, said the city needs to be "like a hotel— you have got to want to stay in it."[80]

One outcome of making cities attractive to the international elite is "gentrification," with the elite as "gentrifiers." Juliet Carpenter and Loretta Lees describe the phenomenon:

> Gentrifiers strive to be distinctive within their own cultural context, and to mark themselves out from others, but internationally they also adhere to a certain conformity, as the symbols used can be read and identified by similar social groups cross-nationally ... Gentrification is thus one expression of the globalization of culture in a Postmodern world, an example of how a process that ostensibly aims to express difference results in a measure of global conformity and a lack of distinctiveness.[81]

While gentrification usually involves the upgrading and, as described by Carpenter and Lees, homogenising of existing often run-down urban districts, Saskia Sassen describes the rest of the urban infrastructure that is required for, what she calls, "the hyperspace of global business" as "state-of-the-art office buildings, residential districts, airports, and hotels."[82]

The consequences are described by an American executive: "I had a two hour flight. I got out of the airport, into a taxi, went into a glass office building, had a meeting and went to lunch at some fancy restaurant within the same building, had a little bit more of a meeting, got out, got into the cab, went back to the airport. I could've been anywhere in the world, really." [83] The global economy and the requirements of the global elite have had a major physical impact on the cities around the world that try to capitalise on the considerable financial benefits of becoming recognised as a "global city."

Global elites and global cities are a product of the economy of the New Global Era. The impact of this economy on the nations in which these cities are located and, indeed, on the other nations which would, as the newspaper *The Economist* said in 2007, "kill for a thriving financial sector that produced highly paid jobs and juicy tax revenues,"[84] has been far-reaching. The status of the nation-state itself and the major cities within it has been transformed, and with that economic and political transformation has come a physical transformation. As Saskia Sassen tells us, "in order to understand the pronounced social and economic changes in major cities today, we need to examine certain fundamental aspects of the new world economy."[85]

References

1. Joseph E Stiglitz. *Globalization and Its Discontents*. London: Penguin, 2002, 133.
2. Jordi Borja & Manuel Castells. *Local and Global, Management of Cities in the Information Age*. London: Earthscan, 1997, 9.
3. Nayan Chanda. *Bound Together: How Traders, Preachers, Adventurers and Warriors Shaped Globalization*. New Haven: Yale University Press, 2007, 254.
4. Martin Wolf. *Why Globalization Works*. New Haven: Yale University Press, 2005, 14–15.
5. Alain Touraine. "The New Capitalist Society." In *Identity, Culture and Globalization*, edited by Eliezer Ben-Rafael. Leiden: Brill, 2002, 270.
6. Jagdish Bhagwati. *Defense of Globalization*. Oxford: Oxford University Press, 2004, 3-4.
7. Quoted by Jan Aart Scholte. "Global Trade and Finance." In *The Globalization of World Politics: An Introduction to International Relations*, edited by John Baylis & Steve Smith. Oxford: Oxford University Press, 2006 (2001), 600.
8. Wolf, op. cit., 14.

9. Peter L. Berger. 'The Cultural Dynamics of Globalisation." In *Many Globalizations: Cultural Diversity in the Contemporary World*, edited by Peter L. Berger & Samuel P Huntingdon. Oxford: Oxford University Press, 2002, 1.

10. Chanda, op. cit., 257–8.

11. Friedrich Schorlemmer. "Der Befund ist nicht alles," Contribution to a debate on Bindungsverlust und Zukunftsangst is der Risikogesellschaft, October 30, 1993, Halle, manuscript, 1.

12. Nelson Mandela. *Long Walk to Freedom* vol. 2. Abacus: London, 2003, 3, 75.

13. Richard Crockatt. "The End of the Cold War." In Baylis & Smith, op. cit., 127–8.

14. Pankaj Ghemawat. *World 3.0: Global Prosperity and How to Achieve It*. Boston, Massachusetts: Harvard Business Review Press, 2011.

15. Ulf Hannerz. "Scenarios for Peripheral Cultures." In *Culture, Globalisation and the World System: Contemporary Conditions for the Representation of Identity*, edited by A King. Minneapolis: University of Minnesota Press, 1997, 107.

16. Anthony McGrew. "Globalization and Global Politics." In Baylis & Smith, op. cit., 22–23.

17. Martin Albrow. *The Global Age*. Cambridge: Polity Press, 1996, 149.

18. Arjun Appadurai. *Modernity at Large: Cultural Dimensions of Globalisation*. Minneapolis: University of Minnesota Press, 1996, 17.

19. Roland Robertson. *Globalization: Social Theory and Global Culture*. London: Sage Publications, 1992, 8.

20. Ulrich Beck. *What is Globalisation?* Cambridge, Polity Press, 1997 (2002), 11–12.

21. Wolf, op. cit., 18.

22. Anthony Giddens. *The Consequences of Modernity*. Cambridge: Polity Press, 1991, 175–6.

23. Ibid., 2.

24. Ibid., 51.

25. Ibid., 176.

26. "I define postmodern as incredulity toward metanarratives." Jean-Francois Lyotard, *The Postmodern Condition: A Report on Knowledge* (1979). Minneapolis: University Of Minnesota Press, 1984, xxiv.

27. Jan Aart Scholte. *Globalisation: A Critical Introduction*. London: Palgrave Macmillan, 2005, 262–3.

28. Albrow, op. cit., 100.
29. Mike Featherstone. *Undoing Culture: Globalization, Postmodernism and Identity*. London: Sage Publications, 1995, 139.
30. Chanda, op. cit., 271.
31. Ronald Niezen. *A World Beyond Difference: Cultural Identity In the Age of Globalisation*. Oxford: Blackwell, 2004, 168–9.
32. John Kavanagh. "Washington Institute of Policy Research." In Graham Balls & Milly Jenkins, 'Too Much for Them, Not Enough for Us." *Independent on Sunday*, July 21, 1996.
33. Joseph E Stiglitz. *Globalization and Its Discontents*. London: Penguin, 2002, 248.
34. Ibid., 214–5.
35. Jeffrey S. Juris. "Networked Social Movements: Global Movements for Global Justice." In *The Network Society: A Cross-Cultural Perspective*, edited by Manuel Castells. Cheltenham: Edward Elgar Publishing, 2004, 341.
36. Niezen, op. cit., 74.
37. Stiglitz, op. cit.
38. Gerard Baker. "Welcome to 'the Great Moderation'." *The Times*, January 19, 2007.
39. http://millercenter.org/president/bush/essays/biography/5 (accessed October 2011).
40. Francis Fukayama. "The End of History?" *The National Interest*, Summer 1989, 4.
41. Naomi Klein. *No Logo*. London: Flamingo, 2000, 116–7.
42. Ibid.
43. Marjory Ruth Lister. "Globalisation and its Inequities." In Globalization and Identity, edited by Alan Carling. London: IB Tauris, 2006, 32.
44. Steven Lamy. "Contemporary Mainstream Approaches: Neo-Realism and Neo-Liberalism." In Baylis & Smith, op. cit., 221.
45. William Pfaff. *Barbarian Sentiments: How the American Century Ends*. New York: Hill and Wang, 1989, 5.
46. A Murray. "The American Century: Is it coming or going?" *The Wall Street Journal*, December 27, 1999, 1.
47. James Davison Hunter & Joshua Yates. "The World of American Globalisers." In *Many Globalizations: Cultural Diversity in the Contemporary World*, edited by Peter L. Berger & Samuel P Huntingdon. Oxford: Oxford University Press, 2002, 350.
48. Ibid., 344–5.

49. Keller Easterling. *Enduring Innocence: Global Architecture and its Masquerades.* Cambridge, MA: MIT Press, 2005, 88.
50. Nederveen Pieterse. "Globalisation as Hybridisation." *International Sociology* 9 (2) (1994): 15.
51. Donald McNeill. "The Global Architect: Firms, Fame and Urban Form." London: Routledge, 2009, 14–15.
52. Ibid.
53. Own research, 2008.
54. Dominic Rushe & Louise Armistead. "The Global Deal Machine." *The Sunday Times*, November 19, 2006, 3–5.
55. McNeill, op. cit. 28.
56. Ibid., 27.
57. Ibid., 27–8.
58. Personal interview with Peter Oborn, Deputy Chairman of Aedas, 2011.
59. Neil Leach. "Hyperhabitat Programming the World." Digital Cities, London Architectural Design 79 (4) July/August 2009, 89.
60. Aaron Seward. 'Making it Big', New York, *The Architects' Newspaper,* June 16, 2010
    http://archpaper.com/news/articles.asp?id=4637
61. Saskia Sassen. *The Global City.* Princeton, NJ: Princeton University Press, 2001, 332.
62. Ibid., 104.
63. Ibid., 244–5.
64. Mike Featherstone. "Postnational Flows, Identity Formation and Cultural Space." In *Identity, Culture and Globalization*, edited by Eliezer Ben-Rafael. Leiden, Brill, 2002, 504.
65. "Four Faces of Global Culture." *National Interest* 49 (1997), 23.
66. Leslie Sklair. "The Transnational Capitalist Class and the Discourse of Globalisation." Cambridge Review of International Affairs, www.theglobalsite.ac.uk, 2000, 2–3.
67. Ibid., 3–4.
68. Leslie Sklair. "The Transnational Capitalist Class and Contemporary Architecture in Globalizing Cities." *International Journal of Urban and Regional Research* 29 (3) (2005): 485–500.
69. Sklair, 2000, op. cit., 3–4.
70. Manuel Castells. *The Rise of the Network Society.* Oxford: Blackwell, 2000, 446–8.

71. Richard Florida. *Cities and the Creative Class*. London: Routledge, 2005, 151.
72. Agnes Heller. "Where are we at Home?" *Thesis Eleven* 41 (1995).
73. McNeill, op. cit., 35.
74. Interview with Rem Koolhaas, 2000. www.indexmagazine.com/interview/rem_koolhaas.shtmln (accessed October 2011).
75. Featherstone, in Ben-Rafael, op. cit., 510.
76. Norman Foster. *Rebuilding the Reichstag*. London: Weidendfeld and Nicholson, 2000, 17.
77. Ann Bernstein. "Can South Africa be more than an Offshoot of the West?" In Berger and Huntingdon, op. cit., 211.
78. Featherstone, in Ben-Rafael, op. cit., pp 497–8.
79. Ian Angell. "The Information Revolution and the Death of the Nation State." *Political Notes* 114. London: Libertarian Alliance, 1995, 2.
80. James Ashton. "On Top of the World." *Sunday Times*, November 11, 2009, 5.
81. Juliet Carpenter & Loretta Lees. "Gentrification in New York, London and Paris: And International Comparison." *International Journal of Urban and Regional Research* 19 (1995): 288.
82. Saskia Sassen. A Sociology of Globalisation. New York: Norton, 2007, 176.
83. Hunter & Yates, op. cit., 333–4.
84. "Magnets for Money." *The Economist*, September 15, 2007, 22.
85. Sassen, 2006, op. cit. 329.

A. Helmond City Library, Helmond, Netherlands; Bolles+Wilson; 2010. Reflexive Modernism: standard modernist architecture, modern by reflecting on the historic modernity of its antecedents.

B. Berlier Industrial Hotel, Paris; Dominique Perrault Architecture; 1990. Supermodernism: neutral modern architecture applied to different building functions

C. *View towards Guggenheim Museum, Bilbao, Spain, Frank Gehry, 1997. Iconic Architecture: extraordinary buildings as city marketing.*

D. *Suitcase House Hotel, Beijing, China; Edge Design Institute; 2002. Critical Regionalism: abstract modernist response to local identity.*

E. *Scottish Parliament, Edinburgh; Enric Miralles; 2004. Metaphoric Architecture: imaginative use of metaphor to suggest local identity.*

F. *View of Pudong, Shanghai, China; redevelopment began 1993. The universal commercial city.*

G. *View of Dharavi, Mumbai, India. Asia's largest slum. The product of rapid urbanisation.*

H. View of Västra Hamnen district, Malmö, Sweden; begun 2001. Contextual Urbanism: sustainable urban design based on the traditional urban plan.

I. Borgo Città Nuova, Alessandria, Italy; Gabriele Tagliaventi; 1990. Traditional Architecture: literal expression of tradition and local culture.

PART III:

HOW GLOBALISATION MAKES THINGS THE SAME

The New Structure of Global Trade

The expanded free movement of capital established in the post-Cold War world of the early 1990s opened up an increasing number of national financial markets for international investment. To benefit the economies of these countries, international financial transactions needed to do more than just speculate on currency variations: there had to be an opportunity to invest in manufacturing and service industries. Additional finance would boost production, the standard of living and tax revenues. To attract such investment, states had to ensure that their industry and companies were structured in a manner that would give investors confidence that their investment was transparently managed without undue political interference and, not only could their capital be invested, but also withdrawn. Such transparency and capital movement would be very hard to achieve under the old communist command economies or other coercive governments with their opaque, state-owned, dictatorial and bureaucratic economic management and crony monopolies and so, with the liberalisation of financial markets, came pressure to conform to the Washington Consensus. The Washington Consensus had ten broad policy principles: low national debts, minimal state subsidy, low taxes, market-based interest rates, open-market exchange rates, an open import regime with no restrictive tariffs, an economy open to foreign investment, none or few nationalised industries, no competition-limiting regulation, and private property rights. It is clear that these principles are both political and economic and, while

they had existed in the North Atlantic economies since the Second
World War, their introduction in emerging economies would shift
the balance of trade and affect the political climate throughout the
world.

****

These trading and political conditions were well established in the
United States and Western Europe. It is, therefore, to be expected
that it would be the companies from these countries that would
benefit the most from seeing their system extended. Taking
advantage of an estimated doubling of available labour as China, India
and the Soviet Union and its satellites entered the market in the early
1990s (rising to what the International Monetary Fund estimated as a
quadrupling of available labour between 1982 and 2007),[1] North
Atlantic companies could expand production and lower costs
dramatically. The low wage levels of these new entrants, good
transport, the Washington-Consensus low-tariff regime and
electronic communications made transnational manufacture and
trading an extremely attractive proposition. As the chairman of the
American Apparel Manufacturers Association said in 1995, "It
doesn't make any difference where you are making the goods, so
long as you can get the right products at the right price at the right
time."[2] Not only could manufactured goods for the large North
Atlantic consumer economies be cheaper, but the same goods could
also be sold on a much expanded market in the emerging economies.
This was the great commercial benefit of a newly globalised world
economy.

The primary beneficiaries were the new or expanded transnational
corporations (TNCs). The United Nations Conference on Trade and
Development defines a TNC as "an enterprise that controls assets of
other entities in countries other than its home country." TNCs had
existed since the English East India Company was founded in 1600
and they have grown steadily since then. Their increase in the New
Global Era has, however, been remarkable (chart 4). In 1980 there

were 7,000 and by 2008 this had grown more than tenfold to 79,000. In 2008 they turned over eleven per cent of global gross domestic product (GDP) with US $13 trillion of annual sales and employed eighty-two million people. Of the largest hundred, seventy-two were from the United States, France, Germany, the UK and Japan—in that order—with twenty-one of these from the United States. In 2001 the output of the leading fifty corporations exceeded that of the GDP of 142 member nations of the United Nations. At the top, they include companies such as General Electric, BP, Walmart, Volkswagen and Nestlé. Small TNCs range from software designers to professional firms.

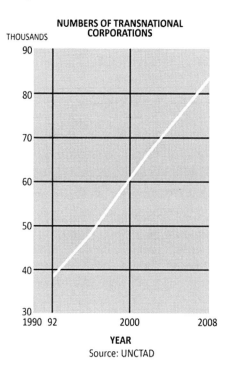

Chart 4. Numbers of Transnational Corporations 1992–2008

The growth and financial power of TNCs has been accompanied by the growth and strengthening of a parallel transnational governing system dedicated to the promotion of global free trade. The principal institutions are the IMF, OECD and the World Trade Organisation (WTO). Each of these institutions were based on the United States-dominated free trading system after the Second World War, and each expanded or adapted to reflect the changed international condition at the start of the New Global Era.

Joseph Stiglitz sets out the founding principles of the IMF in 1945. It was based on "the belief that there was a need for *collective action at the global level* for economic stability, just as the United Nations had been founded on the belief that there was a need for collective action at the global level for political stability" [emphasis in original]. It is controlled "through a complicated voting arrangement based largely on the economic power of the countries at the end of the Second World War. There have been some minor adjustments since, but the major developed countries run the show, with only one country, the United States, having effective veto."[3]

The OECD began as a transatlantic organisation to administer American aid to Europe (the Marshall Plan) in 1948, but in 1961 became a global institution to harmonise trade between democratic nations. Up until 2003 it had thirty-four members, but by 2007 it had engaged with a further ten countries including Brazil, Russia, India and China.

The WTO began life as the General Agreement on Tariffs and Trade (GATT) in 1947, but in 1995 became the World Trade Organisation. GATT originally had twenty-three member nations, almost all outside the Soviet bloc (China also dropped out after the communist revolution), but the WTO now has 153 member nations, with thirty-one observer nations. The only major economy non-member was Russia, which had been trying to join for seventeen years (it was blocked by disputes with former Soviet member-nations, but will enter in 2012). The environmental activist, Colin Hines, believes that "it is not unrealistic to regard the WTO as representing effective world government for the first time in human history."[4] From a quite different standpoint, the economist Martin Wolf agrees, observing that the WTO "system covers almost all trade," and notes that it "has increasingly come to affect what were thought of as purely domestic regulatory decisions."[5]

While the IMF, OECD and WTO are the principal controlling institutions of the world trading system, there are now another 250 Intergovernmental Organisations (IGOs), which range from Interpol and the International Organization for Standardization to the International Maritime Organisation and the Organisation of Islamic Cooperation. These organisations are managed by national governments and control and monitor the workings of the global political and economic system. Their decisions and actions affect us all but, as Stiglitz points out, IGOs "have ... escaped the kind of direct accountability that we expect of public institutions in modern democracies."[6]

Alongside the state-sponsored network of global control and regulation lie a huge number of Non-Governmental Organisations (NGOs), sometimes known as "civil society movements" (the term Non-Governmental Organisation was created by the United Nations in 1945). Many of these are local or national issue-based groups, but since the nineteenth century it has been recognised that many subjects for reform or advancement are international in nature. The first International Non-Governmental Organisation (INGO) was the British and Foreign Anti-Slavery Society, founded in 1839. Others followed such as the International Committee of the Red Cross in 1863, Oxfam in 1942 and Greenpeace International in 1979. It is hard to accurately trace the numbers of such organisations but there seem to have been about two hundred up to the turn of the twentieth century.[7] *The Economist* newspaper puts the number in 1990 at six thousand and estimates for the early part of this century vary between twenty thousand and forty thousand.[8] As Anthony McGrew, a British authority on international relations, says, "In recent decades ... transnational organizations ... advocacy networks ... and citizens' groups have come to play a significant role in mobilizing, organizing, and exercising political power across national boundaries. This has been facilitated by the speed and ease of modern global communications and a growing awareness of common interests between groups in different countries and regions of the world."[9]

The global reach of all these supra-governmental organisations and networks has been facilitated by major developments in Information and Communications Technologies (ICTs)—telephone, television, email and the internet—since the 1980s. Technological advances in ICTs have been an essential ingredient of the New Global Era (chart 5).

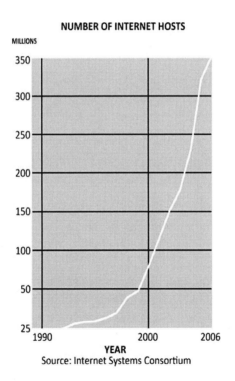

NUMBER OF INTERNET HOSTS

MILLIONS

YEAR

Source: Internet Systems Consortium

Chart 5. Numbers of Internet Hosts 1993–2006

Manuel Castells, scholar and theorist of the rise of communications technologies, traces their influence in the spread of TNCs:

> … when business engaged in its own restructuring process, it took advantage of the extraordinary range of technologies that were available from the new revolution, thus stepping up the process of technological change, and hugely expanding the range of its applications. Thus, the decision to go global in a big way … would not have been possible without computer networking, telecommunications, and information technology-based transportation systems. The network enterprise became the most productive and efficient form of doing business, replacing the Fordist organization of industrialism … the full networking of companies, the digitalization of manufacturing, the networked computerization of services and office work, could only take place, from the 1980s onwards, on the basis of the new information and communication technologies.[10]

Castells identifies "a new form of social organization" created by the "revolution in information and communication technologies … *the network society*" [my emphasis]. He is quite clear that "digital networks … know no boundaries in their capacity to reconfigure themselves. So, a social structure whose infrastructure is based on digital networks is by definition global. Thus, the network society is a global society."[11] He also identifies a new spatial arrangement created by the interconnection between organisations established by ICTs as "the space of flows." "Flows" are information exchanges and interactions through electronic media between individuals and organisations remote from one another. "The space of flows" is "the material form of support of dominant processes and functions in the informational society." Castells identifies three layers of this space: the exchanges—the electronic devices themselves; the nodes and hubs; and the organization of the flows by "managerial elites."[12]

The use of ICTs in IGOs has followed a parallel path to that of the TNCs, but the more radical sector of INGOs has made the most innovative use of communication technology. Internet connection and networking sites can bring together interest groups from different countries with relative ease. The social anthropologist, Jeffrey Juris describes the impact of these new networks:

> Whereas directly democratic forms of participation have historically been tied to local contexts, new networking technologies and practices are facilitating innovative experiments with grassroots democracy coordinated at local, regional, and global scales. Among the more radical global justice activists, networks represent much more than technology and organizational form; they also provide new cultural models for radically reconstituting politics and society more generally. In this sense, grassroots, network-based movements can be viewed as democratic laboratories, generating the political norms and forms most appropriate for the information age.[13]

Tony Juniper of Friends of the Earth calls the internet "the most potent weapon in the toolbox of resistance. ... the Net is more than an organizing tool—it has become an organizing model, a blueprint for decentralized but cooperative decision making. It facilitates the process of information sharing to such a degree that many groups can work in concert with one another without the need to achieve monolithic consensus (which is often impossible, anyway, given the nature of activist organizations)."[14] The use of ICTs means that interest, identity and conviction groups are no longer limited to geographic proximity. Global networks can be created with ease and their influence can range from political action to protest against the effects of globalisation. It is an irony that the primary technological instrument of globalisation can be used to resist the interests of the primary drivers of globalisation.

A Transformed Political Landscape and the Global City

The New Global Era has transformed the political landscape. In 1648, the Treaties of Westphalia defined the nation state as politically autonomous, in control of its laws, citizens and economy, and free to exercise military power against other nation states. The only institutional challenge to this power was the creation of the United Nations and, in particular, the rights given to the individual over the state in which they resided by the Universal Declaration of Human rights in 1948. The United Nations is, however, an organisation of nations, and the legal powers of one major nation over another are in practice limited. The principal challenges to the status of the nation state came not from the planned creation of international institutions, but from a combination of global economic and technological developments. In the nineteenth century nation states had expanded and consolidated to secure the advantages of large economies and powerful military establishments; at the end of the twentieth century, these two pillars of the state collapsed.

The advantages of the free movement of capital and the corresponding liberalisation of trade have drawn governments into a collective surrender of control over national economies. The consequences are explained by Peter Willets, an expert in global governance:

> It is no longer possible to regard each country as having its own separate economy. Two of the most fundamental attributes of sovereignty, control over the currency and control over foreign trade, have been substantially diminished ... When goods move physically across frontiers, it is usually seen as being trade between the relevant countries, but it may also be intra-firm trade. As the logic of intra-firm trade is quite different from intercountry trade, governments cannot have clear expectations of the effects of their financial and fiscal policies on TNCs.[15]

Nuclear proliferation and the costs of the arms race have negated any potential benefit from warfare between economic equals. Since the Second World War, state-sponsored combat has been largely limited to the satellite states of the principal political blocs, or "police" campaigns by major powers against what they claim to be rogue or failed states. The increasing sophistication of armaments and global specialisation in manufacture has also compromised the autonomy of national defence industries. This is explained by David Held, Anthony McGrew, David Goldblatt & Jonathan Perraton, in *Global Transformations: Politics, Economics and Culture*: "In order to sustain a cost-effective military capability the national DIB [defence industrial base] has to be progressively transnationalised, so compromising the very notion of a national DIB and national defence."[16] In 1992, even the "most vaunted weapons" of the greatest industrial and military power, the United States, "literally could not be built without commercially developed Japanese machine tools."[17]

Even control over citizens has been eroded by the formation of transnational networks facilitated by ICTs. The political impact of global networks is outlined by Jonathan Aronson, a specialist in international communications:

> Global networks empowered and vastly increased the numbers of NGOs and even individuals on the international stage. NGOs now create, track, and disseminate information and organize people and groups sympathetic to their goals to pursue specific policy outcomes in areas such as human rights advocacy, environmental protection, and women's rights ... global networks erode the monopoly of information in the hands of governments, democratizing access to breaking information. Firms, journalists, and NGOs often have better information than governments ... global networks provide transparency to everybody, making it difficult for countries unilaterally to take national policy decisions when the problems are global.[18]

The nation state remains, nonetheless, the only source of democratic legitimacy and nation states continue to affect the direction of international affairs through IGOs but, as Held et al. point out: "the locus of effective political power can no longer be assumed to be national governments—effective power is shared, bartered and struggled over by diverse forces and agencies at national, regional and global levels. In other words, we must recognize that political power is being repositioned, recontextualized and, to a degree, transformed by the growing importance of other less territorially based power systems."[19] The sociologist Daniel Bell was right when he wrote in *The Washington Post* in 1988, just before the key events of the New Global Era, that "the nation state is becoming too small for the big problems of life and too big for the small problems of life."[20]

****

Commentators such as Zygmunt Bauman see this new balance of power as a threat to the role of the nation state as the protector of the interests of its citizens: "For their liberty of movement and for unconstrained freedom to pursue their ends, global finance, trade and the information industry depend on the political fragmentation —the *morcellement*—of the world scene. They have all, one may say, developed vested interests in 'weak states'—that is, in such states as are weak but nevertheless remain states."[21] The legendary Mexican revolutionary Zapatista, Subcommandante Marcos, saw it in even more stark terms in 1997:

> In the cabaret of globalisation, the state goes through a striptease and by the end of the performance it is left with the bare necessities only; its powers of repression. With its material basis destroyed, its sovereignty and independence annulled, its political class effaced, the nation-state becomes a simple security service for the mega-companies … The new masters of the world have no need to govern directly. National governments are charged with the task of administering affairs on their behalf.[22]

The growing financial power of the TNCs and the reduced status of the nation state have undoubtedly altered the relationship between the interests of the state and the interests of the business community. As the wealth, independence and mobility of the TNCs grew, the presence and financial activity of these companies could be advantageous to the economies of nation states. If a country wants TNCs to trade within their borders it has to be an attractive location. Political scientist Colin Crouch outlines the problem in the Fabian

Society's publication, *Coping with Post Democracy*: "Large corporations have frequently outgrown the governance capacity of individual nation states. If they do not like the regulatory or fiscal regime in one country, they threaten to move to another, and increasingly states compete in their willingness to offer favourable conditions as they need the investment."[23] When TNCs assess different locations to find the most advantageous tax regime for their activities it is called "regulatory arbitrage." The choice of location is, however, more than purely economic. In 1956, in a classic paper "A Pure Theory of Local Expenditures," the economist and geographer Charles Tiebout, analysed a choice of location by a theoretically fully mobile population according to levels of taxation and the provision of public goods. Tiebout's paper used migration to suburban districts in the USA as his model, and concluded that choice was as much to do with the quality of the place as financial advantage.[24] Martin Wolf explains the implications of his conclusions for genuinely fully mobile global corporations.

> Owners of mobile factors of production would move to the jurisdiction that gives them the combination of taxes and services they prefer. There is no reason to suppose that this location would be the one with the lowest taxes. Even capital, the most mobile of all factors of production, will flee from a jurisdiction so under-taxed that it fails to provide decent and reliable justice. Capital will also be attracted by a jurisdiction with a highly educated labour force or any other complementary asset which raises its prospective return. Self-evidently, the attraction of location-specific public goods will be still greater for workers, who will want to live in places that are safe, have pleasant amenities, offer good public services and enjoy high overall incomes. The question is not where the tax is lowest, but rather where the welfare derived from the bundle of local amenities, income-earning opportunities and taxes is the highest.[25]

Some of these location-specific public goods were listed by *The Economist* newspaper in 2007: "plenty of skilled people, ready access to capital, good infrastructure ... and low levels of corruption." To attract the combination of the local spending power of global corporations and whatever taxation can be gleaned from their multinational activities, countries have to provide a beneficial financial climate together with a living and working environment suitable for the executives who make the choices. *Trader* magazine, a publication aimed at hedge-fund managers and currency traders, ranked world cities according to a series of criteria that included trading infrastructure, taxation, nightlife and recreation facilities. As *The Economist* said: "quality of life is important to highly paid financiers, and successful centres ... are changing constantly to keep delivering what it takes."[26]

The Universal Trading City

Electronic communication should allow a global company headquarters to locate anywhere in a host country, but in practice a number of factors draw them to major city centres. Some of these are the same "agglomeration economies" that draw in the Transnational Capitalist Class or "managerial elites" discussed above. To these must be added regulatory arbitrage and the provision of a living and working environment attractive to key decision-making executives. There can be no doubt of the value to national economies gained from hosting global trading centres. The twenty-three largest cities generate, on average, a GDP eighty per cent higher than the economies of their host countries. The 380 top cities generated fifty per cent of global GDP in 2007.[27] This gives a considerably enhanced status and political power to major cities. Castells confirms that "the reinvention of the city-state is a salient characteristic of this new age of globalization, as it was related to the rise of a trading, international economy at the origin of the modern age."[28] Attracting the Transnational Capitalist Class—and so the transnational corporations that they command—to major cities is now an important part of the economic strategies of nation states and city

Figure 26. View of Hong Kong.

The glass-walled office block, signature of the global trading city.

governments. This has made the design of cities into a strategic instrument of the global economy.

For a city to function as a global centre it must have not only a good workforce, a good transport infrastructure and a favourable fiscal climate, it must also have the right urban ingredients. As with the regulatory system for transnational trade, as Jan Aart Scholte tells us, "the trimmings" will have "a decidedly Western character, with office blocks, business suits and briefcases."[29] Jordi Borja and Manuel Castells, in their book *Local and Global: Management of Cities in the Information Age*, go into more detail: "The setting up of an urban node for advanced services becomes a prerequisite, and it is invariably organized around an international airport, a satellite-telecommunications system, luxury hotels with appropriate security systems, English-language secretarial support, financial and consultancy firms familiar with the region, local and regional government offices capable of providing information and infrastructure to back up international investors and a local labour market having personnel skilled in advanced services and technological infrastructure."[30] The supply of the buildings that support global business has transformed the centres of cities around the world. The new buildings are those that service international and national corporate users and the consumer economy that they promote: office blocks, international hotels, airports and shopping malls.

It has been observed for some time that this kind of new building was giving the cities that house them a uniform appearance. In 1974, the Egyptian architect Hassan Fathy complained that he found "from Baghdad to Benghazi, look-alike blocks of dreary high-rise buildings rose along drab, dusty boulevards."[31] Two years later, at a United Nations Educational, Scientific and Cultural Organization (UNESCO) meeting in Nairobi, in a document entitled, "Recommendations Concerning the Safeguarding and Contemporary Role of Historic Areas," concern was expressed that "at a time when there is a danger that a growing universality of building techniques … architectural forms may create a uniform environment throughout the world."[32] It was partly in response to this sentiment that postmodernist architecture in the 1970s and 1980s had taken on a specifically historical and place-related appearance. The 1990 to 1992 recession that heralded the start of the New Global Era had, however, created a climate of austerity that ran against the more extravagant aspects of Postmodernism and their association with the Reagan-Thatcher economic boom.

Reflexive Modernism

A large portion of the architectural profession had never been happy with the overtly historical aspects of Postmodernism. By the 1980s, all but the oldest architects in the developed world had been trained in architectural schools that taught that, as the British architect Amys Connell had argued in 1934, Modernism is the "inevitable progress of modern civilization."[33] Although many followed the postmodernist fashion of the time, excusing their turn to historical references as ironic, highly-respected architects such as Richard Rogers or I. M. Pei were immovable in their adherence to Modernism. Major figures, such as the German philosopher Theodor Adorno, also took against Postmodernism, declaring in his posthumously published and long-in-the-preparation *Aesthetic Theory* that architecture, "if out of disgust with functional forms and their inherent conformism … wanted to give rein to fantasy, it would fall immediately into kitsch."[34] The prominent American architectural critic, Martin Filler, summed up the feelings of many architects in 1990:

> Emboldened by the laissez-faire atmosphere created by Reaganomics and the most spectacular stock market prosperity since the twenties—as well as a pervasive endorsement of the flagrant display of wealth exhibited in all aspects of consumer behaviour—the major corporate clients of the big architectural firms called for and responded to designs in which assertive forms and showy materials mimicked a hollow grandiosity and unbridled crassness reminiscent of the Gilded Age.[35]

With all the passion of repentant sinners, the turn against Postmodernism was so strong amongst architects that, for the next twenty years, any direct reference to historical architecture on a new building, unless it was abstracted beyond immediate recognition, would be roundly condemned.

Just at the moment when cities across the world entered into a building boom to service and attract the geographically expanding global corporate business sector, architecture had turned to an aesthetic of unembellished simplicity. In the manner of all reactions, the new direction in architecture was defined as much by what it was as by what it sought to replace. If Postmodernism referred to pre-modernist history, the new architecture only drew on modernist history; if Postmodernism was eclectic, the new architecture was simple and rational; if Postmodernism was extravagant and exuberant, the new architecture was spare and calm. The new direction in architecture was widely recognised and described as, variously: Minimalist, High Modern, Soft Modern or Supermodern. Hans Ibelings produced the most comprehensive study of this new style in his 1998 book, *Supermodernism: Architecture in the Age of Globalisation*. Ibelings describes the type:

> Since the early 1990s, more and more buildings have been built worldwide whose sole involvement with their context consists of toeing the building line. For this architecture the surroundings constitute neither legitimation nor inspiration for these are derived from what goes on inside the building, from the programme. This autonomy is in many cases reinforced by the fact that the building has an inscrutable exterior that betrays nothing of what happens inside.
>
> In this respect, too, supermodern architecture is essentially different from the Postmodern variety whose practitioners always tried to find some way of expressing the building's purpose, either by following the conventions of building typology or by adding symbolic pointers. In supermodern architecture this rarely if ever happens. In many instances these buildings look as if they might house just about anything: an office or a school, a bank or a research centre, a hotel or apartments, a shopping mall or an airport terminal.[36]

Ibelings also observed that "the changed attitude towards Modernism. The almost contemptuous aversion to Modernism displayed by postmodernist and deconstructivist architects has given way to a more nuanced view. And although this has not resulted in a genuine revaluation of the architecture that dominated the Western world in the 1950s and 60s, it has led to new interest in the modernist aesthetic and to a revival of the idea that the processes of modernisation are the driving force behind architectural and urbanist innovation."[37]

A desire to return to the old certainties of early Modernism is confirmed by the Japanese architect Tadao Ando, winner of the Pritzker Prize for Architecture in 1995, who wrote in 1991: "The most promising path open to contemporary architecture is that of development through and beyond Modernism. This means replacing the mechanical, lethargic, and mediocre methods to which Modernism has succumbed with the kind of abstract, meditative vitality that marked its beginnings."[38] Bob Allies, a respected British architect, started his career as a postmodernist but, like many others in the late 1980s, turned back to Modernism. Writing in 2006, Allies now sees Postmodernism as an "aberration" and believes that "the social, technical and aesthetic agenda of Modernism continues to provoke and sustain architectural practice."[39] The architect Patrik Schumaker notes the trend in 2010: "The mainstream has, in fact, returned to a sort of pragmatic Modernism with a slightly enriched palette; a form of eclecticism mixing and matching elements from all Modernism's subsidiary styles."[40]

As the British architectural critic Owen Hatherley observes: "Modernism might have resurged, but ... it isn't quite the same Modernism. This is a Modernism that is based on the distance between itself and the everyday. While the Modern design of the 1920s ... was immersed in the quotidian, their equivalents today are the designers of corporate skyscrapers, museums and art galleries."[41] Hatherley, a socialist, bemoans the abandonment of the left-wing agenda in the Modernism he supports, but this train had left the station a long time ago. Modernism had been transformed from its reformist mid-European origins to serve corporate business in the United States in the mid-twentieth century. What was now emerging was the next step in the development of Modernism.

Modernist symbolism was now attached to corporate identity and, in this form, came to represent membership of a successful capitalist system among the new entrants to the global free market, many of them former socialist nations. While the aesthetic vocabulary of glass, geometric composition and lack of decoration was inherited from the 1930s and 1960s, the world had changed. Unlike early Modernism, which was genuinely revolutionary, or post-Second World War Modernism, which was forging a new orthodoxy, the Modernism of the late twentieth and early twenty-first century had become a culturally embedded establishment in the

North Atlantic countries. It was what the sociologists Ulrich Beck, Anthony Giddens and Scott Lash had identified in the wider modern condition in the 1990s, a modernity that had to deal with the achievement of its past objectives and confront the changing circumstances that could undermine them.

Much as the liberal social cohesion sought by early modernisers was breaking down with consumerism and individualism, so the communitarian idealism of early modernist architects was breaking down as architecture served speculative commercial development. This new kind of modernity was given the name "reflexive" by Beck, Giddens and Lash.[42] This apparent revival of Modernism and, what the critic Chris Abel called in 1986, "the crucial battle for the real Modern Movement,"[43] is the architectural manifestation of the same phenomenon—Reflexive Modernism. In 1990, the abandonment of the old certainties of Modernism is eloquently described by Dominique Perrault through his Hotel Industriel in the anonymous outskirts of Paris: "Nothing, less than nothing, no anchorage, no hold, no hook, no soothing theories about the city with-parks-and-gardens but a confrontation with 'our world', that one, the true, the so-called 'hard' world, the world people claim not to want."[44]

When the economy recovered in the early 1990s, Postmodernism had been discarded, and it was this Reflexive Modernism that was the established architectural type of the economies that dominated the newly liberalised global free market. When the emerging nations sought to align themselves with the established capitalist nations, the available symbols were the business suit, the English language and the glass-walled office block—the established commercial type of Reflexive Modernism.

The social idealism of early Modernism may have been fatally compromised but its internationalism survived. The pioneering German modernist, Erich Mendelsohn, had declared in 1919 that the "new architecture" would be part of a new "supra-nationalism" that "embraces national demarcations as a precondition; it is free humanity that alone can re-establish an all-embracing culture."[45] These sentiments were repeated in 1982 by the American philosopher

Figure 27.   Indian Institute of Management, Ahmedabad, India; HCP Design; 2008.

International Reflexive Modernism, modernity by reference to past modernity.

Figure 28.   Museum of Fine Arts,Leipzig; Karl Hufnagel, Peter Pütz and Michael Rafaelian; 2004.

Supermodernism, an anonymous universal modernist style suitable for all building types.

Marshall Berman: "Modern environments and experiences cut across all boundaries of geography and ethnicity, of class and nationality, of religion and ideology: in this sense, modernity can be said to unite all mankind."[46] A year later, the architectural critic Kenneth Frampton repeated the belief that Modernism or "the avant-garde is inseparable from the modernization of both society and architecture."[47] This message was taken up by the emerging economies seeking to modernise. The development of Pudong, the new district of Shanghai and a city of glass skyscrapers, was described by Jiang Zemin, Chinese President and former mayor of Shanghai, as "a microcosm of Shanghai's modernization and the symbol of Chinese reform and opening up"[48] (figure F).

The Symbolism of the Global City

As cities around the world tried to attract the trading benefits of the global economy, or present themselves as modern economic centres, it would seem logical to politicians and planners to remodel them to imitate cities that were already major business centres and home to transnational corporations. In the New Global Era these were almost exclusively North Atlantic cities, Tokyo or the then British colony of Hong Kong (handed back to China in 1997). In China, for example, as Charlie Qiuli Xue and Yingchun Li report, "now that Beijing, Shanghai, Guangzhou and other cities are determined to become 'international metropolises,' they must follow the lead of existing world cities such as London, New York and Tokyo."[49] Above all, much as the dominant economic centre was Wall Street, the iconic image was the cluster of skyscrapers of downtown Manhattan seen from the Hudson River. The magazine *Progressive Architecture* reported in 1995 on "a shift of historic proportions … and architecture is the premier symbol of that transformation … the Chinese, as well as many other Asians, tend to want buildings as tall as possible and in an ostentatiously Modern style as can be found."[50] Existing centres were transformed or new business districts created with clusters of tall

Figure 29. "Where the World Comes to Bank," Emirates Bank advertisement.

Figure 30. View of West Bay, Doha, Qatar. The creation of an anonymous international office environment to attract global business.

Figure 31. World Trade Center, Central Business District, Beijing. Global trading is symbolised by the creation of World Trade Centers as an explicit reference to downtown Manhattan.

The global financial market is represented by the universal global business district.

buildings. If, as in the West Bay area in Doha, Qatar, there were no takers for the new glass towers they were built anyway, as their construction was thought to be attraction enough for incoming TNCs (figure 30). In case the association was not sufficiently clear, groups of glass towers were identified as "World Trade Centers" (always spelt the American way), and these have sprung up in Mumbai, Chennai, Delhi, Hanoi, Beijing, Guangzhou, Moscow, Sao Paulo, Dubai and many other cities (figure 31). New World Trade Centers are under construction in Doha and Abu Dhabi. All are members of the World Trade Centers Association, which has the lost twin towers of Manhattan as its logo. The powerful symbolism of World Trade Center in New York, as the nexus of the global capitalist system, led both to its destruction in 2001 and the undiminished desire of cities around the world to attach themselves to its idea and imagery.

Architectural imitation did not stop at city centre clusters of high rise buildings. In India a series of technology campuses have been created in Chennai, Hyderabad and Thiruvananthapuram.[51] *The Economist* described the new "gleaming campus" of Infosys, "India's third-biggest information technology firm," in Bangalore with "a golf green and a Domino's Pizza as the staff canteen. You might as well be in Silicon Valley."[52] As N.R. Narayana Murthy, Chairman of Infosys, confirms, "Right now, when you come into our campus, you're leaving India behind ... We're living in a make-believe world."[53]

The combination of the turn to reflexive modernist architecture in North Atlantic countries and the adoption of North Atlantic architectural imagery by emerging economies created a global architectural homogeneity that seemed to satisfy the international ambitions of the early modernist pioneers. Ibelings sees his version of reflexive modernity, supermodernism, as "The new frame of reference [that] will no longer be dictated by the unique, the authentic or the specific, but by the universal."[54] Manuel Castells believes this neutrality is the mute herald of the new age:

> The architecture that seems most charged with meaning in societies shaped by the logic of the space of flows is what I call 'the architecture of nudity.' That is, the architecture whose forms are so neutral, so pure, so diaphanous, that they do not pretend to say anything. And by not saying anything they confront the experience with the solitude of the space of flows. Its message is the silence.[55]

The British sociologists, Gerard Delanty and Paul Jones, find that this anonymous architecture represents the "universalistic aspirations of the European modernity ... Instead of epic grandeur and pomposity, the new architectural discourses are of transparency, accessibility and, probably most importantly, a reflexive attitude approach to collective identity."[56] Greek urban theorist, Aspa Gospodini, sees this new Modernism (which she calls by one of its common synonyms, "innovative") as:

simultaneously expressing the specificity of place and the links with
the world beyond … this would facilitate the process of integration
of European cities into the new (global) urban system of Europe …
innovative design schemes, by creating new urban images and new
types of public space while simultaneously offering spatial
membership to all individuals and cultures of the society, may also
generate new forms of "locality."[57]

The Global Suburb

Cities do not consist entirely of city centres, new business districts or
retailing. On the contrary, housing represents by far the largest
volume of built form in any city. In Dubai, which has expanded
rapidly, specifically to attract global business, and where the
expatriates who service the economy constitute eighty-five per cent
of the population, it is not only business premises that must be built
to the standards of North Atlantic corporations: it has also been
necessary to construct an appropriate environment for the family life
of international executives (figure 32). The characteristic North
Atlantic type, a series of low-density, gated suburbs on a North
American pattern complete with supermarkets and residents' clubs,
have been built around the city for incoming executives with names
like "The Meadows," "West Garden" and "Emirate Hills," and have
been described as "the undisputed 'Beverley Hills' of Dubai."

The modern suburb was a nineteenth-century British invention
adopted enthusiastically by the USA in the twentieth century. In
Britain and North America in particular, lending institutions and
home-owning consumerism promoted a market-driven suburban
type, purchased by families and with designs tailored to public taste.
The commonality of the type and the popular taste of the product led
intellectuals and architects to deride suburban development from the
early twentieth century onwards; a phenomenon recorded in detail
by John Carey in his book *The Intellectuals and the Masses*.[58] In free
market democratic countries, however, suburbs remained very
popular, and rings of low-density private housing are now a

characteristic of all North Atlantic cities. As the urban historian
Robert Fishman observed in 1987, notwithstanding the disdain of the
architectural profession and urban elites, the suburban ideal had
"enough support from ordinary people in the real world to transform
the structure of the modern city."[59] The combination of space,
privacy and the social status of personal independence made the type
attractive, not only to itinerant North Atlantic executives, but also to
countries where economic growth created an aspiring middle class.

  Suburban villa developments are now a feature of almost all major
cities. Real estate agents in Beijing record 176 villa developments
under way, "built with nature as a backdrop ... most new villas are
based on a European style."[60] A development called "Grand Hills" has
"North American style villas with private gardens ... in a unique
peaceful and vast living environment." Beijing Eurovillage has
"European country style houses with inspiration [sic] of Beijing
quadrangle." Outside Bangalore in India, VGP Garden Homes has a
series of houses with names like "Hampton," "Wembley" and
"Glendale." "Located in the thick of IT action," the Concorde
Cuppertino development in Bangalore is an "ultra-modern villa
project spread across 12 acres with 182 luxury villas." South
American gated communities, *condominio fechados* in Brazil and *barrios
privados* in Argentina, provide secure suburban housing behind razor-
wire fencing. Outside Jakarta, the Kota Wisata development offers
housing and shopping facilities that would enable people to "go
around the world without [a] passport: Visits to beautiful Indonesia,
jewels of Paris, German masterpiece, romantic Italy, Japanese
heritage, spirit of America, splendour of China."[61] As the political
geographer Peter Taylor observes, "popular suburbia and modern
architecture have represented two very different paths to
modernity." Unlike most architectural and urban designers, he sees
the modern suburb not as a regrettable outcome of the consumer
economy and dependence on the motor car but as "a true monument
of the modern world, the modern equivalent to the great Gothic
cathedrals of the high middle ages in feudal Europe."[62]

Most suburban development is not designed by architects, or if it is, or if the definition of "architect" is less regulated in some countries than others, it is undertaken by architects who are far from the reflexive modernist mainstream. In these suburbs, properties are often sold freehold on the real estate market to individual families. Suburbs which rent or lease individual houses also compete on the open market for custom. The only interest for developers is to gain a competitive edge, and building design is one part of a package that may include security, landscaping, vetted residents, servicing and so on. In higher-value suburbs, lots are often sold freehold and either the developer offers a range of designs which can be "customised" or the purchaser can engage his own architect or designer. Free from the self-referential aesthetic politics of architects, if there is any indication of the design inclinations of the middle classes on a global scale, it will be found here. Some political systems exercise aesthetic control, often administered by the architectural establishment or their associates in the planning professions. This is common in northern Europe, but less common elsewhere. Even in northern Europe, the democratic system can make it hard for an aestheticized minority to impose their taste on an educated home-buying public, although in more regimented societies this does happen.

The physical quality of the product will depend on its scarcity. If the demand for private houses outstrips supply, the quality will be lower, as purchasers concentrate more on obtaining the product than the finer detail. The styles of individual houses are extremely varied, but are often divided into categories by real estate agents and developers to give purchasers a defined range of choices. The choices will reflect the aspirations of the purchasers, if not their aesthetic sophistication. There are a number of "contemporary" or "ultra-modern" designs, but the predominant types have a somewhat free interpretation of a traditional design from somewhere in world—but not necessarily from the location of the house. There are classical houses of an American type, pejoratively called "McMansions" by detractors in the United States; European styles, which are often similar to McMansions but with some specific place reference such as

Figure 32.   View of Dubai suburb.   Creating a North Atlantic family living environment in the desert for global executives.

Figure 33. Poster advertising a new suburb, Kerala, India.

Figure 34.   Suburban villa, Guangzhou, Canton, China. The suburban house is often an interpretation of traditional design, frequently of a North Atlantic type.

The North Atlantic suburban type has a worldwide appeal.

a double-pitched Mansard roof for a French style, or a stepped gable for a Dutch style; a local traditional style will have added details such as a locally distinctive roof design or porch. Many of the traditionally styled houses combine different stylistic elements and modern features. The stylistic eclecticism, if not the architectural irony, of Postmodernism survives throughout the world in these housing schemes and, indeed, in other buildings outside the North Atlantic home of Modernism. It is as if Postmodernism opened up a popular desire to combine modernity with tradition that could not be supressed by a change of heart in the architectural establishment.

Although the designs of the houses are themselves of interest, and it would require a survey of some depth to go beyond empirical observation, the global spread of the suburban type is consistent. The individual house in its individual lot, with similar houses in areas designed to create a semi-rural environment, and often with additional services or facilities, seems to be a universal combination. It will have variations, such as high perimeter walls in Middle Eastern countries or small lot size relative to house size in East Asian countries, but the North Atlantic suburban concept has become a very successful and widespread global type.

Deterritorialisation and the Non-Place

The almost universal combination of glass office towers in city centres, similar apartment towers and American-style suburbs on the periphery give a superficial impression of homogeneity to visitors from North Atlantic countries in particular, who are often disturbed and disappointed to find similarity where they expected to find difference. The Australian landscape urbanist, Catherin Bull, describes the condition as "the dominating trends towards technical standardization, spatial homogenization and off-site decision-making that provide the global context or 'frame', universal and modernizing."[63]

The homogenisation of cities is the subject of frequent comment. Ibelings sees this as a manifestation of Supermodernism:

> Cities and agglomerations around the world have undergone comparable developments and assumed similar shapes. Wherever one looks there seem to be high-rise downtowns, low-rise suburbs, urban peripheries with motorway cultures and business parks, and so on. And everywhere the accompanying architecture has assumed a certain expressionlessness. Nowhere is this trend clearer than in the Asian metropolises, in recent years the subject of numerous reports in professional publications which describe, with a mixture of astonishment and admiration, the feverish development activities in cities like Seoul and Shanghai.[64]

The urbanist and author, John Short, refers to the phenomenon in his 1989 book, *The Humane City*, as the international "blandscape."[65] The

American architect and journalist, Roger Lewis, goes into detail in *The Washington Post* in 2002:

> The experience of strolling through malls at Canary Wharf in London's Docklands, at Potsdamer Platz in Berlin and at Manege Square in Moscow is fundamentally the same.
>
> The global culture of design is supported by architects who study what other architects are creating, no matter where. With fabulous photographs in slick magazines and professional journals, trend-conscious designers can scan and span the globe, sharing high-style concepts rendered in stylish materials. Glass, aluminium, stainless steel, copper, titanium and natural stone are readily available. If they can't be acquired locally, they can be imported.
>
> Thus it's not unusual for a building in New York or Shanghai to be constructed with a sophisticated glass and metal curtain wall made in England or Germany and granite and marble imported from Spain or Zimbabwe. Once this would have been considered prohibitively expensive, but today shipping materials globally has become routine.[66]

The French anthropologist Marc Augé in his important 1995 book *Non-Places: Introduction to an Anthropology of Supermodernity* sets out his theory that "supermodernity produces non-places" and that "a world thus surrendered to solitary individuality, to the fleeting, the temporary and ephemeral, offers the anthropologist (and others) a new object."[67] Augé sees this new uniform condition as a particular characteristic of the modern globalized world and defines his word for the phenomenon, the "non-place":

> … non-places are the real measure of our time; one that could be quantified—with the aid of a few conversions between area, volume and distance—by totalling all the air, rail and motorway routes, the mobile cabins called "means of transport" (aircraft, trains and road vehicles), the airports and railway stations, hotel chains, leisure parks, large retail outlets, and finally the complex skein of cable and wireless networks that mobilize extraterrestrial space for the

purposes of a communication so peculiar that it often puts the individual in contact only with another image of himself.[68]

Augé sees the non-place as somewhere where the transnational "foreigner lost in a country he does not know (a 'passing stranger') can feel at home … in the anonymity of motorways, service stations, big stores or hotel chains."[69] The non-place is both the creation of a uniformity that takes away the unique identity of cities and a special kind of identity appropriate to organisations that belong nowhere in particular.

The American anthropologist, Michael Kearney, in an anthropological review of globalisation and transnationalism links the idea of the non-place to the wider anthropological concept of "deterritorialisation." He uses similar language to Augé: "Deterritoraliation has to do with the construction of 'hyperspaces,' i.e. environments such as airports, franchise restaurants, and production sites that, detached from any local reference, have monotonous universal qualities."[70] In broader anthropological usage, deterritorialisation is "the severance of social, political, or cultural practices from their native places and populations." The term has its origins in the description of the isolation of activities for their removal to another context and was set out in the 1972 book, *Anti-Oedipus*, by the philosopher Gilles Deleuze and the psychotherapist Félix Guattari.[71] Taken on by anthropologists, the expression has been particularised to "a central feature of globalization," and is described by the Spanish social anthropologist Gil-Manuel Hernàndez as "a general cultural condition which derives from the dissemination of global modernity, whose existential implication affects more people than ever, deeply transforming their everyday lives." Hernàndez goes on to describe that effect: "In an intensely deterritorialized context, the globalization of everyday experiences makes it ever more difficult to maintain a stable sense of local cultural identity, including national identity, as our daily life entwines itself more and more with influences and experiences of remote origin."[72]

Figure 35. View of the City of London. Uniform development of city centres creates anonymous urban space.

Figure 36. International Terminal, Dubai airport. Airports, shopping malls and hotels create a worldwide uniform and neutral environment, occasionally decorated with superficial references to their location.

Modernist design and common functions create the same neutral "non-place" around the world.

In reality, most established cities will be complex. Cities will include non-places in their new central business districts, transport hubs and suburbs, alongside relatively unaffected survivors of the pre-global period. In most countries outside the North Atlantic regions, there will be extensive slums, *favelas* or *gandi basti*, described by the American social commentator, urban theorist and activist, Mike Davis, as "the gritty antipodes to the generic fantasyscapes and residential theme parks."[73] Historic areas will often be gentrified with, as the social-anthropologist Julia Nevarez describes them:

> distinctive architectural styles in the patterns of improvement of housing stock and standards of aesthetics. Maintenance, aesthetics, and safety in public spaces even though customized to fit specific locales, follow a general model whereby vernacular, spectacular, and global brands are combined with the particularities of place in urban landscapes. The urban development initiatives of gentrifying areas are closely linked to general economic and cultural patterns of globalization.[74]

Augé sees even this as a manifestation of non-place, as "supermodernity … makes the old (history) into a specific spectacle, as it does with all exoticism and all local particularity."[75]

The more recent and the larger the urban expansion, the greater will be the tendency to uniformity. Nowhere is this more apparent than in Dubai, a city that only started on the massive development process that created the modern city in 1990, the start of The New Global Era. The German urbanist and architectural sociologist Harald Bodenschatz, wrote in 2009:

> Without a doubt marketing Dubai as a "Wonder of the World," a "luxury destination," a "city of superlatives," and "one of the fastest growing cities on earth" was an immense achievement. Founded in 1997, the "Department of Tourism and Commerce Marketing," a governmental organisation headed by the ruler of Dubai, is responsible for city marketing. Unknown even just a few years ago,

Dubai was successfully branded into minds all over the world—with images provided by this gigantic marketing machine.

Bodenschatz goes on to describe the urban outcome:

> The important question for the identity of a real city, asking where the city center might be, cannot be easily answered: the city hall rises in Deira, clusters of high-rises can be found dispersed around the city, the tallest building marks a so-called "downtown," a new 200 hectare district, not, however, the centre of the city. The Central Business District, the economic heart of Dubai, is located at the northern end of the central expressway, in between the meanwhile totally unimposing, ancient (meaning it was opened in 1979) World Trade Center, and the Financial Center, launched in 2002.[76]

In other words, to use Augé's terminology, Dubai is little more than a disconnected collection of non-places. The architect George Katodrytis, from the American University at Sharjah, sees the city as a phenomenon related to the wider consumer economy:

> Dubai … creates appetites rather than solves problems. It is represented as consumable, replaceable, disposable and short-lived. Dubai is addicted to the promise of the new: it gives rise to an ephemeral quality, a culture of the "instantaneous." Relying on strong media campaigns, new "satellite cities" and mega-projects are planned and announced almost weekly. This approach to building is focused exclusively on marketing and selling.[77]

Dubai can be seen as an extreme and self-contained example of the more widespread transformation of city centres into arenas for global consumption. The American urban sociologist Sharon Zukin identified the takeover of public space by commercial interests in her 1995 book, *The Culture of Cities*: "Defining consumption space by its look is especially suited to transnational companies in the symbolic economy, which try to synergize the sale of consumer products, services, and land … The look is the experience of the place.

Controlling the vision brings market power."[78] Ronald Niezen links the anonymity of the non-place to consumer culture:

> The volume, pace, and reach of decontextualized culture is cutting people from their familiar moorings. The relationships between cultures and localities have become abstract, "unnatural." People almost everywhere are subjected to intangibles, objects and ideas that lack a definite place or provenance. Public spaces have been transformed to reflect or accommodate boundaryless commerce. The shopping mall and multiplex cinema are quintessential gathering points of global forces.[79]

The negative impact of global commerce on cities has not escaped anti-globalisation protestors. Reclaim the Streets, "a direct action network for global and local social-ecological revolution," paints a negative picture of the modern city:

> Road schemes, business "parks," shopping developments—all add up to the disintegration of community and the flattening of a locality. Everywhere becomes the same as everywhere else. Community becomes commodity—a shopping village, sedated and under constant surveillance. The desire for community is then fulfilled elsewhere, through spectacle, sold to us in simulated form. A TV soap "street" or "square" mimicking the area that concrete and capitalism are destroying. The real street, in this scenario, is sterile. A place to move through not to be in. It exists only as an aid to somewhere else—through a shop window, billboard or petrol tank.[80]

Consumerism, the Globalisation of Markets and Branding

As the anti-globalists point out, the uniformity of cities in the New Global Era needs to be seen in the wider context of the global expansion of consumerism and its cultural impact.

The homogenising effect of the consumer economy has been recognised for some time. In 1848 Karl Marx wrote in the *Communist*

Manifesto: "National differences and antagonisms between peoples are daily more and more vanishing, owing to the development of the bourgeoisie, to freedom of commerce, to the world-market, to uniformity in the mode of production and in the conditions of life corresponding thereto."[81] As American products and lifestyles were aggressively promoted in the OECD countries after the Second World War, Marx's predictions looked ever more accurate. In 1951, towards the end of an illustrious career, the Spanish-American philosopher George Santayana wrote:

> The authority that controlled universal economy, if it were in American hands, would irresistibly tend to control education and training also. It might set up, as was done in the American zone in Germany, a cultural department, with ideological and political propaganda. The philanthropic passion for service would prompt social, if not legal intervention in the traditional life of all other nations, not only by selling there innumerable American products, but by recommending, if not imposing, American ways of living and thinking.[82]

In an influential essay in 1965, *Universal Civilization and National Cultures*, the French philosopher Paul Ricœur set out the conditions for technical and commercial convergence:

> Thus we are confronted with a *de facto* universality of mankind: as soon as an invention appears in some part of the world we can be sure it will spread everywhere. Technical revolutions mount up and because they do, they escape cultural isolation. We can say that in spite of delays in certain parts of the world there is a single, world-wide technics. That is why national or nationalistic revolutions, in making a nation approach modernization, at the same time make it approach a certain cosmopolitanism. Even if … the scope is national or nationalistic it is still a factor of communication to the extent that it is a factor of industrialisation, for this makes it share in the universal technical civilization … it can be said that throughout the world an equally universal way of living unfolds. This way of living is manifested by the unavoidable standardization of housing and

clothing. These phenomena derive from the fact that ways of living are themselves rationalized by techniques which concern not only production but also transportation, human relationships, comfort, leisure, and news programming as well. Let us also mention the various techniques of elementary culture or, more exactly, the culture of consumption; there is a culture of consumption of world-wide dimensions, displaying a way of living which has a universal character.[83]

In 1983, the American economist Theodore Levitt, in an important article in the *Harvard Business Review*, "The Globalization of Markets," not only popularized the word "globalization" in the American business community, but warned them that, "the globalization of markets is at hand." He wrote:

> Worldwide communications carry everywhere the constant drumbeat of modern possibilities to lighten and enhance work, raise living standards, divert, and entertain. The same countries that ask the world to recognize and respect the individuality of their cultures insist on the wholesale transfer to them of modern goods, services, and technologies ...
>
> In business, this trend has pushed markets toward global commonality. Corporations sell standardized products in the same way everywhere—autos, steel, chemicals, petroleum, cement, agricultural commodities and equipment, industrial and commercial construction, banking and insurance services, computers, semiconductors, transport, electronic instruments, pharmaceuticals, and telecommunications, to mention some of the obvious ...
>
> Nothing is exempt. The products and methods of the industrialized world play a single tune for all the world, and all the world eagerly dances to it.[84]

Levitt concludes: "In the process of world homogenization, modern markets expand to reach cost-reducing global proportions. With better and cheaper communication and transport, even small local market segments hitherto protected from distant competitors now feel the pressure of their presence. Nobody is safe from global reach and the irresistible economies of scale." This article, written as a wake-up call to American corporations, paved the way for a massive expansion of markets with the collapse of the Soviet Union and the liberalisation of the Chinese and Indian economies.

The political dominance of the United States, combined with the experience of its corporations in the largest single national market in the world, and its power over the free-trade economy since 1945, gave its products a head start in expanding global economy after 1992. The spread of North Atlantic consumer products was reinforced by developments in the communication industry and, in particular, in the popular media—film, television and music. While the availability of more varied consumer goods and improved trading opportunities brought widespread benefits to individuals and nations, the cultural impact was not always welcome.

The economists Daniel Yergin and Joseph Stanislaw summarise the problem: "For many countries, participation in the new global economy is very much a mixed blessing. It promotes economic growth and brings new technologies and opportunities. But it also challenges the values and identities of national and regional cultures."[85] As the anthropologist Daniel Miller says, "people are often suspicious of culture defined as a process of consumption, seeing it as somehow less authentic or worthy given its comparative transience and lack of roots ... [but] culture . . . has become increasingly a process of consumption of global forms."[86]

The impact of these global forms on less-wealthy societies is starkly presented by the linguist and counter-development campaigner Helena Norberg-Hodge, drawing on her work with the isolated Himalayan Ladakh community.

Almost everywhere you travel today you will find multi-lane highways, concrete cities and a cultural landscape featuring grey business suits, fast-food chains, Hollywood films and cellular phones. In the remotest corners of the planet, Barbie, Madonna and the Marlboro Man are familiar icons. From Cleveland to Cairo to Caracas, Baywatch is entertainment and CNN news ... all around the world, villages, rural communities and their cultural traditions, are being destroyed on an unprecedented scale by the impact of globalising market forces. Communities that have sustained themselves for hundreds of years are simply disintegrating. The spread of the consumer culture seems virtually unstoppable ...

Today, the Western consumer conformity is descending on the less industrialised parts of the world like an avalanche. "Development" brings tourism, Western films and products and, more recently, satellite television to the remotest corners of the Earth. All provide overwhelming images of luxury and power. Adverts and action films give the impression that everyone in the West is rich, beautiful and brave, and leads a life filled with excitement and glamour.

In the commercial mass culture which fuels this illusion, advertisers make it clear that Westernized fashion accessories equal sophistication and "cool." In diverse "developing" nations around the world, people are induced to meet their needs not through their community or local economy, but by trying to "buy in" to the global market ...

For millions of young people in rural areas of the world, modern Western culture appears vastly superior to their own.[87]

It is not seen this way by the corporations that export North Atlantic products. American culture in particular is seen by Americans through the lens of the freedom of the individual, and freedom to trade is frequently conflated with political and religious freedom. As the sociologists James Davison Hunter and Joshua Yates explain:

[M]oral authority is grounded in the *language of universal individual rights and needs.* Whether selling soft drinks, fast food, running shoes, hybrid crop fertilizer, or financial investments or providing technical assistance for Third World health clinics, environmental protection advocacy, or biblical principles for a strong family, the American globalizers all understand their efforts as a fulfilment of rights and needs basic to human existence [emphasis in original].[88]

Human rights to individual freedom are, in this way, translated into free choice for the consumer. The vice president for International

Public Relations at AT&T said that the outcome will be "a place of massive consumer choice when the global capital markets make fabulous product choices available, the accessibility of technology and information, virtual travel, and it's a place where the consumer as king is extraordinary."[89] There is a similar kind of presumption in this statement by a consultant for the huge American agricultural produce conglomerate, Archer Daniels Midland: "One thing globalization has done is transfer the power of governments to the global consumer. It is the consumer who dictates what we produce, how much we produce, and essentially what price we get paid for our efforts."[90] Global consumerism is nevertheless spectacularly successful. In the one part of the world where political events might have turned the population against anything that emanated from the North Atlantic nations, and in particular the United States, in a 2002 poll eighty-three to ninety-four per cent of the Arab respondents criticised US policy but they stated that they love American music, movies, clothes, democracy and freedom.[91] A Filipino, interviewed in 2003, confirms the dissociation of the product from its place of origin: "I used to go on anti-American rallies when I was a student, but I never thought about the [American] brand of clothes and shoes I wore!"[92] As Davison, Young & Yates note: "The ATM, basketball, hamburger, skateboard, cell phone, computer, computer hacker, sneakers, baseball cap, laundromat, candy bar, microwave oven, parking meter, camera, jukebox, the modern passenger airplane, convenience store, greeting card, ice cream, sports drink, blue jeans, rap music, chewing gum, credit card, skyscraper, and the like, are virtually everywhere. Indeed, so much of what we know as globalization is, in both source and character, undeniably American."[93]

The picture of all parts of the world submerged by North Atlantic consumer products is an over-simplification of a more complex relationship between cultures, which are never static, and influence from other cultures, which has always existed. Nonetheless, the penetration of these products in a relatively short space of time does give the widespread impression that, as Jan Aart Scholte says, "Global products inject a touch of the familiar almost wherever on earth a person might visit."[94] A measure of the seriousness of this impression is that, in Paris in 2001, UNESCO felt the need to publish a *Universal Declaration on Cultural Diversity* which, in the institution's typically guarded language, both stated the problem and suggested the solution. The Declaration considered that "the process of globalization, facilitated by the rapid development of new information and communication technologies, though representing a challenge for cultural diversity, creates the conditions for renewed dialogue among cultures and civilizations"[95]

The impression of global uniformity is most forcefully symbolised by the techniques that are used to sell retail products in diverse markets to global consumers with complex cultural preferences, and where there is a wide range of choices, both local and international. The most effective way to do this is to offer something more than just prepared food, an item of clothing or a motor car. Since the parallel development of the consumer economy, mass media and in particular television in the North Atlantic countries in the 1950s, the old phenomenon of trademarking has grown into the major marketing tool of branding. As the marketing industry became more sophisticated, brand names became more significant until a high point was reached in 1988 when Philip Morris purchased Kraft for six times its book value. It was believed at the time that the high price was to obtain the well-established Kraft brand.

The use of brands provides product differentiation, gives confidence in consistency of quality and, if well managed, can give the added bonus of status to the purchaser. Products are thereby given a personality and "every element, in every advertisement, in every advertising campaign, must develop that identity with a cumulative repetitive force."[96] Research has indicated "that places and countries don't matter to consumers any more. The media is the cultural glue that binds world society together and the media is selling brands ... Brands in turn represent a cluster of values—the BMW man, the Nike man—which define people, not places."[97] The vice president of Nike sees the brand as a direct approach to the consumer: "We always describe the brand as a person. So who is the person? … what we are really trying to do is build up a personality. It is more like building a person than building a brand."[98] With branding, the product is directed to the consumer over the heads of nations and individual cultures and, with the globalisation of trade, branding takes on a new significance as more and more businesses have to trade at a distance and consumers are offered products owned and manufactured from multiple sources. The brand itself can no longer be culture-specific, and marketing firms recognise that "the laser-like clarity of a single, distinctive positioning is … the product's only chance of cutting through the indifference of the consumer, the chaos of the marketplace and the clutter of the media."[99] It will inevitably follow that the brand will have a universal, homogenising character. However hard companies try to differentiate their product for local markets, the mere fact that the brand is consistent and international gives it a global character.

There is a sort of innocence in the protest of a Coca-Cola executive: "The cultural anthropologists who would suggest that we're advancing one way of life over the other, I would ask them to understand why it is that Coca-Cola would be able to broadcast an optimist point of view unless it exists already. Trying to change the nature of cultures is not part of our success criteria. I don't even understand what would be the motivation."[100] Whatever the corporate philosophy, the combination of trading power, massive differentiation in personal income and the fact that, as the advertising executive turned activist Jerry Mander points out, the "globalisation of television transmission via satellite and the *ubiquitousness* of advertising enabled Western industrial corporations to spread commodity culture and Western material values everywhere, even to non-developed countries that had no roads,"[101] [emphasis in original] will inevitably project the values and lifestyles of the dominant economic power. It is no accident that of the top ten global brands in 2010, all but one (Nokia) originate from the United States; and of the top one hundred, fifty-three originate from the United States; and of the remainder, thirty-nine are from western Europe, with another eight from Japan and South Korea, and one from Mexico.[102]

The power of global brands is attested by research undertaken by Douglas Holt, John Quelch and Earl Taylor: "Like entertainment, stars, sports celebrities, and politicians, global brands have become a lingua franca of consumers all over the world. People may love or hate transnational companies, but they can't ignore them. Many consumers are awed by the political power of companies that have sales greater than the GDPs of small nations and that have a powerful impact on people's lives as well as the welfare of communities, nations and the planet itself."[103] Consumers see brands as a guarantee of quality and many are attracted by their global reach. As Holt et al. report a Costa Rican saying, "local brands show what we are; global brands what we want to be."[104]

We can also measure the symbolic success of branding by the strength of feeling of those who oppose it. The vice president of Corporate Communications at McDonald's asserts that "Over 80 per cent of our products and packaging in France are French. We're a French company there. We contribute an enormous amount to the French economy. We employ tens of thousands of French people. We support French farmers and buy French agricultural products."[105] But however much McDonalds' executives may protest their local credentials, McDonalds has become a powerful symbol of, as the former French president Jacques Chirac said, allowing "one single power ... to rule undivided over the planet's food markets."[106] José Bové, the university-educated agricultural activist, became a national hero when he was imprisoned for wrecking a McDonalds restaurant in the French market town of Millau in 1999. As Holt, Quelch and Taylor confirm: "Brands like Coca Cola, McDonalds, and Nike have become lightning rods for anti-globalisation protestors."[107]

In 2007, after an internet campaign led by the Chinese TV personality Rui Chenggang protesting that Starbucks' presence in Beijing "undermined the solemnity of the Forbidden City and trampled on Chinese culture" drew half a million signatures, Starbucks agreed to move out. The company was offered the option of remaining but without its brand name, but that was a step too far, and the vice-president for Greater China Eden Woon said: "We decided at the end that it is not our custom worldwide to have stores that have any other name, so therefore we decided the choice would be to leave."[108] The problem was not the brand *as* a brand but the foreign provenance of the brand. China too recognises the economic power of brands and, as President Hu Jintao said at the 17th Party Congress of the Communist Party in 2007, "We must accelerate the growth of Chinese multinational corporations and Chinese brand names in the world markets."[109]

Tourism Redefined and the Branding of Cities

As cities compete for global trade by providing what they see to be the right built environment for transnational corporations and aspiring national firms they have, as we have seen above, tended to create places that are superficially similar. In the global marketplace for the attraction of transnational business, cities must also look for ways of differentiating themselves from one another.

If a city is historic, it has an identity by which it may be already be known or which it can develop and market. If there is a history of artistic culture this is an additional benefit and, if there is not, it is possible to add and promote themed museums or performance buildings. These are well-established methods for attracting tourism, a quintessentially global activity.

The income from tourism can be substantial. The Global Policy Forum records international tourist arrivals increasing from 400 million per annum in 1990 to 925 million in 2008. By 1992, according to the World Tourist Organisation, it had become the world's largest industry in terms of most of the standard economic indicators, including employment, gross output and capital investment. In 2010 the industry generated US $919 billion in export earnings, which is six per cent of the world total. On this basis alone, the economic benefits of having a location which will attract tourists are worthwhile.

As the New Global Era has progressed, low-cost travel has expanded, and formerly restrictive regimes have not only opened their markets, but have also opened their borders to outbound travel. Outbound tourism tends to follow other global indicators. In 2002 John Urry recorded that the forty-five most highly developed countries in the world account for three-quarters of outbound tourism.[110] Since then, Chinese outbound tourism has grown dramatically from 4.5 million in 1995 to more than 50 million in 2009, while the USA and Germany (the largest country for outbound tourism) remained comparatively static in the same period at around 60 million and 80 million respectively. The nature of tourism has also changed. In the 1940s the accepted definition of tourism excluded any "earning activity." By 1998 the OECD definition included business activities as part of tourism, but excluded anything "activity remunerated from within the place visited." The United Nations World Tourist Organisation (UNWTO) now defines tourism as travel outside the traveller's usual environment and includes "business or other purposes"—without qualification.

The concept of the tourist has been transformed. The philosopher Agnes Heller calls them "united tourists," as:

> not only "tourists" are tourists. So are international businessmen, jetting lecturers, and regular conference participants, people who constantly move around the globe, jumping from hotel to hotel, from business dinner to business dinner. But to be a member of the club of the united tourists is not linked to high professionalism or a substantial income. Moving from the countryside to the city, from the city to the suburbs, or from the suburbs to another city, transforms a person into a tourist in his or her home country.[111]

To this list could be added retirement migration, what the gerontologist C. J. Guilleard calls "the longest holiday of the lifetime."[112] John Urry sees these trends as part of a more general "dissolving of the boundaries, not only between high and low cultures, but also between different cultural forms, such as tourism, art, education, photography, television, music, sport, shopping and architecture." Using the expression he coined, "the tourist gaze," Urry sees that tourism is "increasingly bound up with, and is partly indistinguishable from, all sorts of other social and cultural practices. This has the effect, as 'tourism' *per se* declines in specificity, of universalising the tourist gaze—people are much of the time 'tourists' whether they like it or not."[113]

As a consequence, the use of tourism for the promotion of cities to create market differentiation has a much wider application than just the attraction of leisured visitors, profitable though that may be. Richard Lloyd and Terry Clarke, in their paper *The City as an Entertainment Machine*, describe the new condition: "Workers in the elite sectors of the postindustrial city make 'quality of life' demands, and in their consumption practices can experience their own urban location *as if tourists*, emphasizing aesthetic concerns. These practices impact considerations about the proper nature of amenities to provide in contemporary cities"[114] [emphasis in original]. As the sociologist Bella Dicks says in *Culture on Display*, "globalization has … heightened economic competition amongst localities, and set local governments the task of advertising their particular qualities in order to lure in capital investment … Cultural display has been a vital means of manufacturing and promoting this place-identity."[115] Dicks sets out the ingredients of "visitability":

> Places today have become exhibitions of themselves. Through heavy investment in architecture, art, design, exhibition space, landscaping and various kinds of redevelopment towns, cities and countryside proclaim their possession of various cultural values— such as unchanging nature, the historic past, the dynamic future, multiculturalism, fun and pleasure, bohemianism, artistic creativity or simply stylishness. These cultural values have come to be seen as a place's identity, the possession of which is key to the important task of attracting visitors. And this identity is expected to be easily accessed by those visitors or, to use a currently favoured term in urban design, to be legible. Places whose identity seems

inaccessible, confusing or contradictory do not present themselves
as destinations. They do not, in other words, seem visitable. An
identity that is not pointed to in the form of well-restored or
beautifully designed buildings, artworks, shopping plazas, streets,
walkways or gardens does not compose itself into a view nor offer
itself as an "experience." To avoid such a fate, places should "make
the most of themselves"—rather like the well-toned body promoted
in healthy living magazines. In this way, they can find their niche in
the new cultural economy of visitability.[116]

The marketing of historic places to enhance "visitability" creates a
dilemma, identified by the sociologist John Allcock:

> On the one hand, the touristification of localities typically calls into
> question local identities, as these are drawn into global markets ...
> as the international corporations who manage tourism development
> impose a measure of standardization upon the tourist product ...
> On the other hand, the specific features of local identities are among
> the most important resources available in the competitive marketing
> of tourism. The realization of the significance of this asset leads to a
> codification of this cultural inventory, and to its self-conscious
> promotion as a marketable asset.[117]

In the same way as the global retail product must be uniformly
attractive but made distinctive by branding, so the physical identity
of the historic city becomes a consumer product in its own right,
tidied up to be acceptable to as many potential occupiers as possible
but distinctive enough to be more attractive than the next place.

The outcome is more often than not a kind of packaged heritage
where, as Heller observes, "there are the same hotels, the same
menus, and the same cinemas. Also there is a kind of English spoken
everywhere, yet all places also offer their 'specialities,' their mostly
artificially kept local traditions."[118] Cities do, however, have other
means of boosting their identity. These include special events such as
sporting occasions from football matches to the Olympics, concerts
or festivals, and international exhibitions (Expos). As Urry says, by
staging these events cities "have the power to transform themselves

Figure 37. Palace of the Arts Reina Sofia, Valencia; Santiago Calatrava; 2004.

The architecture of cultural display.

from being mundane places ... into being these special 'host city' sites that come to occupy a new distinct niche within global tourism."[119]

These events need accommodation such as stadia, athlete's housing, exhibition halls or, for Expos, striking temporary structures (sometimes made permanent). As with the construction of other cultural buildings such as museums or galleries, if there are no suitable historic facilities, the new buildings can be used to add to the distinctiveness of the city. Dean MacCannell identifies two strategies for the provision of

cultural productions ... (1) it may add to the ballast of our modern civilization by sanctifying an original as being a model worthy of copy or an important milestone in our development, or (2) it may establish a new direction, break new ground, or otherwise contribute to the progress of modernity by presenting new combinations of cultural elements and working out the logic of their relationship.[120]

Figure 38. Beijing National Stadium (Bird's Nest); Herzog & de Meuron with Ai Weiwei; 2008.

International events as architectural display.

The architecture of culture and events attract international tourism and promote cities on the global stage. This second option would have wider beneficial effects, according to Aspa Gospodini (in a European context): "The impact of innovative design of space on the development prospects of cities, and smaller peripheral cities in particular, is related to their potential to be placed on the new urban map of Europe as places attractive to new enterprises, residents and especially to urban tourists."[121] This sentiment has led to the one of the most distinctive products of the New Global Era, the iconic building as a city brand.

The Birth of the Iconic Building
and the Bilbao Effect

Cities have long been represented by distinctive buildings. In the ancient world, Ephesus was notable for the Temple of Artemis, and Alexandria for its lighthouse or pharos. In the medieval period, churches and their towers or steeples gave cities their distinct identities. More recently, the Eiffel Tower and the Empire State building became symbols of Paris and New York City respectively. The first attempt to create a new symbol for a modern city was the Sydney Opera House. The design was won at competition in 1957 by Jørn Utzon after a controversial selection process. It did not open until 1973, ten years late and fourteen times over budget, following major constructional and structural problems. In the creation of a modern iconic building, however, this was to become a familiar pattern and, indeed, all of this was put to one side when Utzon was awarded the top architectural award, the Pritzker Prize, in 2003. The citation for the prize said, "There is no doubt that the Sydney Opera House is his masterpiece. It is one of the great iconic buildings of the 20th century, an image of great beauty that has become known throughout the world—a symbol for not only a city, but a whole country and continent."

The Sydney Opera House had the characteristics that were necessary for a city icon, distinctiveness and an instantly recognisable form. The word "icon," originating in the Greek Orthodox religious images venerated as "windows into heaven," had come to mean any "important or enduring symbol." There have been a number of more detailed definitions of the building-as-icon as the idea spread in the 1990s. An eleven point series of defining characteristics were proposed in by the critic Aaron Betsky in the catalogue of an exhibition at the San Francisco Museum of Contemporary Art in 1996, *Icons as Magnets of Meaning*, which included "wow' syndrome" and "enigmatic character … exerting a hypnotic quality in their sense of otherness."[122] Charles Jencks followed a similar line saying that, while they must of course be distinctive and recognisable, they will also be enigmatic or "a giant iconostasis asking to be decoded,"[123] as well as a metaphor—presumably an as-yet-uncoded metaphor. The British cultural commentator Stephen Bayley takes a different and more straightforward view, and recognises the critical point that an architectural icon will fulfil "the demands of powerful branding— instant recognition, zero ambiguity."[124] Bayley's definition accurately identifies the relationship between the attempt to create an icon and branding, two clearly related phenomena. Jencks' and Betsky's meanings do not contradict this: the idea that this is something that is an enigma or needs to be de-coded is the typical concern of historians or professional commentators. While the whole phenomenon has been a great opportunity for commentators and analysts, city icons are not made for them, they are made to deliver a clear and simple message: "This city is important, know it."

While the Sydney Opera House set the standard, the fashion for city branding through the commissioning of special buildings is a distinctive feature of the New Global Era. Just prior to the new era in 1982, the French President, Francois Mitterand, anxious both to leave a legacy in the particular manner of French politicians and to boost the image of Paris, launched the *Grands Projets*, commissioning international architects to design high-profile buildings. These began to come to completion at the end of the 1980s. At this time, the Guggenheim Museum in the north-Spanish city of Bilbao, the definitive building of the emerging New Global Era, was conceived (figure C), and all subsequent attempts to boost the reputation and incomes of cities through the imagery of architecture would refer to this project. As the Californian architect Frank Gehry confirmed, the brief for the building was itself to be "an equivalent to the Sydney Opera House."[125]

The story begins in New York in 1988 when the Guggenheim Museum appointed a dynamic new curator, Thomas Krens. The famous Frank Lloyd Wright museum building was in need of repair, there was insufficient space to display its collection and it was short of funds. Krens sold three important works for US $47 million, raised another US $54 million by selling public bonds and announced his intention to expand the museum as an international brand. There was already a branch of the Guggenheim Museum in Peggy Guggenheim's former home in Venice, and Krens began negotiations with Venice and Salzburg for new buildings. The former Director of the National Centre for Exhibitions for the Spanish Ministry of Culture, Carmen Gimenez was, however, employed in 1989 as a curator by the Guggenheim in New York and started negotiations in 1991 with the Basque government in Bilbao.

Bilbao is the capital of the Basque region, an ethnically and linguistically distinct area on the Spanish Atlantic coast that spreads into southern France, and has had a strong and, in its extreme form, terrorist, separatist movement since the nineteenth century. It was a major industrial port but suffered significant decline and urban decay in the twentieth century. The democratisation of Spain in 1975 led to a significant degree of financial autonomy for the Basques and, when Spain joined the European Union in 1986, the deprivation and poverty of the region attracted grant aid. In 1991 the Strategic Plan for the Revitalisation of Metropolitan Bilbao was adopted and in 1992 the public society, *Bilbao Ria 2000* was created. That year *Bilbao Ria 2000* engaged the well-known Argentine-American architect Cesar Pelli to master plan the derelict port area. The city's infrastructure and the condition of historic buildings were upgraded, and a series of famous international architects were commissioned for new projects in the city: Santiago Calatrava for a footbridge, Norman Foster for a series of new subway stations, and Stirling and Wilford for a transport interchange.

An important museum on the regenerated port area would act as a centrepiece for the regenerated city and the financial independence of the region allowed it to negotiate directly with Thomas Krens. This led to an immediate pledge of US $20 million for the Guggenheim name and expertise, plus US $100 million for the building, plus sums for running costs and the collection. Part of the deal by Krens was that an internationally-renowned architect would design the building and he engaged Frank Gehry to help to select the site. In the three-firm competition that followed the selection, Gehry was the winner.

Frank Gehry is a Canadian-born architect who moved to California for his professional education and stayed there for the rest of his career. He started on his own in 1962, but early projects were unremarkable. His own house, an apparently disordered assembly of found elements on an existing bungalow started in 1978, gave him a reputation (that he denied) as a follower of the philosophy of deconstruction (discussed earlier). A number of higher profile buildings in California followed, including an aquarium and gallery, all with what was becoming a trademark randomness in the exterior design. By 1991, buildings like the Chiat/Day Building (which included the extraordinary Claes Oldenburg giant binoculars at the entrance) gave him a reputation beyond the USA. He had, however, only completed one building outside the USA, a small gallery to exhibit furniture at the Vitra furniture company in Weil am Rhein, Germany. By 1991, he was an architect who might have been internationally known by critics and academics, but he could not yet be called an international architect.

His career was transformed by his selection for the Bilbao Guggenheim Museum and, indeed, the role of new architecture as a branding device for cities was transformed when the building was completed in 1997. The extraordinary abstract sculptural form of curved intersecting planes of titanium sheets on a promontory in the Nervion River was a huge success. The building was much more the exhibit than its rather mediocre contents, and became so famous that it was better known than the city it was intended to promote. In 1998 it was estimated that the museum generated an additional €150 million GDP and €27 million tax revenue for the city, figures that have held up or improved in the subsequent decade.[126] While the total disconnection of the building form from its internal function ran against established modernist thinking and made many architects very uneasy, its *avant garde* credentials were clear. Ken Shuttleworth, leader of Norman Foster's architectural team which built London's iconic "Gherkin," or 30 St. Mary Axe, confirmed this in 2009: "The

Guggenheim Bilbao has led to a time of exploration and the pursuit of a new expressive language, which is free from the shackles of the past … it is the single most influential building of the last 20 years."[127]

The Guggenheim project reflects with remarkable clarity some of the primary forces of the time: the aggressive promotion of an American brand abroad; the disengagement of local city-based economies from national economies (albeit in this case with an unusual political background); the significance of the new tourist economy; the use of culture for the branding of the city; and the global engagement of other players from the established free-market economies—the other architects engaged by the city or participating in the competition were from the USA, Austria, Spain, Britain and Japan. This resonance with the political and economic direction of the New Global Era not only contributed to its success it also ensured that there would be numerous attempts to re-create what was now known as the "Bilbao Effect" worldwide, including the character of the architecture.

****

Other cities sought the benefits of the Bilbao Effect. As Sharon Zukin says in her 1995 book *The Culture of Cities*: "City boosters increasingly compete for tourist dollars and financial investments by bolstering the city's image as a centre of cultural innovation, including restaurants, *avant garde* performances, and architectural design."[128] The iconic or *avant garde* building was seen as a major component in the promotion of cities. As Beriatos & Gospodini claim: "Irrespective of the particular functions and activities accommodated in space, it is *avant-garde* design of both buildings and open spaces that can make urban space morphology in itself and of itself a sightseeing, a tourist resource."[129] A report in the magazine *Building Design* in 2003 summed it up: "Cities are competing against each other for icons and are using international architects to drum up that 'something different.' In Chongqing … city authorities are racing to create the necessary public buildings. Rather in the manner of a shopping spree, they say they want 10 and have decided half should go to foreign architects."[130]

Cities all over the world have commissioned extraordinary buildings. In 1993, in the burgeoning Chinese city of Guangzhou, the mayor Lin Shusen planned a new opera house in the Central Business District that would, as Jiang Xu and Anthony G.O. Yeh say, "be a new expressive icon that integrates with urban strategy to create new cultural significance to the city."[131] This was designed by Zaha Hadid and completed in 2011 (figure 39). In Baku in Azerbaijan, the Korean firm Heerim have designed a crescent-shaped hotel that is, as the architects claim, "set to become the symbol of Azerbaijan, and also an icon to help people the world over think of the country as the gateway between the past and the present, and between the East and the West."[132] In Abu Dhabi, the government are assembling a collection of iconic buildings. On September 29, 2011 the *Kaleej Times* reported that the thirty-five-storey Capital Gate Hotel, described by the state-owned developer as "an icon for Abu Dhabi," had entered the Guinness Book of Records as the "furthest leaning manmade tower"[133] (figure 40).

Figure 39.   Opera House, Guangzhou, China; Zaha Hadid; 2011. A cultural building by a star architect to enhance the cultural credentials of a fast-growing Chinese city.

Figure 40 (left). Capital Gate Hotel, Abu Dhabi; RMJM; 2011. Hotel and office block, certified as the world's furthest leaning man-made tower.
Figure 41 (right). Burj Khalifa, Dubai; Skidmore, Owings and Merrill; 2010. Iconic status by height. The world's tallest building — for now.

Iconic buildings: promotional architecture for global city status.

The global search for status through the construction of architectural icons has drawn in some surprising participants. Paris, a city which not only includes one of the world's best-known icons, the Eiffel Tower, but is itself an icon of European civilization, launched a new plan for *Grand Paris* in 2009. President Nicholas Sarkozy announced that, with this plan Paris would "rival London, New York, Tokyo or Shanghai" and be a "global city, open and dynamic, attractive, a creator of wealth and jobs." Regulations that have protected Paris against intrusion from tall buildings would be waived, "provided they are beautiful." The head of La Defense development, Philippe Chaix, said, "Greater Paris will be revolutionary. It will change our image on the world stage." [134] At the other end of the scale the phenomenon descends to a level beyond parody. In 2004 the declining English industrial town of Middlesbrough commissioned a British second-tier star architect, Will Alsop, to master plan a new development in a redundant dock area called Middlehaven. The mayor sent out a press release that said, "Gateshead [a nearby English town] may boast the glittering Sage; Sydney the spectacular Opera House, but we will offer up a whole field of dreams ... why shouldn't Middlesbrough be up there with the likes of Boston or Bilbao? ... Why shouldn't we be the ones to lead the way into the future?"[135]

Iconic Architecture: Practice and Theory

The established and simplest way of making an impact with buildings is simply to rely on height. As architecture critic and author Ada Louise Huxtable says of the tall building: "For better or for worse, it is the measure, parameter, or apotheosis of our consumer and corporate culture ... It romanticizes power and the urban condition."[136] The new appeal of tall buildings as global symbols was idiosyncratically summarised by the Australian developer Bruno Grollo when he proposed a tower for Melbourne in 1994 which, at 678 metres, would have been the highest in the world at that time. It was never built. Grollo declared that "it would be a golden building for a golden city for the golden times to come ... it has to put the city on the world map." The tower would have "to do something for Melbourne that did what the pyramids did for Egypt, or the Colosseum did for Rome, or the Opera House and Harbour Bridge did for Sydney."[137]

Branding by height had the additional advantage of an association with the acknowledged financial capital of the world, downtown Manhattan. The city of Beijing had set a target of 300 towers in its central business district. There are over 230 in the Pudong district of Shanghai, and new towers continue to be constructed. Downtown Manhattan has 289 towers. The iconic effect of groups of towers, even when some of those in the group are themselves considered to be icons, is of less significance than simply being the biggest. This is, however, an unavoidably expensive and often short-lived ambition. The twin Petronas Towers in Kuala Lumpur in Malaysia, designed by Cesar Pelli, were commissioned in 1991 as a symbol of the "Tiger Economy" of Malaysia, and completed seven years later. They remained the tallest buildings in the world until the Taipei 101 tower, in Taipei, Taiwan, designed by the Taiwanese architect C.Y. Li, was completed in 2004. This record was finally overtaken when the Burj Khalifa, in Dubai, designed by the American architects SOM, was completed in 2010 (figure 41).

The impact of the unusual form of the Guggenheim Museum in Bilbao, however, set a standard for designs that should not necessarily be large (although they often are) but be distinctive by being different. Rem Koolhaas described the pressures of these demands in 2002: "It is really unbelievable what the market demands [from architecture] now. It demands recognition, it demands difference and it demands iconographic qualities."[138] The differences were not to be an expression of differences in the location of the buildings, the icons were not for local consumption, and the established character of the place was not of any consequence. As Hans Ibelings points out: "Modern architects have always regarded it as more important that their work should be in keeping with the age than in harmony with the surroundings."[139] Clients seeking iconic buildings felt much the same. Xie and Liu report that in the competition for Tomorrow Square in Shanghai, it was the Chinese jury members that preferred something "abstract modern" rather than anything with specific references to Chinese architecture.[140] Pio Baldi, President of the MAXXI Foundation that commissioned Zaha Hadid for the MAXXI Gallery in Rome, said of the new building: "It doesn't seem to be in Rome, it seems to be in another part of the world, New York, London. This is very positive; Rome needed a building like this." [141]

****

In the 1970s and 80s a number of established architects, besides Frank Gehry, had developed a style that answered this demand. Pre-eminent amongst these was Peter Eisenman, with a design technique that involved the explicit introduction of apparently non-functional contradictions in the plan, complicating the design. In Austria, Wolf Prix, who founded Coop Himmelblau, engaged in a similar but more randomised process. Other architects such as Steven Holl and Richard Meier from the USA, and Toyo Ito from Japan, had developed other less extreme versions of deliberate but expressive complication of building exteriors.

A second generation of architects was also waiting in the wings. In 1989 Daniel Libeskind won the competition for the new Jewish Museum in Berlin, but work was delayed by political controversy until 1992. This complex and deliberately disturbing design gave Libeskind, who had been teaching and writing up that point, the opportunity to build, and brought him into prominence. In 1991 the Vitra company in Germany, who had also commissioned Frank Gehry for his first foreign building, engaged the Iranian-born British architect, Zaha Hadid, to design a new fire station. Hadid had also been teaching and exhibiting up to that point, and this was her first building. It was designed as a dramatic series of intersecting volumes with angular sculptural detail that had little to do with practical functional requirements. In 1994 she won a major competition for a new opera house in Cardiff in Wales, to be funded by the British National Lottery. Her design, presented in a series of paintings, was also sculptural and dramatic, and its cost and difficulty of construction became a political debate. It was cancelled, but the controversy and the support given to her by the British architectural establishment enhanced her reputation as an *avant garde* architect. In 1988, the Dutch architect Rem Koolhaas won his first major commission, the Nederlands Dans Theater. It was an original and diverse assembly of volumes and materials combined with a wilfully abstract arrangement of cladding. Koolhaas had made his reputation with the publication of a theoretical work on architecture and urbanism, *Delirious New York*, published in 1978.[142]

By 1990 Koolhaas was the oldest of this group at forty-six: Libeskind was forty-four, and Hadid forty. Each had spent their early careers teaching, writing and exhibiting, but by the 1990s their ideas and radical forms had developed free from the pragmatic limitations of everyday practice. The buildings were conceived as sculptural form first and buildings second which, when combined with extreme geometrical complexity, made them hard to build, difficult to budget and frequently more expensive than their original cost estimates. Nonetheless, the demand for the product, the natural limitation on the numbers of producers and the deep pockets of many of the purchasers, made what would have been a business disaster in any other branch of the profession, irrelevant. Zaha Hadid's partner, Patrik Schumacher, explains their unique position which led to stellar success, large practices and huge profits in the following two decades:

> The *avant-garde* segment has quite a bit more space to manoeuvre than the mainstream commercial segment. This is because our work is considered to be a kind of multiplier. Economically our buildings operate as investments into a marketing agenda—city branding, for instance—with a value that might at times considerably exceed the budget allocated to the project itself. Although we have budgets to work within, our projects are usually not measured in terms of industry standards of cost-effectiveness. They are paid for by funds that have been extracted from the cycle of profit-driven investment—either as public tax money or as sponsorship money administered by a cultural institution's board of trustees. Obviously such funds too are indirectly contributing to an overall business rationale. But as designers we can enjoy and utilize the relative distance from concerns of immediate profitability to further our experimental agenda. We understand that this position is peculiar to a rarefied segment of the profession.[143]

****

The experimental character of these buildings demands a considerable degree of artistry and sophisticated three-dimensional conceptual thought. The subsequent construction information, not undertaken by the designer, is difficult to process. Frank Gehry designs with three-dimensional modelling in increasing levels of complexity. Peter Eisenman uses complex three-dimensional mathematics, maps of the site and preserved accidents to create spaces that respond to a series of apparently contradictory influences on the design. Zaha Hadid continues to develop designs through sketches, as her partner Patrik Schumacher explains: "She also sketches abstractly, irrespective of projects ... We can begin to map or match abstract stimulations across a number of projects—through sketches, interesting organisation, interesting formal possibilities."[144] Daniel Libeskind works with models and drawings. By the time the real boom in demand for iconic buildings was in full flow, when the success of the Bilbao Guggenheim was clear for all to see, advances in computer modelling had made the post-conceptual design process very much easier to manage.

The development of three-dimensional digital modelling with Computer Aided Design (CAD) had reached a level of development in the 1990s that facilitated the presentation and construction of these unusual designs. In 1985 MiniCad, the first specialist architectural program with three-dimensional modelling, was launched by the German software designers Nemetschek AG for use with the Macintosh platform. In 1989 Pro/Engineer launched a three-dimensional modelling system which could be manipulated into different forms while maintaining fixed dimensional criteria, or parameters. This was combined with operator-friendly features such as drop-down menus and icons to make it available to a wider range of users. At about the same time the French company Dassault Systèmes re-wrote its three-dimensional modelling CATIA programs for the widely-used UNIX operating system. Dassault Systèmes was a subsidiary of the French aircraft manufacturer Avions Marcel Dassault, which had developed CATIA in the 1970s for the design and manufacture of the Mirage fighter jet, leading to its adoption in the automotive, shipbuilding and other industries. The use of the programs was limited in the early 1990s, but soon after Windows 95 was released, Microstation, an established interactive graphics design system, was applied to its operating system. In 1998 a group from ProEngineer developed the Revit program, which offered the first parametric building modeller specifically for the building design and construction industry. The following year a more sophisticated version of MiniCad was developed under the brand name Vectorworks. In the same year Dassault Systèmes took over Matra Datavision and its CASCADE system for modelling, visualization and computer-aided manufacture (CAM).[145]

Architects did not at first use these programs directly for design purposes, but came into contact with them through their engagement of specialists in the production of computer generated imagery (CGI) and the engineers responsible for executing their complex designs. In the late 1980s the photorealism of CGI became an important marketing tool for architects, and by the mid-1990s clients were demanding sophisticated visualisations for the rapid presentation of design options for major projects.[146] Engineers had been using computing since Ove Arup and Partners pioneered the digital calculation of complex forms in the early 1960s for the Sydney Opera House. It was not until the late 1990s, and the development of appropriate user interfaces, that architects began to use the technology directly, often less for the design than to document and detail the complex forms that had been designed with physical models and drawings. Foster+Partners were early users of Microstation for the calculation of complex geometries. Frank Gehry used the CATIA system and in 2002 created a stand-alone business, Gehry Technologies, to develop and market a specialist architectural version of CATIA. Zaha Hadid also uses CATIA and her partner, Patrik Schumaker has developed a comprehensive architectural theory around the use of parametric geometry (see below). Daniel Libeskind uses Vectorworks.

****

The publicity given to major iconic projects had created a demand for unusual buildings that could not be met by the naturally limited supply of by-now famous established practitioners. Commercial architects stepped in to fill the demand. With younger architects fully conversant with CAD and CAM, commercial practices could conceptualise and model forms of a similar complexity to those of the leading iconic architects. Parallel advances in product manufacture made the use of small-unit variations to create dramatic exterior effects on large-scale buildings much more affordable. The opportunity was not only created by technological advances, it was part of the underlying culture. As Charles Jencks points out, "We live in a permissive, radical egalitarian era when any building type can be an icon."[147] As the type proliferated, it was inevitable that the quality would decline. As James Madge complained in an article posthumously published in 2007:

> When 3D visualisation software enables students of architecture, unaware of the sophisticated concepts deployed by serious workers in this field, to present the images of hitherto unimagined shapes whose confidently rendered surfaces belie the absence of any knowledge of, or interest in what lies behind, the notion of architecture as nothing more than the invention of new shapes neither needs nor deserves any further encouragement.[148]

By the start of the new millennium, the architectural icon was a recognised and established phenomenon. In 2005 three books on the subject were published almost simultaneously: *The Last Icons: Architecture Beyond Modernism* by Miles Glendenning; *Iconic Buildings: The Power of the Enigma* by Charles Jencks; and *Edifice Complex: How the Rich and Powerful Shape the World*, by Dejan Sudjic. To these can be added *Great New Buildings of the World* by Ana G. Cañizares, published in the same year, and which largely illustrates iconic buildings.

Numerous city redevelopments or large planning projects now included a building or buildings of an unusual shape or with novel features. Architects working on often quite mundane developments were now asked to include "iconic designs" to brand the project.

With large buildings in particular, almost any form seemed possible and the diversity of shapes and structures became almost a riot. Many architects found this stylistic free-for-all disturbing. The ideological anchor of Modernism, with its legacy of social responsibility and a logical response to function and form derived from the nature of building materials, was conspicuously absent. The prominent British architect, Graham Morrison, spoke for many in the profession when he attacked iconic buildings in *The Guardian* newspaper in 2004: "Each image has to be more extraordinary and shocking in order to eclipse the last. Each new design has to be instantly memorable— more iconic. This one-upmanship was, and is, a fatuous and self-indulgent game."[149]

Even for their followers, the new star practitioners at times justified their work with barely comprehensible statements inherited from the obscure philosophical legacy of Deconstruction. When Libeskind describes the Jewish Museum as "not a collage or a collision or a simple dialectic, but a new type of organization which is organized around a center which is not, around what is not visible,"[150] or Rem Koolhaas says that "at first sight, the activities amassed in the structure of Bigness demand to interact, but Bigness keeps them apart,"[151] they may be profound, but they are not offering enough clarity or cohesion to provide any basis for a coherent philosophy around which architects could assemble.

Patrik Schumacher, who studied philosophy as well as architecture, has presented a unified philosophy for these buildings based on the opportunities presented by the computer aided design process. Schumacher has called his theory "parametricism"—a word, borrowed from mathematics, for a computing algorithm that maintains consistent relationships between elements as a computer model is manipulated:

> There is a global convergence in recent *avant-garde* architecture that justifies its designation as a new style: parametricism. It is a style rooted in digital animation techniques, its latest refinements based on advanced parametric design systems and scripting methods.

Developed over the past 15 years and now claiming hegemony within *avant-garde* architecture practice, it succeeds Modernism as the next long wave of systematic innovation. Parametricism finally brings to an end the transitional phase of uncertainty engendered by the crisis of Modernism and marked by a series of relatively short-lived architectural episodes that included Postmodernism, Deconstructivism and Minimalism. So pervasive is the application of its techniques that parametricism is now evidenced at all scales from architecture to interior design to large urban design. Indeed, the larger the project, the more pronounced is parametricism's superior capacity to articulate programmatic complexity.[152]

The formal outcome of Parametric theory is made clear: "Instead of classical and modern reliance on rigid geometrical figures—rectangles, cubes, cylinders, pyramids and spheres—the new primitives of parametricism are animate geometrical entities—splines, nurbs and subdivs. These are fundamental geometrical building blocks for dynamical systems like 'hair', 'cloth', 'blobs' and 'metaballs' that react to 'attractors' and can made to resonate with other via scripts." It is put forward as a proper response to contemporary social and economic forces: "Parametricism aims to organize and articulate the increasing diversity and complexity of social institutions and the life processes within the most advanced centre of post-Fordist network society."[153]

These theories are directed solely to architects and critics and would mean little to anyone outside the profession. Behind the designs of many of iconic buildings there are ideas that are much more intelligible for commissioning clients or committees. The association of a building with some other image, a metaphor, can be a source of inspiration and it can also be an effective way to describe an otherwise difficult and apparently abstract design.

The work of Gehry, being hard to interpret, has often been given nicknames such as the "Fred and Ginger" building in Prague (a reference to the appearance of two dancing figures called after Fred Astaire and Ginger Rogers), and his up-and-coming UTS building in Sydney, Australia, has already been named the "big paper bag."

Gehry has said, however, that "I probably do use that metaphor in my work—though not consciously," [154] and does not always take kindly to the jokes—"there's always some smartarse."[155]

Others of his generation are more literal and open minded. Steven Holl's 1988 Martha's Vinyard House was "derived conceptually from a whale's skeleton."[156] The later generation seems more open to the idea of metaphor. Zaha Hadid's buildings are inspired by, variously: a coral reef, for an art museum in Cagliari in Italy; waves, for the MAXXI building in Rome; and, for the Regium Museum in Reggio Calabria, also in Italy, either a ship or a starfish (the ship was reported to the journalist Hugh Pearman,[157] the starfish is on Hadid's website). Daniel Libeskind will often claim a direct analogy, such as a broken sphere for his Manchester Imperial War Museum North (figure 42) or the concrete walls at his New York Ground Zero design as a metaphor for "democracy unbowed by terrorism," but often his accounts of his inspiration are famously obscure. He describes the thinking behind his unbuilt extension to the Victoria and Albert Museum in London: "This emblem of a heterogeneous and open system of organization for the artefacts and exhibitions provides a diversity of experiences woven into a net of similarities and differences—an aggregate of traces about unexpected topics still to be explored."[158]

Claims for inspiration in metaphor have become both more literal and more commonplace. Modernism had from its foundation relied on a metaphorical relationship with industrial products that symbolised modernity. Le Corbusier used the ocean liner in the 1930s, and Kasimir Malevich the aeroplane. Later there were more literal metaphors: Eero Saarinen used wings in flight at the TWA Flight Center at JFK Airport in New York, and Jørn Utzon used sails as his inspiration for Sydney Opera House. These were metaphors of the architect's choice as a source of inspiration and, for modernists, would be rarely if ever taken from previous buildings—this would be traditional or, after the 1980s, postmodern. In the North Atlantic countries, where Modernism originated, the use of metaphor may have been of interest but was not a major factor in the acceptance of a design. Where Modernism was not an established type, however, the Modernism of the building was not justification enough in itself; something else was needed to persuade the client or client group that the design had some relevance. In this new market, the metaphor became not just a means of selling the design but a branding tool for the client.

Outside the North Atlantic countries, these metaphors become more and more literal. When the French architect Jean Nouvel was commissioned to design the new National Museum in Qatar, he was asked to use the desert rose (a geological formation) as a source for his design.[159] Nouvel now describes his building as a "bladelike petal of the desert rose."[160] The design for the Arabian Performance Venue on a man-made island by the international architects Aedas is surrounded by a series of "petals or leaves" housing apartments and hotel accommodation.[161] The Danish architect Henning Larson's design for the Batumi Aquarium in Georgia is a very literal "iconic rock formation" washed up on the lake shore.[162] The Dutch architects MVRDV's winning design for a lakeside apartment development in Albania is distinctive because, "clad in local stones the buildings turn into a series of rocks, the Tirana Rocks."[163] The British architects RMJM's winning design for the Russian Gazprom tower in St Petersburg is designed as giant gas flame, loosely based on the company's logo (figure 43). The Flame Towers in Baku, Azerbaijan, a mixed development of three flame shaped towers of thirty-nine storeys designed by the London office of the American architects HOK are described by a director of the firm: "Azerbaijan's long history of fire worship provided the inspiration for HOK's iconic design."[164]

As the designs move from metaphor to representation, clients can capitalise directly on their image for branding. The visual concept of the Bird's Nest Stadium for the Beijing Olympics was under the control of the Chinese organisers (figure 38), not the architect. Jacques Herzog of the architects Herzog de Meuron complained that, "Before we had even finished the building, it had become a global icon … It has been used and misused in commercials, on TV… in many ways that we cannot control any more and we have no hold on."[165] Even the pioneer of High-Tech architecture and its claim to functionalism, Norman Foster, has been drawn into the world of the metaphor. His Beijing Airport is described on Foster+Partners' website as a "dragon-like form." The metaphor was suggested by his clients during the design process, and China's CCTV network enthusiastically took up the idea: "The Dragon's head, body and tail are the main buildings of the terminal," while "the ball that the Dragon is playing with is the distributing centre, including parking areas and subway terminal."[166] Now, without prompting, Foster+Partners' CITIC Headquarters tower in the Chinese city of Hangzhou is presented as a design that "draws inspiration from the shape of the ancient 'dou' or 'ding' vessel, a traditional symbol of wealth, dignity and stability."[167] (figure 44).

Star Architects

The most distinctive architectural development of the New Global Era has been the institutionalisation and eventual corruption of the idea of the iconic building based on unique and unusual designs, following in the footsteps of the Guggenheim Museum in Bilbao. The idea has been firmly linked to the concept of the star architect—the "starchitect"—as the designer. Indeed, in the English-language *Beijing Today* in 2010 the two ideas were conflated when Frank Gehry was described as "a genius and an architectural icon."[168] As the global status of the architect could be as important as the status of the building, the iconic design could be less radical. Architects who had become established internationally in the 1980s such as Norman Foster, Richard Rogers, Renzo Piano and Tadao Ando, could build much more conventional buildings primarily made iconic by the fame of the architect.

Figure 42.   Imperial War Museum North, Manchester, England; Daniel Libeskind; 2002. A design based on shards of a shattered globe to represent the destruction of war.

Figure 43.   Project for Gazprom Building, St Petersburg, Russia; RMJM; winning competition entry 2006.   Tower block as a gas flame for the world's largest gas company.

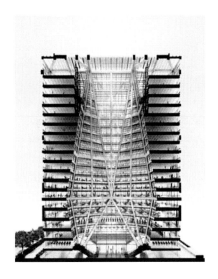

Figure 44. Section of CITIC HQ project, Hangzhou, China: Foster+Partners; construction commenced 2011. Office building with an atrium shaped as ancient Chinese porcelain jar.

Reflexive Modernism animated with the use of metaphor.

The term "starchitect," probably of journalistic origin, describes the small group of celebrity architects that became well known in the New Global Era. There have always been architects famous enough to be drawn abroad by their international reputation. The Italian architect Sebastiano Serlio was invited to France by Francis I in the sixteenth century, and Frank Lloyd Wright was asked to Japan to design the Imperial Hotel in Tokyo in 1916. Since the 1990s, however, the novelty of iconic buildings and their prominence in the branding of cities and corporations made their architects famous, and the press has treated them as celebrities. The definition of who is or who is not a starchitect is variable. Newspapers occasionally publish lists and some names appear consistently: Frank Gehry (probably the original), Norman Foster, Zaha Hadid, Rem Koolhaas and Daniel Libeskind will almost always appear. Peter Eisenman, Robert Stern, Rafael Moneo, Renzo Piano, Richard Rogers, Toyo Ito, Richard

Meier, Rafael Viñoly and Jean Nouvel may also be included. Others will depend on the opinion or nationality of whoever is preparing the list. If it is a British commentator, it is likely that Will Alsop and Future Systems will be included. If an American is making up the list, David Childs and Steven Holl may appear. If the commentator is Italian, Massimiliano Fuksas will most likely be added.

If the architects are indeed to be stars and have names known by interested observers outside the architectural profession, or even instantly recognised by most practicing architects, the number will naturally be limited and will change from time to time. The only qualification is to have built a memorable building or buildings, be well known, and be in practice. While a recent book by the Spanish critic Julio Fajardo Herrero, *Starchitect: Visionary Architects of the Twenty-First Century*[169] lists seventy-five, this personal choice is too many to maintain star status. It is possible to use the winners of the Pritzker Prize as a guide. Known as the Nobel Prize for architecture, it is an award founded in 1979 in the USA for a "living architect whose built work demonstrates a combination of those qualities of talent, vision and commitment, which has produced consistent and significant contributions to humanity and the built environment through the art of architecture." The winner of the $100,000 award is chosen by a panel of nine "experts." Pritzker Prize winners still in practice currently number twenty-six, but do not include accepted stars such as Toyo Ito or Peter Eisenman.

To be a starchitect, whether voluntarily or otherwise, is to be a global brand, and star architects are chosen to give their brand value to projects. As the British international architect David Chipperfield says, "It's easier to know about architects than architecture. A banker won't know about architecture but will know that 'Zaha Hadid' or 'Rem Koolhaas' is a brand."[170] When the city state of Abu Dhabi announced in 2007 that it was to build a new cultural district of Saadiyat Island, it chose star architects to give the project instant status: Norman Foster will design the National Museum, there will be museums by Tadao Ando, Jean Nouvel and Zaha Hadid, and even a golf course by the star course designer, Gary Player. A "Biennale

Park" will have pavilions designed by junior entrants to the star architect system such as the Russian designer and architect Yuri Avvakumov and the Chinese architect Pei Zhu.

The star architect brand can be attached to their buildings to add value. In Manhattan there is the "Nouvel Chelsea" designed by Jean Nouvel; one block is called "New York by Gehry" (figure 45); another "Blue by Bernard Tschumi"; and there is "Herzog & de Meuron's 40 Bond St." As Ada Louise Huxtable, architecture Critic of the *Wall Street Journal*, said, "Now that there is celebrity in architecture, they find they can sell more, faster, if they have a name attached to it."[171] Global retail brands also recognise the value of global architectural brands. Prada, a brand that trades on its exclusivity, has launched a series of Fashion Flagship Stores in major cities: amongst them, Koolhaas's firm OMA has designed shops in Beverley Hills and New York, and their stores in Tokyo are designed by Herzog de Meuron and Toyo Ito. Rem Koolhaas also designed the "Prada Transformer," a rotating pavilion that first appeared in Seoul, Korea, in 2009. In 2008 Zaha Hadid designed a mobile pavilion for Chanel that has finally been given a permanent home in Paris. Daniel Libeskind has been taken on by Swarovski Crystals to design a chandelier in a shopping mall in Berne, Switzerland. Dior's couture collections have been presented as "inspired by Frank Gehry," but the firm's owner, Bernard Arnaud, was less fortunate when Parisian pressure groups managed to block his proposed Gehry-designed art gallery.

There is both irony and a hint of hypocrisy when the architects most frequently called "starchitects" are unhappy with the description. To be identified in this way is only a recognition of the commercial value of a name as a brand, and it serves the architects who are so named very well. When Zaha Hadid won a master plan competition outside Istanbul, it was admitted that "Zaha's international standing played a role" in the judges' decision as it would "create high investor interest."[172] Under these circumstances, it is disingenuous to pretend that you are just an ordinary architect. Frank Gehry, for many the archetypical star architect, is often vociferous about his dislike of the expression. One example of many similar protests is in a *Playboy* magazine interview: "I hate the word starchitect. Stuff like that comes from mean-spirited, untalented journalists. It's demeaning. It's derisive, and once it's said, it sticks. I get introduced all the time, 'Here's starchitect Frank Gehry …' My reaction: 'What the fuck are you talking about?'"[173] Peter Eisenman recognises that "the media people are the people who have changed the role of the architect," and that "the clients want media … they want the stars," and he thinks it has nothing to do with the quality of architecture.[174] Rem Koolhaas is not happy about the expression, but is more perceptive: "I think it's a name that is actually degrading to the vast majority of people it is applied to. And it really is a kind of political term that for certain clients is important because they use star architects."[175]

Figure 45.   Apartment tower, 8 Spruce Street, New York: Frank Gehry; 2011. Marketed as "New York by Gehry."

The fame of star architects can be used to add real-estate value to development.

Notwithstanding these protests, and by whatever name is given to them, there is little doubt that they are indeed a discrete group. Many of them have attended one or more of three key North Atlantic educational institutions, either as students or teachers. The Architectural Association in London has hosted Richard Rogers, Zaha Hadid, Rem Koolhaas, Steven Holl, Will Alsop, Daniel Libeskind and Bernard Tschumi. The Harvard Graduate School of Design has had Rafael Moneo, Rem Koolhaas and Herzog & de Meuron as teachers. The Yale School of Architecture has Norman Foster, Richard Rogers and David Childs as alumuni, and Frank Gehry, Peter Eisenman, Daniel Libeskind, Zaha Hadid, Tadao Ando, Richard Meier, Bernard Tschumi, Cesar Pelli and Bob Stern are present or recent faculty members. The connections go beyond education to employment. Zaha Hadid worked for Rem Koolhaas, and Koolhaas himself was a scholar at the New York Institute for Architectural and Urban Studies when it was run by Peter Eisenman. Daniel Libeskind was also briefly at the Institute for Architectural and Urban Studies and worked for Richard Meier. The group are also almost all from the old free-trade countries. All but three of the thirty-four Pritzker Prize winners come from countries inside this area, the exceptions being Luis Barragán from Mexico, and Oscar Niemeyer and Paulo Mendes da Rocha from Brazil. All the architects most frequently listed as star architects come from the developed economies. Even late entries from the emerging economies, such as the young Chinese architect Ma Yansong, trained at Yale and had a Royal Institute of British Architects' International Fellowship.

Global Architects

The iconic building and the starchitect are both distinct features that have emerged as a direct product of the New Global Era. The star architect group are made up of a very small number of architects and their buildings are, in any global perspective, very few. Most architects are tied to their countries of residence and work under the normal constraints of local clientele and limited budgets. Nonetheless, as is evident from the international fashion for unusual buildings and aspiration to iconic status, the work of these architects has been highly influential. Both the architects and their work have all the power and status of global brands. They are recognised and sought out by cities and corporations for their brand value. They are widely admired by their fellow professionals, even if there are dissenters, and win national as well as international prizes. Their work is regularly published in the national newspapers, all aspects of their practice are news and their projects are studied in detail in professional publications. They are seen by other architects as creative and successful, and as high earners. Their work, their attitude to built form, their use of digital modelling and their ideas have had a profound influence on architecture and architects throughout the world.

References

1. David Smith. "Workers Count Cost of a Global Labour Flood." *The Sunday Times*, April 29, 2007, 4/3.
2. "AAMA convention to focus on sourcing, exporting. (American Apparel Manufacturers Association)." *Daily News Record*, May 4, 1995.
3. Joseph E Stiglitz. *Globalization and Its Discontents*. London: Penguin, 2002, 12.
4. Colin Hines. *Localization: A Global Manifesto*. London, Earthscan, 2000, 131 & 134.
5. Martin Wolf. *Why Globalization Works*. New Haven, Yale University Press, 2005, 207.
6. Stiglitz, op. cit., 52.
7. Union of International Associations, database, 2005. David Held, Anthony McGrew, David Goldblatt and Jonathan Perraton, *Global Transformations: Politics, Economics and Culture*. Cambridge: Polity Press, 1999, 81.
8. Union of International Associations, database, 2005. Helmut K. Anheier, Marlies Glasius & Mary Kaldor, eds. *Global Civil Society 2001*. Oxford: Oxford University Press, 2001.

9. Anthony McGrew. "Globalization and Global Politics." In *The Globalization of World Politics: An Introduction to International Relations*, edited by John Baylis and Steve Smith. Oxford: Oxford University Press, 2006 (2001), 33.

10. Manuel Castells. "Informationalism, Networks, and the Network Society: A Theoretical Blueprint." In *The Network Society: A Cross-Cultural Perspective*, edited by Manuel Castells. Cheltenham: Edward Elgar Publishing, 2004, 21–22.

11. Ibid., 22–3.

12. Manuel Castells. *The Rise of the Network Society*. Oxford: Blackwell, 2000, 442–6.

13. Jeffrey S Juris. "Networked Social Movements: Global Movements for Global Justice." In Castells op. cit.

14. Naomi Klein. *No Logo*. London: Flamingo, 2000, 396.

15. Peter Willetts. "Transnational Actors and International Organizations in Global Politics." In Baylis & Smith, op. cit., 430.

16. David Held, Anthony McGrew, David Goldblatt & Jonathan Perraton. *Global Transformations: Politics, Economics and Culture*. Cambridge: Polity Press, 1999, 138.

17. J. Stowsky. "From Spin-off to Spin-on: Redefining the Military's Role in American Technology Development." In *The Highest Stakes*, edited by Wayne Sandholtz, Michael Borrus, John Zysman, Ken Conca, Jay Stowsky, Steven Vogel, Steve Weber. Oxford: Oxford University Press, 1992, 140.

18. Jonathan D. Aronson. "Causes and consequences of the communications and Internet revolution." Baylis & Smith, op. cit., 628–9.

19. David Held & Anthony McGrew, op. cit., 447.

20. Daniel Bell. "Previewing Planet Earth in 2013." *Washington Post*, January 3, 1988, B3.

21. Zygmunt Bauman. *Globalization: The Human Consequences*. Cambridge: Polity Press, 1998, 67–8.

22. Subcommandante Marcos. "The Fourth World War has Begun," Piece no. 5, Zapatista National Liberation Army, Chiapas, Mexico, 1997.

23. Colin Crouch. *Coping with Post-democracy*. London: Fabian Society, 2000, 20.

24. Charles M Tiebout. "A Pure Theory of Local Expenditures." *The Journal of Political Economy* 64 (5) (1956): 416–424.

25. Martin Wolf. *Why Globalization Works*. New Haven: Yale University Press, 2005, 263–4.
26. "Magnets for Money." *The Economist*, September 15, 2007, 3–22.
27. *Urban World: Mapping the Economic Power of Cities*, McKinsey Global Institute, 2011.
28. Manuel Castells. *The Power of Identity*. Oxford: Blackwell, 2004, 423.
29. Jan Aart Scholte. *Globalisation: A Critical Introduction*. New York: Palgrave Macmillan, 2005, 376.
30. Jordi Borja & Manuel Castells. *Local and Global, Management of Cities in the Information Age*. London: Earthscan, 1997, 17.
31. Hassan Fathy. "Architect for the Poor." *Time*, September 30, 1974, 1.
32. *Recommendations Concerning the Safeguarding and Contemporary Role of Historic Areas*, UNESCO, Nairobi, November 26, 1976.
33. Sir Reginald Blomfield & A D Connell. "For and Against Modern Architecture." *The Listener*, November 28, 1934, 886.
34. Theodor Adorno. *Aesthetic Theory*, trans Robert Hullot-Kentor. New York: Continuum, 1997, 41.
35. Martin Filler. "Hierarchies for Hire: The Impact of the Big Firms Since 1976." In *Thinking the Present: Recent American Architecture*, edited by K. M. Hays & C Burns. Princeton: Princeton University Press, 1990, 25.
36. Hans Ibelings. *Supermodernism: Architecture in the Age of Globalisation*. Rotterdam: NAi Publishers, 1998, 88.
37. Ibid., 129.
38. Harriet Schoenholz Bee, ed. *Tadao Ando*. New York Museum of Modern Art, 1991.
39. Bob Allies. "Contamination Kept Modernism Interesting." *Building Design*, March 31, 2006, 11.
40. Patrik Schumacher. "Parametricism." *The Architects' Journal*, May 6, 2010, 45.
41. Owen Hatherley. *Militant Modernism*. Winchester: O Books, 2008, 12–13.
42. Ulrich Beck, Anthony Giddens, Scott Lash. *Reflexive Modernization: Politics, Tradition and Aesthetics in the Modern Social Order*. Cambridge: Polity Press, 1994.
43. Chris Abel. "Return to Craft Manufacture." In *Architecture and Identity: Responses to Cultural and Technological Change*, edited Chris Abel. Oxford: Architectural Press, (1997) 2000, 46–7.
44. Ibelings, op. cit., 133.

45. Erich Mendelsohn. "The Problem of a New Architecture." Reprinted in *Programmes and Manifestos on 20th-Century Architecture*, edited by Ulrich Conrads. Cambridge, MA: MIT Press, 1970 (first publ. in German 1964), 55.

46. Marshall Berman. *All That is Solid Melts into Air: The Experience of Modernity*. New York: Verso 1983 (1982), 15.

47. Kenneth Frampton. "Towards a Critical Regionalism, Six Points for Architecture of Renaissance." Reprinted in *The Anti-Aesthetic, Essays on Post-Modern Culture*, edited by Hal Foster. New York: The New Press 1998 (Bay Press 1983), 19.

48. John Naisbitt & Doris Naisbitt. *China's Megatrends: The 8 pillars of a New Society*. London: Harper Collins, 2004, 93.

49. Charlie Qiuli Xue, Yingchun Li. "Importing American Architecture to China: The Practice of John Portman and Associates in Shanghai." *The Journal of Architecture* 13 (3) (2008): 317.

50. Philip Langdon. "Asia bound." *Progressive Architecture*, March, 1995, 44, 66.

51. Keller Easterling. *Enduring Innocence: Global Architecture and its Masquerades*. Cambridge, MA: MIT Press, 2005, 14–34.

52. "A Survey of India's Economy." *The Economist*, May 31, 2003.

53. Mark Landler. "Hi, I'm in Bangalore (but I Can't Say So)." *New York Times*, March 21, 2001, 1A.

54. Ibelings, op. cit., 134.

55. Castells, 2000, op. cit., 449–50.

56. Gerard Delanty & Paul R. Jones. "European Identity and Architecture." *European Journal of Social Theory* 65 (4) (2002): 453 & 457.

57. Aspa Gospodini. "European Cities and Place-Identity." Discussion Paper Series 8 (2), Dept of Planning and Regional Development, Thessaly, University of Thessaly, March 2002, 33–4.

58. John Carey. *The Intellectuals and the Masses*. London: Faber and Faber, 1992.

59. Peter J Taylor. *Modernities: A Geohistorical Interpretation*. Cambridge: Polity Press, 1999, 60–61.

60. Capital Realty, Beijing.

61. Hsin-Huang Michael Hsiao. "Cultural Globalisation and Localisation in Contemporary Taiwan." In *Many Globalizations: Cultural Diversity in the Contemporary World*, edited Peter L Berger & Samuel P Huntingdon. Oxford: Oxford University Press, 2002, 45–6.

62. Taylor, op. cit., 59–60.
63. Catherin Bull, Darko Radovic & Claire Parin. "Conclusion: Urban Design For a Cross-Cultural Future." *Cross-Cultural Urban Design*, edited by Catherin Bull et al. London: Routledge, 2007, 210.
64. Ibelings, op. cit., 67.
65. John Short. *The Humane City: Cities as If People Matter*. Oxford: Basil Blackwell, 1989.
66. Roger K Lewis. "Will Forces of Globalization Overwhelm Traditional Local Architecture." *Washington Post*, November 2, 2002.
67. Marc Augé. *Non-Places: Introduction to an Anthropology of Supermodernity*. New York: Verso, 1995, 77–8.
68. Ibid., 79.
69. Ibid., 106.
70. M Kearney. "The Local and the Global: The Anthropology of Globalisation and Transnationalism." *Annual Review of Anthropology* 24 (1995): 553.
71. Gilles Deleuze & Félix Guattari. *Anti-Oedipus*. London: Continuum International Publishing Group Ltd, 1972.
72. Gil-Manuel Hernàndez i Martí, "The Deterritorialization of Cultural Heritage in a Globalized Modernity." *Journal of Contemporary Culture*, Institut Ramon Llull, Barcelona, 2006.
73. Mike Davies. "Planet of Slums." In *Feelings are Always Local*, edited by Joke Brouwer et al. Amsterdam: V2 Publishing/NAi Publishers, 2004, 30.
74. Julia Nevárez, "Locating the Global in Harlem, NYC: Urban Development Initiatives, Public Space, and Gentrification." In *On Global Grounds: Urban Change and Globalisation*, edited by Julia Nevárez & Gabriel Moser. New York: Nova, 2009, 141.
75. Augé, op. cit., 110.
76. Harald Bodenschatz. "Dubai: Wonder of the World in Crisis." *Bauwelt* 23 (2009): 17 & 23.
77. George Katodrytis. "Dubai: Tourism and the End of Public Space," 2006. http://katodrytis.com/main/72/Gulf-first-urban-planningand-development-conference
78. Sharon Zukin. *The Cultures of Cities*. Oxford: Blackwell, 1995, 64–5.
79. Ronald Nitzen. *A World Beyond Difference: Cultural Identity in the Age of Globalisation*. Oxford: Blackwell, 2004, 38.
80. Klein, op. cit., 323.

81. Karl Marx. *Selected Writings*. Oxford: Oxford University Press, 2000, 235–6.

82. George Santayana. *Denominations and Powers: Reflections on Liberty, Society and Government*. New York: Augustus M Kelly, 1972, 459.

83. Paul Ricoeœur. *Universal Civilization and National Cultures, History and Truth*, trans. Charles A Kelbley. Evanston, IL, Northwestern University Press, 1965, 271–84.

84. Theodore Levitt. "The Globalization of Markets." Cambridge, MA: *Harvard Business Review*, May/June 1983, 92–102.

85. D. Yergin & J. Stanislaw. *The Commanding Heights: The Battle Between Government and the Marketplace that is Remaking the Modern World*. New York: Simon and Schuster, 1998, 10.

86. Daniel Miller. "Introduction: Anthropology, Modernity and Consumption." In *Worlds Apart: Modernity Through the Prism of the Local*, edited by D. Miller. London: Routledge, 1995, 4, 8.

87. Helena Norberg-Hodge. "The March of the Monoculture." *The Ecologist* 29, May/June, 1999, 194–6.

88. James Davison Hunter & Joshua Yates. "The World of American Globalisers." In Berger and Huntingdon, op. cit., 338–9.

89. Ibid., 330–1.

90. Ibid., 345.

91. Margaret K Nydell. *Understanding Arabs: A Guide for Modern Times*. London: Intercultural Press, 2006, 122.

92. Douglas B Holt, John A Quelch & Earl L Taylor. *How Global Brands Compete*. Cambridge, MA: Harvard Business Review, September 2004, 4.

93. Hunter & Yates, op. cit., 323–5.

94. Jan Aart Scholte. "Global Trade and Finance." In Baylis & Smith, op. cit., 607.

95. *Universal Declaration on Cultural Diversity*, UNESCO, Paris, November 2, 2001.

96. John Frain. *Introduction to Marketing*. Plymouth, Macdonald and Evans, 1983, 127.

97. Ann Bernstein. "Can South Africa be more than an Offshoot of the West?" In Berger & Huntingdon, op. cit., 216.

98. Hunter & Yates, op. cit., 351.

99. Simon Anholt. *Places: Identity, Image and Reputation*. London: Palgrave MacMillan, 2010.

100. Hunter & Yates, op. cit., 350–1.
101. Jerry Mander. "Metatechnology, Trade, and the New World Order." In *The Case Against Free Trade, GAT, NAFTA, and the Globalisation of Corporate Power*, edited by Ralph Nader. San Francisco and Berkeley, CA: Earth Island Press and North Atlantic Books, 1993, 14–15.
102 Inter Brand Website: www.interbrand.com (accessed November 2011).
103. Holt, Quelch & Taylor, op. cit., 2.
104. Ibid., 3.
105. Hunter and Yates, op. cit., 330.
106. "Chirac Slams US Food Domination." BBC News, September 16, 1999.
107. Holt, Quench & Taylor, op. cit., 1.
108. "Forbidden City Starbucks Closes." BBC News, July 14, 2007.
109. Naisbitt, op. cit., 191.
110. John Urry. *The Tourist Gaze*. London: Sage Publications, 2002 (1990), 5.
111. Agnes Heller. *A Theory of Modernity*. Oxford: Blackwell, 1999, 189–90.
112. Quoted in Vicente Rodriguez. "Tourism as a Recruiting Post for Retirement Migration." *Tourism Geographies* 3 (1) (2001): 52–63.
113. Urry, op. cit., 74.
114. Richard Lloyd & Terry Clark. "The City as an Entertainment Machine." *Annual meeting of the American Sociological Association,* Washington DC, 2000. Research Report no. 454.
115. Bella Dicks. *Culture on Display: The production of Contemporary Visibility*. Milton Keynes: Open University Press, 2003, 35.
116. Ibid., 1.
117. John B. Allcock. "International Law and the Former Yugoslavia." In *Globalization and Identity*, edited by Alan Carling. London: IB Tauris, 2006, 165–6.
118. Heller, op. cit., 188–9.
119. Urry, op. cit., 154.
120. Dean MacCannell. *The Tourist: A New Theory of the Leisure Class*. New York: Schocken Books, 1976, 26–7.
121. Gospodini, op. cit., 30–1.
122. Aaaron Betsky. "Icons: Magnets of Meaning," San Francisco Museum of Contemporary Art, 1996.

123. Charles Jencks. *Iconic Building: The Power of Enigma*. London: Frances Lincoln, 2005, 182.

124. In discussion with the author, December 2011.

125. Jencks, op. cit., 12.

126. Impact of the activities of the Guggenheim Museum Bilbao on the Basque regional economy in 2010, Guggenheim Museum Bilbao Foundation.

127. David Taylor, "Simply the Best." Paris, *MIPIM Preview*, 2010, 41.

128. Zukin, op. cit., 2.

129. Elias Beriatos & Aspa Gospodini. "'Glocalisation' and Urban Landscape Transformations: Built Heritage and Innovative Design versus non-competitive morphologies – the case of Athens 2004." *Discussion Paper Series* 9 (24), Dept of Planning and Regional Development, Thessaly, University of Thessaly, August 2003, 552–553.

130. Robert Booth. "Fortune Cookie." *Building Design*, November 7, 2003, 10.

131. Jiang Xu & Anthony G. O. Yeh. "City Repositioning and Competitiveness Building in Regional Development: New Development Strategies in Guangzhou." *International Journal of Urban and Regional Research* 29 (2) (2005).

132. Heerim website description: www.heerim.com (accessed December 2011).

133. "Capital Gate wins prestigious Cityscape Awards." Dubai, UAE, *Khaleej Times*, September 29, 2011.

134. "Greater Paris: Wider and Still Wider." *The Economist*, December 5, 2009, 43–4.

135. "Brave New World." Tees Valley Generation Press Release, Tees Valley Unlimited Website, April 16, 2009, no longer available.

136. A. L. Huxtable. *The Tall Building Artistically Reconsidered*. New York: Pantheon, 1984, 11.

137. Kim Dovey. "The Global Edifice Complex: Melbourne Australia." In Nevárez & Moser, op. cit., 99.

138. For discussion see Reinier de Graaf & Rem Koolhaas. "€-conography." In *Content : Triumph of Realization*, edited by Rem Koolhaas & Brendan McGetrick. Cologne, Taschen, 2004.

139. Ibelings, op. cit., 45.

140. Charlie Qiuli Xue & Yingchun Li. "Importing American architecture to China: the practice of John Portman and Associates in Shanghai." *The Journal of Architecture* 13 (3) (2008): 328–9.

141. Culture Show, London, BBC2 TV, October 22, 2010.

142. Rem Koolhaas. *Delirious New York: A Retroactive Manifesto for Manhattan.* Oxford: Oxford University Press, 1978.

143. Patrik Schumacher. "Ten Questions for Thinkers about the Present and Future of Design." *Harvard Design Magazine* 20, Massachusetts, 2004, 18–19.

144. Hugh Pearman. "Quick, fetch me a pencil …" *RIBA Journal*, March 2008, 35.

145. Personal interview with Professor Paul Richens, University of Bath November 2011; additional information on users from PhD student Roly Hudson of University of Bath.

146. Personal interview with John Hare, October 2011.

147. Jencks, op. cit., 40.

148. James Madge. "Type at the Origin of Architectural Form." *The Journal of Architecture* 12 (1) (2007): 25.

149. Graham Morrison. "Look at me!" *The Guardian*, July 12, 2004.

150. Daniel Libeskind. Munich, Radix-Matrix Prestel-Verlag, 1997, 34.

151. Rem Koolhass. "Bigness: Or the Problem of Large." *In Rem Koolhaas & Bruce Mau, S,M,L,XL.* New York: Monacelli Press, 1995, 515.

152. Patrik Schumacher. "Parametricism: A New Global Style for Architecture and Urban Design." *Digital Cities,* London, Architectural Design, Edition 79 (4) July/August 2009, 15.

153. Schumacher 2010, op. cit., 43.

154. "How Genius Works." *The Atlantic Magazine*, May 2011.

155. David Neustein. "Frank Gehry's crumpled vision for Sydney." *Australian Design Review*, December 22, 2010.

156. Joseph Masheck. "Steven Holl." *Bomb, Architecture*, no. 79, spring 2002.

157. Pearman, op. cit., 35.

158. Daniel Libeskind. *The Space of Encounter.* London: Thames & Hudson, 2001, 157.

159. Personal Interview with the Director of the National Museum, Qatar, 2009.

160. Karen Cilento. "National Museum of Qatar / Jean Nouvel" www.archdaily.com, March 31, 2010.

161. Description on Aedas' website: www.aedas.com (accessed December 2011).

162. Description on Henning Larson's website: www.henninglarsen.com (accessed December 2011).

163. Description on MVRDV's website: www.mvrdv.nl (accessed December 2011).

164. Quotation from HOK's website: www.hok.com (accessed December 2011).

165. Christine Murray. "Beijing's Cuckoo's Nest." *Architects' Journal* April 17, (2008): 50–52.

166. Quoted by Claire Wrathall. "Beijing Airport: China shows Heathrow How it Should be Done." Englewood Cliffs, N.J, CNBC Business, May 2008.

167. Description on Foster+Partners' website: www.fosterandpartners.com (accessed December 2011).

168. Han Manman. "Imagining Beyond Form—Frank Gehry Brings First Exhibition to Beijing." Information Office of the Beijing Municipal Government, *Beijing Today*, October 22, 2010.

169. Julio Fajardo Herrero. *Starchitect: Visionary Architects of the Twenty-First Century*. New York: Harper Design, 2010.

170. Marcus, J. S. 'Designer Cities: The Development of the Superstar Urban Plan." *The Wall Street Journal*, July 5, 2008.

171. Stephen Zacks. "Starchitect Condos—2005." *Metropolismag*, March 20, 2006.

172. Marcus, op. cit.

173. "Frank Gehry: Playboy Interview." *Playboy Magazine*, January 2011.

174. "Architetti Invervisti, Peter Eisenman." Floornature, Modena, Italy, Fiornano Modenese, 2004.

175. "Living Differently." Anjali Rao interview with Rem Koolhaas. *CNN Talk Asia*, June 24, 2009.

PART IV:

HOW GLOBALISATION KEEPS THINGS DIFFERENT

The Breakdown of the Nation State and Revived Identities

The similarity and international character of consumer products, the ubiquity of brands and the internationalisation of design have become recognised symbols of globalisation. This is often experienced as an unease with the power of transnational corporations and frustration with the seeming lack of democratic accountability of global organisations, ranging from international financial institutions to regional political and trading collectives. While the nation state remains the primary democratic unit on a legislative scale and in *inter*-national affairs, as we have seen above, its traditional powers have been eroded by the free movement of capital, the huge destructive power of armaments, global financial regulation, supra-national organisations, and the growth of transnational corporations. While these high-level global phenomena sit above the disempowered nation state, a plethora of issue-based International Non-Governmental Organisations have come in from below. Other seismic political events have also affected the position of the nation state.

When the global fifty-year military stand-off of the Cold War ended in 1989, the pressure to persuade or coerce large populations to remain loyal to a political system or a defined territory was relaxed. This was felt immediately with the collapse of the Soviet Union. Known in the West by its dominant nation—Russia—the Union of Soviet Socialist Republics celebrated the different ethnic and peasant cultures across its vast territory, but communism and state-wide institutions created a single military and political bloc. When this union descended into financial crisis and the communist infrastructure collapsed, internal tensions and aspirations came to the surface and the Soviet Union rapidly broke up into its constituent parts. A series of nations established themselves as fifteen independent states, from the relatively small Baltic States in the west to the vast, sparsely populated Kazakhstan in the east, to the ancient nation of Georgia to the south.

This very conspicuous state fragmentation was only part of a greater worldwide assertion of local identities and the decline of the power base of the nation state.

The nation state as a monolithic institution actively promoted its distinctive identity and demanded loyalty or, as Arjun Apppadurai puts it, created the "spatial and social standardization that is prerequisite for the disciplined national citizen."[1] In historical terms this was a relatively recent phenomenon. David Held, Anthony McGrew, David Goldblatt and Jonathan Perraton describe the history of modern state formation:

> ... the historical record suggests that even where a proto-sense of the nation existed prior to the eighteenth century—for example in France, Sweden or England—it was always but one identity or point of allegiance. It necessarily competed with larger transnational identities and more particularistic, local and regional identities ... Nations emerged as distinctive collective social actors only when proto-nations were transformed by the economic, social and political changes of the long nineteenth century.[2]

Zygmunt Bauman points out how the process of nation formation affected minorities: "The establishment of any sovereign state required as a rule the suppression of the formative ambitions of many lesser populations—undermining or expropriating however little they might have possessed of inchoate military capacity, economic self-sufficiency and cultural distinctiveness."[3] This apparent unity turned out to be fragile when the power of the state diminished.

Manuel Castells describes how the underlying tensions could lead to fragmentation:

> Once a nation became established, under the territorial control of a given state, the sharing of history did induce social and cultural bonds as well as economic and political interests, among its members. Yet, the uneven representation of social interests, cultures, and territories in the nation-state skewed national institutions toward the interests of organizing elites and their geometry of alliances, thus opening the way for institutional crises when subdued identities, historically rooted or ideologically revived, were able to mobilize for a renegotiation of the historical national contract.[4]

Pressures to change this "historical national contract" had been on the rise since the 1970s. The transnational north European Sami were given their first ethnic parliament by Finland in 1973, and Quebec Province was recognised as a "distinct society" within Canada in 1987. In the 1990s, however, there was a dramatic increase in the reassertion of subdued identities.

The collapse of the Soviet dominance of Eastern Europe had an immediate impact. Yugoslavia violently split into its constituent parts based on the ethnic and religious divisions that had been supressed in the early twentieth century. Czechoslovakia peacefully split into the Czech Republic and Slovakia. Other European nations began to divide internally. In Spain, the Catalan Nationalist Party came to play a major role in Spanish politics in the 1990s, and since 1991 a united Basque nationalist movement has governed the Basque Region. Separatist movements have become stronger. Belgium has been threatening to divide into Flanders and Wallonia for some time, but in 1993 Belgium became a fully federal state. The *Lega Nord*, seeking to establish the new state of Padania, an independent state in northern Italy, entered the Italian coalition government in 1994. In the United Kingdom, following referendums in 1997, limited legislative power was given to two constituent nations: Scotland and

Wales. The Scottish Nationalist party is in power today and still seeks complete independence.

The violent separatism experienced by Yugoslavia was more common outside Europe. Tamil separatists pioneered suicide bombing in Sri Lanka. The Free Papua Movement continues to fight for independence from Indonesia. Civil war in Sudan, and the creation of the new nation-state of South Sudan were only resolved by international intervention. Liberation or separatist conflict has been one of the major sources of conflict since atomic weapons curtailed conventional warfare between major states.

Satisfying the aspirations of minorities within nation states has been managed more peacefully by granting powers and rights to provinces and ethnic and indigenous groups. In 1988 the Brazilian Constitution granted its twenty-seven States "semi-autonomous sub-national" powers. In 1993 the European Union set up the Committee of the Regions to provide some place for extra-national communities in the EU's institutional framework. Chinese decentralisation began when Deng Xiaoping declared in 1980 that provinces should "eat in separate kitchens rather than from a common pot," leading to province-based taxation in 1993, and provincial independence in the management of foreign direct investment in 2009. Uganda decentralised in 1993, in the process restoring the ancient identity of the Kingdom of Buganda. In 1992 the 74th amendment to the Indian Constitution gave greater powers to its twenty-five States to create "vibrant democratic units of self-government." In 1999 Canada created the new territory of Nunavut with its own legislative assembly, a two million square kilometre area with a largely Inuit population of 30,000.

The creation of new nation states, micro-states and the increased power of regions are only part of a rise of identity politics stimulated by political and social changes in the New Global Era. The forging of political identities in the old nation states was described by the political scientist Benedict Anderson in 1983 as, "an imagined political community—and imagined as both inherently limited and sovereign."[5] As "imagined" national communities broke down in the

1990s, the fundamental need for identity began to be directed elsewhere. The geographer David Hooson describes the problem: "The urge to express one's identity, and to have it recognised tangibly by others, is increasingly contagious and has to be recognised as an elemental force even in the shrunken, apparently homogenizing, high-tech world of the end of the twentieth century."[6]

In 1964 philosopher and critic Marshall McLuhan had predicted the transfer of communal identity to an "electrically contracted" global village.[7] This was an optimistic prediction. By the mid-1980s it was clear to many that identity could not be readily allocated to any such large and anonymous concept. The American poet, essayist and academic, Wendell Berry, summed it up in 1977:

> There can be no such thing as a "global village." No matter how much one may love the world as a whole, one can live fully in it only by living responsibly in some small part of it. Where we live and who we live there with define the terms of our relationship to the world and to humanity … A culture is not a collection of relics or ornaments, but a practical necessity, and its corruption invokes calamity.[8]

By the turn of the millennium, even the eminent advocate of cosmopolitanism, Kwame Anthony Appiah, admitted that it "is not that we can't take a moral interest in strangers, but that the interest is bound to be abstract, lacking in the warmth and power that comes from shared identity. Humanity isn't, in the relevant sense, an identity at all."[9]

The disorientation created by expanded global horizons and the increasing irrelevance of nationalist mythologies have encouraged individuals to re-examine, and if necessary redefine, their identities. As the philosopher Simone Weil said, "To be rooted is perhaps the most important and least recognized need of the human soul."[10] Identity politics are based on the search for what Edmund Burke famously called the "little platoon" that we "belong to in society" that is "the first principle (the germ as it were) of publick affections."[11] As Zygmunt Bauman says, poetically:

And what are the abandoned, desocialised, atomised, lonely individuals likely to dream of, and given a chance, do? Once the big harbours have been closed or stripped of the breakwaters that used to make them secure, the hapless sailors will be inclined to carve out and fence off their own small havens where they can anchor and deposit their bereaved, and fragile, identities. No longer trusting the public navigation network, they will jealously guard access to such private havens against all and any intruders.[12]

Cultural Rights and the International Response

Localisation and the search for a particular identity that characterises the New Global Era contradicts the modernisation theories of the 1960s—transferred to globalisation theory in the 1990s—which envisaged the convergence of societies to a North Atlantic type as they developed similar levels of prosperity. As Marc Augé says: "At the very same moment when it becomes possible to think in terms of the unity of terrestrial space, and the big multinational networks grow strong, the clamour of particularisms rises."[13] In 2008 the United States National Intelligence Council recognised this as a new political condition: "Intrinsic to the growing complexity of the overlapping roles of states, institutions, and nonstate actors is the *proliferation of political identities,* which is leading to establishment of new networks and rediscovered communities" [emphasis in original].[14]

Identity politics are as much a witness to the impact of globalisation as the power of transnational corporations and come in many forms.

Threats to the identity of ethnic groups, seen through the lens of Jacques Rousseau's noble savage as a precious survival of our uncorrupted selves, tend to elicit particular sympathy and regret. The assertion of ethnic identity has led the way in the growth of identity politics. In 1994 the anthropologist J McIver Weatherford observed:

For a long time it appeared that ethnic groups were slowly being absorbed into the nations in which they lived. They were viewed as holdovers from another era, and it was thought that gradually as the people modernized, they would naturally abandon their ethnic identity in favour of a national one ... Instead, ethnic identities have grown stronger in the modern world.[15]

The need to assert a particular identity, however, goes beyond primordial ethnicity. The French sociologist Alain Touraine points out:

> ... we see today that in many parts of the world, new actors, both individual and collective, are claiming new cultural rights. They aspire to combine their participation in the economic world with the retention or reinterpretation of their cultural heritage and cultural projects. The strength of these new movements re-establishes the role of political action and endows actors with the capacity to make choices, to feel free, and to take responsibility for their own experience. One may, moreover, distinguish between what is commonly called identity politics—through which individuals and groups strive to protect social attributes, like sex, age, craft, creed, ethnicity or religion—and the demand for cultural rights, which is best defined as the defence of the "subject."[16]

The demand for cultural rights may be an assertion of the individual's right to cultural choice or a collective assertion of social rights, but in either case it is based on a global dynamic. As the British sociologist Roland Robertson points out: "It is crucial to recognize that the contemporary concern with civilizational and societal (as well as ethnic) uniqueness—as expressed via such motifs as identity, tradition and indigenization—largely rests on globally diffused ideas."[17]

The international spread of this concern is witnessed by a series of reports and declarations by supra-national organisations. The first initiatives come from International Non-Governmental Organisations. For example, the Inuit Circumpolar Council was set up in 1977 with the objective of, *inter alia*, the "preservation and evolution of Inuit culture."[18] In 1984 the World Council of Indigenous Peoples issued "The Declaration of Principles of Indigenous Rights" in Panama which included the principle that, "The cultures of indigenous peoples are part of mankind's cultural patrimony" as part of the "minimal rights to which indigenous Peoples are entitled."[19]

By the 1990s the international community, as represented by the United Nations, had taken up the cause.

In 1992 the General Assembly of the United Nations adopted the "Declaration on the Rights of Persons Belonging to National, Ethnic, Religious and Linguistic Minorities," where Article I stated that: "States shall protect the existence and the national or ethnic, cultural, religious and linguistic *identity* of minorities" [my emphasis].[20] In the same year the Council of Europe issued the "European Charter for Regional and Minority Languages" which sought "the protection of the historical regional or minority languages of Europe, some of which are in danger of eventual extinction," and which contribute "to the maintenance and development of Europe's cultural wealth and traditions."[21] In 1994 the European Union established the Committee of the Regions which, as part of its mission statement, seeks to "respond to the challenges of globalisation" and "make the very most of [Europe's] territorial, cultural and linguistic diversity."[22]

The United Nations expanded its interest to a wider view of cultural diversity beyond ethnicity. In the "Vienna Declaration on Human Rights" of 1993, cultural diversity was inserted within the now almost sacred ambit of the 1948 Declaration of Human Rights, stating that the "international community" must bear in mind "the significance of national and regional particularities and various historical, cultural and religious backgrounds," and that "persons belonging to minorities have the right to enjoy their own culture."[23] In 1996 UNESCO issued "Our Creative Diversity. Report of the World Commission on Culture and Development," which warns of the powerful "global pressures of so-called 'global' popular cultures" and declares that "every community has its cultural and spiritual affiliations reaching back symbolically to the dawn of time," and that "these cultural patterns play an irreplaceable role in defining individual and group identity."[24]

By the time UNESCO brought out the "Universal Declaration on Cultural Diversity" in 2001, the international institutional response to the culturally particular had become very clear. It stated that "cultural diversity is as necessary for humankind as biodiversity is for nature … it is the common heritage of humanity and should be recognized and affirmed for the benefit of present and future generations."[25] It went beyond necessity: "The defence of cultural diversity is an ethical imperative."[26] The means of expression of this cultural diversity were also to be protected and were identified: "All persons have … the right to express themselves and to create and disseminate their work in the language of their choice, and particularly in their mother tongue."[27] And "heritage in all its forms must be preserved, enhanced and handed on to future generations as a record of human experience and aspirations."[28]

Identity Politics and the Complexity of the Global Condition

There is an irony in the implication that for cultures to be protected from transnational cultural contamination, they require the recognition of an authoritative transnational organization. These protective resolutions seem, furthermore, to be based on the assumption that minorities under threat are territorially located and should survive much as ancient monuments should be protected as authentic records of past cultures.

The Italian sociologist, Raimondo Strassoldo, expands the search for cultural security beyond surviving minority groups: "Contemporary globalization has … often reinvigorated more localized solidarities. When faced with a seemingly vast, intangible and uncontrollable globality, many people have turned away from the state to their local 'home' in hopes of enhancing their possibilities of community and self-determination."[29] Home is not, however, necessarily static, singular or vulnerable. The French sociologist, Michel Wieviorka, points out that "cultural specificities function in all sorts of spheres, some of which are local and small scale, and others at global level, some being totally confined within a national context, and others extending beyond it, for example in diaspora model."[30] Furthermore, as the anthropologist Fredrik Barth says: "People participate in multiple, more or less discrepant, universes of discourse; they construct different partial and simultaneous worlds in which they move; their cultural construction of reality springs not from one source and is not of one piece."[31] These are what Zygmunt Bauman calls "cloakroom communities ... conjured into being, if in apparition only, by hanging up individual troubles, as theatregoers do with their coats ... patched together for the duration of the spectacle and promptly dismantled again once the spectators collect their coats from the hooks in the cloakroom."[32] As Bauman implies, our relationship with our cultural identity has become increasingly complex. This is described by the British political philosopher John Gray:

> We all of us belong to many communities, we mostly inherit diverse ethnicities, and our world-views are fractured and provisional whether or not we know it or admit it. We harbour a deep diversity of views and values ... The reactionary project of rolling back this diversity of values and world-views in the pursuit of a lost cultural unity overlooks the character of our cultural inheritance as a palimpsest, having ever deeper layers of complexity.[33]

In this complexity sit the "desocialised, atomised, lonely individuals" Bauman identified in us all.

Ajun Appadurai discusses the new insecurity as it is experienced by second generation migrants:

> Many people suddenly find themselves to be minorities when they didn't know they were minorities. ... This is being discovered now by younger migrants throughout the world. They are very much part of the societies in which they live, and indeed have lost various connections to their home societies, and often have come very far from their own parents and grandparents. They have struggled ... but their struggles have an added burden, because they also have to deal with a kind of outside force of image-making.[34]

As the political scientist W. James Booth says: "Gone are the days when there was a seamless web of memory uniting the entirety of the national community in a common narrative of the past."[35] The sociologist Peter Berger sees this as a fundamental aspect of modern society: "Modern man has suffered from a deepening condition of homelessness … It goes without saying that this condition is psychologically hard to bear. It has therefore engendered … nostalgias … for a condition of 'being at home' in society, with oneself and, ultimately, in the universe."[36]

In order to achieve some stability of identity— to "be at home"— in an alien or unstable condition, societies may adapt their changed circumstances to create new hybrid cultural forms that have the reassurance of traditions. In *The Symbolic Construction of Community* the sociologist Anthony Cohen describes this process:

> It has long been noticed that societies undergoing rapid, and, therefore, de-stabilizing processes of change often generate atavistically some apparently traditional forms, but impart to them meaning and implication appropriate to contemporary circumstances. Such reactions to change may be a syncretistic marriage of tradition and modernity in language, technology, religion and so forth. They are also sometimes manifest as a deliberate maintenance of the forms of customary practices in changed circumstances which now render their earlier rationales anachronistic. These syncretic techniques appear to be means of rendering alien practices into a familiar and, therefore, acceptable form. They may be regarded as vernacular translations and modifications of extrinsic social influence.[37]

This established technique for the manipulation of tradition to re-establish cultural identity took on a modern form as global media and international communication rendered all places familiar and altered our perception of what was local. The Cambridge sociologist John B. Thompson outlines how we have expanded the ways we can use tradition to create the familiarity of belonging to a place or a community.

... with the development of the media, traditions were gradually uprooted; the bond that tied traditions to specific locales of face-to-face interaction was gradually weakened. In other words, traditions were gradually and partially *de-localized*, as they became increasingly dependent on mediated forms of communication for their maintenance and transmission from one generation to the next.

The uprooting or "de-localization" of tradition had far-reaching consequences ... It enabled traditions to be detached from particular locales and freed from the constraints imposed by oral transmission in circumstances of face-to-face interaction. The reach of tradition—both in space and in time—was no longer restricted by the conditions of localized transmission. But the uprooting of traditions from particular locales did not lead them to wither away, nor did it destroy altogether the connection between traditions and spatial units. On the contrary, the uprooting of traditions was the condition for the re-embedding of traditions in new contexts and for the re-mooring of traditions to new kinds of territorial unit that exceeded the limits of shared locales. Traditions were de-localized but they were not de-territorialized: they were refashioned in ways that enabled them to be re-embedded in a multiplicity of locales and re-connected to territorial units that exceed the limits of face-to-face interaction.[38]

Personal and Social Identity

Identity has always been an essential element in human society but, as it becomes increasingly fragmented and contested and takes on an enhanced political and social dimension, it is important to understand at a fundamental level what lies behind the need for identity in social and personal life.

Identification is fundamental to all human perception. We have to identify phenomena in order to understand them and interact with them. We identify things as the same and different. As humans we give a common identity and name to groups of things we categorise as similar, and to do so we must identify a group of things as different from other groups of things. We can also identify social groups. Each person seeks their identity as an individual and does so through the social groups to which they belong. Identity is established through sameness and difference: in the sense of sameness with groups of people who it is assumed share this sense; in the sense of difference from other groups. As the political scientist Jan Aart Scholte explains, this goes to heart of self and community:

> Understanding and affirming the self— both as an individual and as a group member—is a prime motivation for, and major preoccupation of, social interaction. People seek in social relations to explore their class, their gender, their nationality, their race, their religious faith, their sexuality, and other aspects of their being. Constructions of identity moreover provide much of the basis for social bonds, including collective solidarity against oppression. Notions of identity underpin frameworks for community, democracy, citizenship and resistance. In short, identity matters (a great deal).[39]

Group identity is a fundamental part of human behaviour. In 1970, the psychologist Henri Tajfel[40] conducted a series of experiments which reduced the identity of a series of individuals, one to another, to the absolute minimum by identifying only similar scores in trivial tasks. These individuals, knowing no more about their relationship with the others than a correspondence of score, consistently gave preferential treatment to those whose scores came closest to their own. This is known as Social Identity Theory and establishes the principle that for each of us there is an "in-group," which we favour, and "out-groups," which we do not.

The social psychologist Marliynn Brewer puts this into an evolutionary perspective:

> ... our ancestors chose cooperation rather than strength, and the capacity for social learning rather than instincts. As a result humans are characterized by obligatory interdependence ... Clear group boundaries provide a compromise between individual selfishness and indiscriminate cooperation or altruism. In effect, defined in-groups are bounded communities of mutual obligation and trust that delimit the extent to which both the benefits and costs of cooperation can be expected ... If human survival depends on bounded communities

of mutual, obligatory interdependence, then humans must also have
evolved psychological characteristics that support functioning in
such a social context. The capacity for symbolic self-representation,
the need for belonging and contingent, group-based trust are all
cognitive and motivational mechanisms that support and maintain
interdependent group living. Similarly, social identity and the need
for positive distinctiveness can be viewed as psychological
mechanisms that bind individuals to groups and commit them to the
preservation of intergroup boundaries.[41]

From our evolutionary origins in small social groups or tribes of
about 150 (Dunbar's number),[42] joined together for mutual benefit
and survival, we have now expanded a genetic predisposition to in-
group identity into a much wider field. From an existence where
there was mutual recognition and shared activities to a modern life in
a nation state or global group, where we can share carefully
protected, created and even enforced identities with populations
numbered in the millions, we find ourselves in a much more
complex condition in which we must find our identity. In both tribes
and nation states, this complexity is managed through the use of
symbols. In *The Symbolic Construction of Community*, Anthony Cohen
shows that "the consciousness of community has to be kept alive
through manipulation of its symbols. The reality and efficacy of the
community's boundary—and, therefore, of the community itself—
depends upon its symbolic construction and embellishment."[42] We
can recognise these symbols from the ceremonials of state to the use
of distinctive language and dress amongst social groups.

Much as communities do not spring from nowhere, the symbols
that define them are not spontaneous but are often traditional:

As sets of assumptions, beliefs and patterns of behaviour handed
down from the past, traditions provide some of the symbolic
materials for the formation of identity both at the individual and at
the collective level. The sense of oneself and the sense of belonging
are both shaped—to varying degrees, depending on social
context—by the values, beliefs and forms of behaviour which are
transmitted from the past. The process of identity formation can

never start from scratch; it always builds upon a pre-existing set of symbolic materials which form the bedrock of identity.[43]

As they are traditions rather than history, these symbols are not fixed. They can evolve with the community and even be invented[44] but, in all cases, their effectiveness as traditional symbols requires a convincing pedigree, real or imagined.

As the scale and variety of community expands, identity becomes less clear cut. As social psychologist Judith Howard points out:

> At earlier historical moments, identity was not so much an issue; when societies were more stable, identity was to a great extent assigned, rather than selected or adopted. In current times, however, the concept of identity carries the full weight of the need for a sense of who one is, together with an often overwhelming pace of change in surrounding social contexts—changes in the groups and networks in which people and their identities are embedded and in the societal structures and practices in which those networks are themselves embedded.[45]

And indeed, it is not necessary to choose any single one of these and for most of us "individual identification is revealed as, to a considerable extent, a customized collage of collective identifications."[46] Salman Rushdie can therefore ask of the modern condition: "Do cultures actually exist as separate, pure, defensible entities? Is not melange, adulteration, impurity, pick'n'mix at the heart of the idea of the modern?"[47]

As we have seen, in the New Global Era identity can be a problem. As Jan Aart Scholte says:

> Globalization has tended to increase the sense of a fluid and fragmented self, particularly for persons who spend large proportions of their time in supraterritorial spaces, where multiple identities readily converge and create "lost souls." In more globalized lives, identity is less easily taken for granted; self-definitions and associated group loyalties are much more up for grabs. Hybrid identities present significant challenges for the construction of community. How can deep and reliable social bonds

be forged when individuals have multiple and perhaps competing senses of self—and indeed often feel pretty unsettled in all of them?[48]

If group identity is, as the evidence suggests, a fundamental human need necessary for the proper function of family, community and nation, this rootlessness could undermine all these essential pillars of society. It is perhaps at this moment that the identity of place becomes particularly significant. Manuel Castells describes how people try to manage threats to their identity: "When the world becomes too large to be controlled, social actors aim to shrink it back to their size and reach. When networks dissolve time and space, people anchor themselves in places, and recall their historic memory … These defensive reactions become sources of meaning and identity, constructing new cultural codes out of historical materials."[49]

If society is fluid and symbolic markers of identity are ambiguous, almost all of us have at least somewhere we call home. As psychologist Stephanie Taylor points out: "Discussions of place and identity, whether among academic theorists or research participants, almost inevitably return to the concept of home."[50] Home is a place that is at least geographically stable; as the anthropologist Gordon Matthews says, "one's home is where in the world one most truly belongs."[51] The art and cultural historian Anthony King puts the concept on home into its physical and architectural context:

> This dwelling or residence always involves different levels of choice, in terms of location, neighbourhood, cost, size, typology, image, it is also part of our identity—whether that identity is professional, class, social, ethnic, cultural or, in particular places, racial. The location and dwelling where we live is one (important) way of how we either choose to, or are seen to, represent ourselves to others.[52]

Image consultant Simon Anholt describes how, as the secure foundation of our identity of place, home is the bedrock of all other geographic identities:

> The identity and image of the places we inhabit are really a seamless extension of the identity and image of ourselves; it is a natural human tendency for people to identify themselves with their city, region or country. Our sense of self isn't bounded by our own bodies: it extends out into family, neighbourhood, district, region, nation, continent, and ultimately to the human race.[53]

The tremendous significance of the places we call home makes any challenge to the security or stability of place identity particularly critical. The sociologist Tom Gieryn puts it most starkly: "To be without a place of one's own—*persona non locata*—is to be almost non-existent."[54]

"Glocalisation" and New Trading Conditions

The protection and assertion of community or individual identity can range from the benign preservation of threatened languages to, what Zygmunt Bauman calls, "identification wars." While reference to an idealised and localised past may be a strategy for counteracting the homogenising or threatening aspects of globalisation, the fact that it is set in motion by globalisation unavoidably links the two phenomena. Bauman makes the connection: "The frantic search of identity is not a residue of the pre-globalization times not-yet-fully-extirpated but bound to become extinct as the globalization progresses; it is, on the contrary, the side-effect, and by-product of the combination of globalizing and individualizing pressures and the tensions that spawn. The identification wars are neither contrary nor stand in the way of the globalizing tendency: they are a legitimate offspring and natural companion of globalization and far from arresting it, lubricate its wheels."[55] The sociologist Mike Featherstone goes one step further to say that "it is not helpful to regard the global and local as dichotomies separated in space or time; it would seem that the processes of globalization and localization are inextricably bound together."[56]

Trading practices, concerned only with the most effective means of marketing goods, provide practical evidence. Global outreach and local marketing were combined in the portmanteau word, "glocalisation." The word seems to have had its origins in papers in the *Harvard Business Review* by Japanese authors which used the Japanese term *dochakuka*, roughly meaning "global localization," in the late 1980s.[57] Translated to "glocalisation" by running together globalisation and localisation, it had become, according to the *Oxford Dictionary of New Words* in 1991, "one of the main marketing buzzwords."[58] In marketing terms, it means that the globalization of a product or service is more likely to succeed when the product or service is adapted specifically to each country in which it is marketed.[59] More cynically, economists Winfried Ruigrok and Rob van Tulder define "glocalisation" as: "A company's attempt to become accepted as a 'local citizen' in a different trade bloc, while transferring as little control as possible over its areas of strategic concern"[60] The word "glocal" so succinctly summarised the widely observed combination of the global and local in the 1990s that it has now been expanded to mean more simply: "relating to the connections or relationships between global and local businesses, problems, etc."[61] and has passed into more general use.

One of the most potent symbols of global homogenisation, the worldwide success of McDonalds, is based not just on the status of the McDonalds' hamburger as an American global product, but on its approach to different local markets. In Japan, for example, a country uniquely open to outside cultural influence and with a high-quality indigenous culinary culture, the Japanese conglomerate Fujita Shoten brought McDonalds to their national market with a quite different profile to the low-cost product in the United States by targeting middle class customers, thereby establishing a global-local position as a locally fashionable high status foreign product.[62]

MTV, promoter of that most distinctly and globally influential North Atlantic product—popular music—had to learn the hard way. Launched by Viacom in the United States in 1981, transforming "promotional clips" into the new creative medium of music video, it was highly successful in its home market. In 1989 MTV successfully exported its formula to fellow North Atlantic countries in Europe. In 1992 Viacom partnered with Satellite Television Asian Region

(STAR) TV to create MTV Asia. In India, as in other Asian countries, STAR TV realized that its success would rely on adapting its broadcasts to the culture of its audiences, but MTV refused to comply and the partnership in India ended. In 1997, struggling to re-enter the Indian market, MTV re-launched as an Indian channel, broadcasting in Hindi and English featuring Hindi-pop music alongside Western popular music. By 1999 its policy was to "Indianize, humanize, and humorize" its programming.[63] It has become the most popular music channel in India and now, the lesson learnt, the Vice-President of MTV can claim: "We're one of the very few brands who have nailed the notion of being able to be global and local at the same time."[64]

The process of expansion through mergers and acquisitions offers another route to local and global identity. Kodak, for example, entered the Chinese market through the purchase of seven Chinese film companies and, by doing so, became one of the two major film companies in China. Its CEO could tell Chinese audiences that the China Kodak Company aimed to become "a first-rate Chinese company." [65]

In 1995, Ian Angell, professor of information systems at the London School of Economics saw this as the future:

> … globalization is resulting in a trend towards *localization* or, as Morita [Akio Morita, co-founder of the Sony Corporation] calls it, "global localization." Global companies are setting themselves up within *virtual enterprises,* at the hub of loosely knit alliances of local companies, all linked together by global networks, both electronic and human. These companies assemble to take advantage of any temporary business opportunity; and then separate, searching for the next major deal. Apart from local products, local companies also deliver local expertise and access to home markets for other products created within the wider alliance. Companies and countries outside such networks have no future.[66]

The Local and the Global in Environmentalism

The most significant global-to-local issue of the end of the twentieth, and the start of the twenty-first century (and beyond) is widely considered to be environmental damage caused by the use of fossil fuels.

It has long been known that industrialisation polluted the air and the environment. It first came to a crisis in the UK, where the industrial revolution began. The industrialised West Midlands became known as the "Black Country" in the nineteenth century due to pervasive soot blackening. London became famous for its "pea-souper" fogs, which came to a climax in 1952 when some 4,000 people died, largely from respiratory conditions. This led to the first modern legislative air-quality controls—the British Clean Air Acts of 1956. Industrialisation was, however, linked to an increase in general prosperity, and rapid economic expansion after the Second World War made industrial pollution into a global problem. This first became an international issue in the 1970s when Canada and the Scandinavian countries protested at the wind-blown pollution from adjacent industrial countries that led to the destruction of woodland from "acid rain" (although the phenomenon had been observed for a century, the term was first coined in 1972). This led to the first broad international agreement on pollution in 1979, the Convention on Long-Range Trans-Boundary Air Pollution.

In 1972 the United Nations called the Conference on the Human Environment, the first major conference on international environmental issues. This was followed by the World Commission on Environment and Development in 1983 (the "Brundtland Commission") which called for a response to growing concern "about the accelerating deterioration of the human environment and natural resources and the consequences of that deterioration for economic and social development."[67] It was followed by the publication of "Our Common Future" in 1987, more commonly known as the "Brundtland Report," which includes the definition of sustainability most commonly used to this day.[68] In the following year, the United

Nations and the World Meteorological Organization founded the Intergovernmental Panel on Climate Change (IPCC), which produced its first report in 1990, with a supplement for the United Nations Conference on Environment and Development—also known as the "Earth Summit"—held in Rio de Janeiro in 1992. 172 countries participated, 108 heads of state attended, and about 2,400 representatives of Non-Governmental Organisations were present. This firmly institutionalised a desire to remedy environmental deprivation, and the control of natural resources as a global objective for nation states and, at the same time (and unusually), established similar objectives for environmental activists. The IPCC's reports on the warming of the earth's surface by the release of carbon dioxide from the activities of industrial society, and the popularisation of the term "greenhouse effect," focused global environmental interest onto climate change—although other critical issues such as water supply remained as issues of international concern.

As *The Economist* reported in 2009: "Climate change is the hardest political problem the world has ever had to deal with. … At issue is the difficulty of allocating the cost of collective action and trusting other parties to bear their share of the burden. … climate change has been a worldwide worry for only a couple of decades. Mankind has no framework for it."[68] While most states recognise in principle their responsibility to take action on the reduction of dependence on fossil-fuels, the efficiency and continuing availability of these fuels, together with a popular reluctance to accept either a lower standard of living or, in the case of emerging economies, restraint on growth that would keep their populations below the standards of developed countries, often make the impact of the measures required politically unacceptable.

China's Deputy Minister of the Environment, Pan Yue, spoke of the environmental dangers of the Chinese economic miracle to the German magazine *der Spiegel* in 2005:

> This miracle will end soon because the environment can no longer keep pace. Acid rain is falling on one third of the Chinese territory,

half of the water in our seven largest rivers is completely useless, while one fourth of our citizens does not have access to clean drinking water. One third of the urban population is breathing polluted air, and less than 20 per cent of the trash in cities is treated and processed in an environmentally sustainable manner. Finally, five of the ten most polluted cities worldwide are in China.[69]

In 2011 the Chinese Prime Minister Wen Jiabao unwittingly expressed the dilemma of the state when he vowed "to meet the people's growing material and cultural needs, and make the lives of commoners better and better," while stating that China "absolutely must not any longer sacrifice the environment for the sake of rapid growth and reckless roll-outs."[70] If a government free from a short-term electoral mandate cannot control the balance between its own accepted need for environmental control with the economic aspirations of its citizens, the problems for the liberal democracies must be commensurately greater.

The inherently global nature of environmental damage and reform is matched by the fact that it is the everyday actions of individuals at a local scale that, in aggregate, has the most significant impact on the environment. Power generation and fossil fuel retrieval only amount to about one third of greenhouse gas emissions. The remainder are made up of discretionary and lifestyle activities such as transport, construction and industrial production. The leading British environmental activist Jonathan Porritt makes the interdependency of the global and the local—the glocal—quite clear:

> That which can be delivered locally and coordinated regionally, should be. The sustainability benefits (as in reduction of damaging environmental impacts) are substantial … But … [a] strictly rational, function-based commitment to regionalism and localism does not need to be accompanied by some automatic ideological abhorrence of appropriate models of globalisation … the inherently global nature of challenges such as climate change, demand an unprecedented

commitment to global institutions and processes without which no
solutions can possibly be forthcoming.[71]

In the search for remedies to the damaging effects of our energy-
consuming ways of life, commentators frequently make reference to
the local for inspiration or solutions. The same Gro Brundtland who
provided us with our default definition of sustainability in 1987, in
her later role as Director-General of the World Health Organization
in 1999, looks to indigenous peoples to:

> teach us about the values that have permitted humankind to live on
> this planet for many thousands of years without desecrating it ...
> Indigenous peoples thus collectively represent a corrective to the
> environmental and social abuses of modernity; and indigenous
> identity tells us as much about widely held concerns over the global
> impact of reckless industrialization as it does about the people and
> communities most directly endangered by it.[72]

In the same year, in a Guide to the World Trade Organisation, the
Canadian human rights lawyer, Steven Shrybman, associates
environmental sustainability with cultural diversity: "Diversity is the
characteristic of nature, and the basis of ecological stability. Diverse
ecosystems give rise to diverse life forms and diverse cultures. The
co-evolution of culture, life forms and habitats has conserved the
biological diversity of the planet. Cultural diversity and biological
diversity therefore go hand in hand."[73]

As the source of environmental reform moves from the global to
the local, the community itself becomes the object of the concept of
sustainability. Gabriel Chanan, Alison West, Charlie Garratt and
Jayne Humm define a sustainable community in *Regeneration and
Sustainable Communities* in 1999:

> A sustainable community could be described as one in which there
> exists, from a mixture of internal and external sources, a self-
> renewing basis of economic viability, quality of services and social
> capital sufficient to support a good quality of life for all inhabitants,
> improve conditions and opportunities where they are inadequate,

face new problems creatively as they arise, and pass on to future inhabitants the tangible and intangible assets to achieve the same or higher standards.[74]

Critical Regionalism: the Modernist Response to Localism

Reflexive Modernism, with its conscious reference to the legacy of Modernism, lacked a ready means for expressing local identity. The invention of the term the "International Style," although largely dropped by the 1960s, did nonetheless express an underlying belief in the universal nature of technologically-driven progress and its uniform outcomes. It was, as Alfred Barr said in 1932, a "contemporary style, which exists throughout the world ... unified and inclusive."[75]

There was, nonetheless, a strand of Modernism that was concerned with local or regional expression. This has been carefully recorded and classified by the husband-and-wife architectural historians Alexander Tzonis and Liane Lefaivre.

The tension between the universal aspirations of Modernism and the idea of something particular to a place that would necessarily have an historical character was recognised by one of the earliest exponents of modernist regionalism, Lewis Mumford, the notable historian of technology, architecture and urbanism. In 1931, writing on regional planning, Mumford identified:

> ... two elements in every architecture ... one of them is the local
> ... which adapts itself to special human capacities and
> circumstances, that belongs to a particular people and a particular
> soil and a particular set of economic and political institutions. Let us
> call this the regional element ... The other element is the universal:
> this element passes over boundaries and frontiers ... Without the
> existence of that universal element, which usually reaches its highest
> and widest expression in religion, mankind would still live only at
> the brute level.[76]

Ten years later, he was very careful to make sure that the expression of the local that "belongs to a particular people" had to be seen in relation to, what he called, "The great lesson of history … that the past cannot be recaptured except in spirit," going on to make it quite clear that with any expression of regionalism, "our task is not to imitate the past, but to understand it, so that we may face the opportunity of our own day and deal with them in an equally creative spirit."[77]

Even this explicitly modernist stipulation was not enough to convince many of the more dogmatic internationalists. One of the fathers of Modernism, Walter Gropius, referred to Mumford's regionalism in 1948 as based on "chauvinistic sentimental national prejudice."[78] In 1959, an attempt by the British-Swedish architect Ralph Erskine to create an architecture adapted to sub-arctic conditions would be attacked by the British Brutalist architect, Peter Smithson, saying: "In your work you should endeavour to be a bit less like Walt Disney, for instance, and a bit more like Charles Eames."[79] For modernists, there was an ever-present danger of unwittingly interpreting local or regional features too literally. To avoid an accusation of sentiment or imitation, even regionalists would have to display originality and, to the uninitiated, this could disguise their regionalist intentions. The Turkish architectural historian, Suha Ozkan ,wrote in 1985 that:

> Compared to buildings and projects of the architectural *avant-garde*, the referential tendency of some regionalist practices has given regionalism something of a conservative reputation. Such is the power of the new and modern culture's drive toward it at any cost, including the need for continuity. This often makes architects reluctant to promote themselves as regionalists.[80]

In spite of professional criticism, there was a feeling amongst some modernists, such as Ernesto Rogers and Richard Neutra, that their architecture could and should be capable of expressing something particular to the region in which it was built. In 1981 Tzonis & Lefaivre, in their essay "The Grid and the Pathway," called this localising tendency "Critical Regionalism." They added the word "critical" specifically to guard against the idea of regionalism being "transported back to its obsolete, chauvinistic outlook."[81] It was important for them that "regionalism is seen as an engagement with the global, universalizing world rather than by an attitude of resistance."[82]

Figure 46. Torre Velasca, Milan; Ernesto Rogers; 1958.

International Modernism was occasionally moderated to make explicit references to local character.

When Postmodernism and its particular use of historical elements became fashionable in the 1980s, the use of historical elements in the name of local identity created the kind of architecture that the modernist regionalists had feared. Postmodernists, such as Michael Graves, promoted a more literal interpretation of the architecture that belonged to, what Mumford had called, "a particular people."[83] Graves wrote in 1982: "It is crucial that we re-establish the thematic associations invented by our culture in order to fully allow the culture of architecture to represent the mythic and ritual aspirations of society."[84] In the following year the critic Kenneth Frampton sought to re-claim regionalism for Modernism. He took up the expression "Critical Regionalism" from Tzonis and Lefaivre in an influential paper, "Towards a Critical Regionalism: Six Points for an Architecture of Resistance."[85]

Frampton's paper was inspired by his reading of an essay by the French Philosopher Paul Ricœur, "Universal Civilization and National Cultures," first published in English in 1965. Ricœur wrote and was quoted by Frampton: "There is the paradox: how to become modern and to return to sources; how to revive an old dormant civilization and take part in universal civilization."[86] To solve this paradox, Frampton tried to steer a middle route "which distances itself equally from the Enlightenment myth of progress and from the reactionary, unrealistic impulse to return to the architectonic forms of the preindustrial past."[87] The former was, of course, conventional Modernism and the latter the more literally historical elements of Postmodernism, very much to the fore at the time of writing. Over time he would be less equitable. In later versions of his paper he shifted in the direction of Modernism, saying: "There remains a solid and liberating heritage lying within the complex culture that we generally subsume under the term the Modern Movement. It is nothing short of reactionary folly to abandon the liberative, critical, and poetic traditions of this century on the ground of a retardaire fashion." He wanted to be clear that "regionalism should not be sentimentally identified with the vernacular."[88]

For Frampton:

the fundamental strategy of Critical Regionalism is to mediate the impact of universal civilization with elements derived *indirectly* from the peculiarities of a particular place. It is clear from the above that Critical Regionalism depends on maintaining a high level of critical

self-consciousness. It may find its governing inspiration in such
things as the range and quality of local light, or in a tectonic derived
from a peculiar structural mode, or in the topography of a given site
[emphasis in original].[89]

Regionalism, in this interpretation, is to design specifically for the
location inspired by, rather than imitating, what was found in the
locality. It may only express "history in ... a geological and
agricultural sense." He believes that "'in-laying' the building into the
site, has many levels of significance, for it has a capacity to embody,
in built form, the prehistory of the place, its archaeological past and
its subsequent cultivation and transformation across time." He is,
parenthetically, anxious to ensure that "the idiosyncrasies of place
find their expression without falling into sentimentality."[90]

For many architects, when Modernism was re-emerging as the
dominant philosophy and Postmodernism was in decline, Frampton's
Critical Regionalism provided a welcome counterbalance to an
emerging awareness that globalisation was delivering a disturbing
worldwide uniformity. It has become quite routine for architects to
describe their work as locally responsive, whether or not they make
any reference to Frampton.

The Malaysian ecological architect Ken Yeang and the British
modernist Alison Brooks are quite explicit about the relationship of
their work to Critical Regionalism. Other architects, such as the
Australian Glen Murcutt and the Indian architect Raj Rewal, while
heralded by Critical Regional theorists, use the same language as
Frampton without specifically identifying themselves in the same
terms. Murcutt, influenced by Mies van der Rohe and Alar Aalto,
describes his work as:

> addressing the hydrology, it's addressing the geomorphology. It's
> addressing the typography, the wind patterns, light patterns,
> altitude, latitude, the environment around you, the sun movements.
> It's addressing the summer, the winter and the seasons in between.
> It's addressing where the trees are, and where the trees are will tell
> you about the water table, the soil depth, climatic conditions.[91]

Figure 47. Menara Mesiniaga Tower, Kuala Lumpur; Ken Yeang; 1992. The first "bioclimatic" tower that provides regional identity by responding to regional climatic conditions.

Figure 48. Indian Parliament Library, New Delhi; Raj Rewal; 2003. Modernist design that seeks to express the essence of the region while avoiding past historical styles.

Critical Regionalism, a modernist acknowledgement of local character that relies on a response to site-specific features while avoiding direct references to past architecture.

Rewal says, "We have to re-invent modernity in terms of our own traditions and cultural heritage. It is an important task to search for a modern architectural language, which responds to our requirements, lifestyle, climate and building materials."[92]

Tzonis & Lefaivre continue to catalogue the architects and projects that they believe conform to the principles of Critical Regionalism.[93] The list is wide and sometimes surprising. It ranges from the Italian pioneer of High Tech architecture, Renzo Piano and the Spanish star architect, Santiago Calatrava, to the Israeli contextualist, Moshe Safdie, and the Texan modern traditionalist, Leslie Elkins. Although many architects will not define themselves as Critical Regionalists, Tzonis & Lefaivre have clearly identified an ideological undercurrent in Modernism that, boosted by the polemical work of Frampton, has come to prominence in the New Global Era as architects seek to retain the formal heritage and production of unprecedented outcomes that they inherited from Modernism, while responding to the call for local distinctiveness.

Sustainability and Locality

Critical Regionalism gives a potential theoretical framework to the use of the energy-saving aspects of design and the adaptation of the building to local climatic conditions.

As international attention came to focus on the detrimental effect of the use of fossil fuels on the environment and the likely impact on the climate, many architects became enthusiastic promoters of sustainable building practice. This filled the moral vacuum that had existed in the profession since the loss of confidence in Modernism of the 1970s and 1980s. Figures claiming that buildings consume between thirty per cent and fifty per cent of total fossil-fuel energy in the developed world were, and continue to be, widely quoted,[94] encouraging a sense of guilt and a desire to make amends. Presented in this form the figures misrepresent the role of new building. It is primarily the activities that take place in the built environment that consume this level of energy rather than the act of construction. As much human activity takes place within buildings, the figure is hardly surprising. Unoccupied buildings would consume very little if any energy. Nonetheless, new construction and the performance efficiency of buildings have their part to play in the consumption of fossil fuels and the output of carbon dioxide.

While environmental issues had been an international concern since the first "Earth Day" in 1970, the 1992 UN Earth Summit in Rio de Janeiro put sustainability on the international political agenda. Following the Summit, Agenda 21 was published which included the Rio Declaration on Environment and Development. This loosely worded portmanteau document included Principle 4: "In order to achieve sustainable development, environmental protection shall constitute an integral part of the development process and cannot be considered in isolation from it."[95] Sustainable development became a definitively global concern and subsequent research, conferences and reports had an increasing impact on architects around the world.

A UK government agency, the Building Research Establishment (BRE), produced the world's first comprehensive environmental assessment method for buildings in 1990, called the BRE Environmental Assessment Method (BREEAM). Two years later the Earth Summit was attended by the newly-elected president of the American Institute of Architects (AIA), and environmental sustainability became a mainstream mission for American architects. The International Union of Architects and AIA conference in 1993 was themed on sustainability, and the AIA played a key role in President Clinton's symbolic "Greening of the White House" in the following year. The US Green Building Council was formed and undertook five years of research before it launched the Leadership in Energy and Environmental Design (LEED) as a "voluntary, consensus based, market-driven" energy efficiency rating system.

Other nations took up the cause. LEED was adopted in a number of other countries. There are nineteen associated national Green Building Councils applying the same system. Canada and Mexico, two countries in NAFTA (the North American Free Trade Agreement), have joined. Others range from India and Russia to

Brazil and Argentina and include six European countries, South Korea and Turkey. BREEAM has been taken on in six European countries and Israel. The BRE has signed a memorandum of agreement with the French *Centre Scientifique et Technique du Bâtiment* (CSTB) to align BREEAM standards and methodologies with the CSTB's *Haute Qualité Environnementale* (HQE) which was initiated in 1996. Australia has introduced its own system, Green Star building rating, and New Zealand adopted the same measures with local modifications.

In Germany, in common with many north European countries, high insulation standards had been in place since the 1970s and are administered through a complex series of State regulations, *Landesbauordnungen* (Building Code of the States), guided by the Federal *Musterbauordnung* (Model Building Code). In 1988, however, Professor Bo Adamson from Sweden, and Wolfgang Feist of the *Institut für Wohnen und Umwelt* (Institute for Housing and the Environment, Germany) began work on a much more comprehensive "*Passivhaus*" standard, funded by the German State of Hesse. The Passivhaus-Institut was created in 1996 to promote and control Passivhaus standards. This sophisticated system has been widely used for domestic buildings in German-speaking and other European countries.

These environmental tests for new building construction were voluntary. Their development was part of a growing concern at the scientific information that was being released about greenhouse gasses, pollution and climate change. By the late 1990s the professional enthusiasm for sustainable building meant that few architects would risk opprobrium by challenging the need to build more sustainably, and many architects took on or proclaimed a positive commitment to reducing greenhouse gasses.

This visionary phase of environmentalism entered a new stage when the international political community agreed to take collective action to address the dangers of global warming. Following the 1992 Rio Earth Summit it was agreed that the signatories of the "Framework Convention on Climate Change" would meet at a series of "Conferences of the Parties" to work on the implementation of the Convention's objectives. In 1997, at the third of these conferences in Japan, the Kyoto Protocol was drawn up.[96] The Protocol was signed by 160 countries and, by 2011, had been joined by another 31; the USA refused to commit. The document was to come into force in 2005 and, in order to achieve "stabilization of greenhouse gas concentrated in the atmosphere," required the developed-nation signatories to reduce their greenhouse gas emissions collectively to levels 5.2 per cent below the 1990 level—the quantity varying considerably between nations. While there is no specific reference to building design or construction, the Protocol includes a requirement to "implement policies and means to promote sustainable development,"[97] and notes that "adaptation technologies and methods for improving spatial planning would improve adaptation to climate change."[98] From 1997—but most particularly since 2005— environmental sustainability in building design and construction changed from being a voluntary activity supported by enthusiasts to a regulatory requirement.

In spite of the very public professional enthusiasm for sustainability in architecture and the genuine commitment of some firms that have taken it on as a speciality, the significance of the phenomenon has not been matched by a significant change in aesthetics. It has become almost routine for designs to be presented as sustainable and, in recent years in some countries, it has become an obligation. Architects were, however, reluctant to change their aesthetic preferences. Catherine Slessor, in her book *Eco-Tech*, observed that environmental performance is "not so evident in the physical form of architecture, but in its attendant technologies, whether in the development of new materials and products, or in the use of traditional materials in different ways."[99] Improved energy conservation is often due to the engagement of talented environmental engineers who devise complex mechanical and passive systems without affecting the architect's conventional design principles.

It is, for example, well established that glass-walled buildings have poor environmental characteristics[100] and are likely to be harder to build as environmental regulations increase. Professor Steve Rayner, researching technology and climate changes at Oxford, has predicted that "making buildings out of glass is going to become a historical phenomenon ... big glass office buildings will become pariah buildings."[101] The glass wall is, however, a definitive characteristic of modernist buildings and will not be surrendered easily. Catherine Slessor notes that "since the technical and commercial development of large-scale glass envelopes during the second half of the nineteenth century, the notion of transparency has exerted a seductive hold on the architectural imagination."[102] A director of the British architects ORMS said, in response to the unsuitability of glass façades in 2010, "Architecture needs to be optimistic as well as sustainable, and glass in its widest sense is one of the most exciting materials we have."[103]

A new glass-walled tall building in New York, 1 Bryant Park Tower (figure 49), has achieved the highest level of LEED certification by its innovative engineering rather than its architecture:

> The new building employs a system for rainwater catchment and reuse, greywater recycling, energy efficient building systems, and high performance glass which maximizes day-lighting and minimizes solar heat gain and loss ... the state-of-the-art, onsite 4.6-megawatt cogeneration plant ... provides a clean and efficient power source for the building's energy requirements, significantly reducing its reliance on the NYC grid. The system also perfectly complements a ... cooling system that produces and stores ice during off-peak hours, and then uses the ice phase transition to help cool the building during peak load. Another .... innovation is the air purification system not only is the air entering the building purified to a high standard, but the air exhausted is also cleaned.[104]

Frank Gehry, who is critical of the LEED system, boasts of his use of glass in Switzerland by relying only on local regulations: "We built it entirely out of glass and cooled it with a geothermal system."[105]

As with glass, the tall building as an expression of technological advancement has been a definitive modernist product from its theoretical origins. The opportunities for high-impact and iconic status have made the form particularly attractive in the New Global Era. Anthony Wood of The Council on Tall Buildings and Urban Habitat (CTBUH) confirms that "the skyline is seen as an important symbol to portray that a country has arrived on the scene and is a First World country." The CTBUH record that the previous decade had been the single greatest period on tall building construction in history, with 350 skyscrapers constructed since 2001.[106] David Scott of Arups, the international engineers and architects, reported in 2006, that it is "a very interesting, important time for tall building design." At first sight, these large, highly engineered, energy dependent, air-conditioned buildings would seem to be the antithesis of energy-saving design. For architects wishing to maintain their sustainable stance, it is, therefore, important to reconcile these apparently opposing positions. As David Scott goes on to claim: "new technologies, and a greater understanding of how these buildings perform under normal and extreme conditions, are making tall buildings more robust, more efficient and more sustainable."[107] If leading architects are to compete in this market and maintain their position on sustainability they have an urgent interest in promoting the environmental performance of tall buildings. Norman Foster's 1997 Commerzbank Headquarters in Frankfurt is often listed for its use of natural light and opening windows, whereas some of these were Frankfurt regulatory requirements.[108] Foster's 30 St Mary Axe office building in London (figure 50) is described on his website as "London's first ecological tall building." He states that "the higher the building, the more viable it becomes ... by bringing together different functions, we can balance energy needs across these uses, generating even greater environmental benefits."[109] Renzo Piano defends the design of the tallest building in Europe in London, called "The Shard of Glass"— which houses eighteen floors of luxury hotel, twelve floors of high-value apartments, three floors of restaurants and twenty-four floors of offices—on its small land-take by saying that "the earth is fragile and must be defended. The first thing to defend is land."[110] SOM describe their seventy-one storey Pearl River Tower in Guangzhou in southern China as a design that "redefines what is possible in sustainable design by incorporating the latest green technology and engineering advancements."[111]

Figure 49. Bank of America Tower, 1 Bryant Park, New York; Cook + Fox Architects; 2009. A glass tower block with highest US energy sustainability rating.

Figure 50. 30 St Mary Axe (the Gherkin), London; Norman Foster, 2004. Iconic tower promoted as sustainable architecture.

**Engineering ingenuity and energy-loss measurement protocols
have enabled conventional modernist building types to claim high
levels of sustainability.**

These are not universally accepted views. Sources with no vested interest in the promotion of tall buildings have reached different conclusions. A comparative analysis of buildings of different heights in Melbourne in 2001 discovered that, "the two high-rise buildings have approximately 60 per cent more energy embodied per unit gross floor area (GFA) in their materials than the low-rise buildings."[112] There are no universally accepted measurements for embodied energy or longevity (the energy required to make and bring all the parts of a building to the site and the time before the exercise has to be repeated) and so they are often missed out of energy-use calculations. A special report for the British Government in 2002 concluded that: "The proposition that tall buildings are necessary to prevent suburban sprawl is impossible to sustain. They do not necessarily achieve higher densities than mid or low-rise development and in some cases are a less-efficient use of space than alternatives ... Tall buildings are more often about power, prestige, status and aesthetics than efficient development."[113]

Adaptation of these and other buildings to improve environmental performance has, nevertheless, had some impact on the way conventional modernist elements are designed. The loose principles of Critical Regionalism, whereby any adaptation to the conditions of the site can be an expression of regional character, gives an opportunity for the architect to make a more or less abstracted gesture to the locality of the building.

To avoid the solar heat gain that affects glass-walled buildings, the glass itself can be covered with a coating or opaque pattern, or perforated shading screens can be placed in front of the glass. These features give opportunities for decorative patterns that have some local inspiration. Arata Isosaki has a geometric screen around his Liberal Arts and Sciences Building in Doha, Qatar, as an interpretation of Islamic tile patterns. Foreign Office Architects' John Lewis Store in the English city of Leicester has an abstracted lace pattern to signify the historic lace production from the area (figure 51). Jean Nouvel's One New Exchange office building in London has a pattern of applied patches, or frits, with a colour range inspired by the surrounding buildings.

Nothing more than the response to orientation, local shading or climate can be sufficient for the architect to claim that a new building responds to the locality. Ken Yeang has said: "The local and climactic response is the local identity. Every site is different and by responding to the locality we create a natural identity."[114] Lee Polisano, when design director of Kohn Pederson Fox, stated that "Local form becomes local by the manifestation of local circumstances. When the building is designed for orientation and climate, when the front and back are in the local context, we create a new local context into which other buildings can be built."[115] Peter Oborn, Deputy Chairman of Aedas Europe, combines both climate and shading screen when he describes his firm's response to local identity. He believes that "sustainability becomes a form of localism."[116] Aedas's twin towers of the Abu Dhabi Investment Council Headquarters have sophisticated active shading screens and these "reflect the cultural identity of the Middle East with a rationalised geometry based on traditional screens placed around a contemporary design, which is based on a climatic response."[117]

Identity and Reflexive Modernism

Any response to what is locally distinctive must be a response to the identity of the place. The desire to make a new building something that adds to the identity of where it is built is an almost universal desire for any architect who wants to create something that will be other than invisible. This will make the new building or complex of buildings *identifiable* and it may also—but not necessarily—reinforce the *identity* of the place in which it is built. The identity of the surroundings of a new building is, unless it is part of the construction of an entirely new place, something that exists. To respond to this identity positively is to enter into some relationship with it. This has become a stated intention of many architects, often reacting consciously or unconsciously to the observation that much modern architecture ignores, compromises or destroys the identity of established towns and cities.

In 2002, Larry Oltmann, London design director of the American architects SOM, declared that he is "adamant that as international architects we should bear the responsibility for helping to preserve cultural identities."[118] In 2007, Alejandro Zaera-Polo, the Spanish partner of the British architects Foreign Office Architects, describes his approach to different locations: "We territorialise ourselves, try to become locals in each place," and compares each project to how "a particular grape will grow in ways that will produce different flavours."[119] In 2009 the British international architect, David Chipperfield, tells us that "certain contexts spark something that is resonant."[120] In the same year, the Finnish architect, Juhani Pallasmaa

Figure 51. John Lewis Store, Leicester, England; Foreign Office Architects; 2008. Glass-walled department store given local identity by applying a decorative screen outside the glazing with a pattern based on the town's historic lace industry.

Figure 52. Apartment building, Johannisstrasse in Mitte, Berlin: J. Mayer H; 2012. Local identity drawn from the imaginative interpretation of the architect.

Architects can include their personal interpretation of the locality in their designs and apply it in an abstracted form.

says, "I speak for an architecture that arises from an acknowledgement of its historical, cultural, societal and mental soil."[121]

This widely expressed concern is often a direct reaction to the potentially negative impact of large or iconic buildings. The Malaysian-British architect C. J. Lim is "concerned about the impact of large projects on human habitation, culture and tradition."[122] The German architect Stefan Benisch believes that "one of the biggest errors of international architecture is that we thought that we could build the same thing everywhere" and tells us that, "we are now more concerned with the cultural context, the climate, the geography and so on."[123] It is clear that the interest of these architects is with something beyond the powerful impact of iconic architecture that makes it simply *identifiable*. The intention seems to be to go further and address the way that the *culture* of people is tied to the *identity* of their locality. While they may seek to preserve the cultural identity of places, they are generally clear that they do not, in the words of Pallasmaa, "support architectural nostalgia or conservatism,"[124] and, as Zaera-Polo has said, will "look at local specificities in a way that is not bound by tradition."[125]

The intention behind these architectural principles is to respond to the relationship between the identity of a locality and the way local people identify with their surroundings in the design of new buildings. It is also, in accordance with modernist thinking, something more than a simple physical similarity with the existing surroundings. This sets up a potentially complex relationship between the way that architects interpret local identity and how the population take their identity from their locality

In the predominant architectural culture of Reflexive Modernism a methodology and outcome that goes beyond simple physical similarity will be adopted. There seem to be two current techniques: the spirit of place or "site-specific design," and "symbolic identity" or the architect's personal discovery of local symbolism. The two techniques can be used independently or in combination but the process behind each of them is distinct.

Site-specific design is Critical Regionalism. Ken Yeang of Llewellyn Davis Yeang calls this "systemic identity."[126] The British Architect, Alison Brooks, described this succinctly as an abstract reaction to "found conditions."[127]

Symbolic identity is the choice of a symbolic aspect of a design that seems to be in some way relevant to the location. This was described by the Berlin conceptual architect, Jurgen Mayer, as finding "certain elements that are local that we could interpret and make into something architecturally new"[128] (figure 52). The choice of symbolism is usually personal. Brooks believes that she must "bring her own personal obsessions" to her designs.[129] Mayer says that, while there always a client and city, "the architect has to make the proposal."[130] Yang tells us that "the only way you can get through the complexity of design is to be intuitive."[131] Zaera-Polo resorts to "the sublime, a physically exciting form to project the things around to a higher level."[132] In none of these responses is there any reference to an attempt to analyse or discover the way the relevant community or communities see the identity of their place. On the contrary, Sheila O'Donnell of the Irish firm, O'Donnell and Tuomey, tells us that "We find that people want the details [of their town] but we want to look at the way people *did* things in the past—the landscape, the climate" [emphasis as spoken].[133]

The design of the Scottish Parliament building in 1998 brought together with remarkable clarity the political, social and architectural issues of the identity of place, architecture and community in the New Global Era.

The Parliament building was commissioned to house the new Scottish Parliament following the devolution of limited legislative powers from the United Kingdom to the Scottish nation as a result of a referendum in 1997. While a neo-classical building had been fitted out for a Scottish parliament at the time of a previous but failed referendum in 1979, the inaugural holder of the new position of First Minister of Scotland and champion of devolution, Donald Dewar, dismissed this as a "nationalist shibboleth." A decision was made that a modern building should be built, in the words of the Devolution

Minister Henry McLeish, as "a forward-thinking modern Parliament for the new Millennium." Dewar wanted the building to be "a tangible symbol of this new democratic adventure."[134]

Dewar announced a limited competition for the design of the new building, to be placed opposite the Royal Palace of Holyrood, so that there would be "world-class creative talent brought to bear on developing a Parliament building that is fit for the Millennium and beyond."[135] The competition was won by the Catalan architect, Enric Miralles y Moya with a design that, according to Dewar, "sits in the land because it belongs in the land."[136] Miralles' design for the complex of buildings did not make an assertive physical presence but sat low within the landscape of surrounding hills. It was, nonetheless, intended to be an icon for the newly assertive Scottish nation.

The choice of a Catalan architect had a particular, possibly accidental, significance. Catalonia was also a nation within a state that was actively seeking autonomy. At this time, the Catalonian capital, Barcelona, was also the most fashionable city in Europe since its dramatic regeneration before and after the 1992 Olympic Games under its visionary mayor, Pasqual Maragall. (Maragall had not only made the city a major tourist destination, he had employed so many star architects that in 1999 the Royal Institute of British Architects broke a 150-year tradition when, instead of awarding its annual Gold Medal for architecture to a famous architect, it was given to the City of Barcelona).

Sadly, both Dewar and Miralles died two years later when the building work had just begun. Fortunately for the project, Miralles and his wife and architect-partner, Benedetta Tagliabue, had completed the design before his death.

In 1999 Miralles said, "We don't want to forget that the Scottish Parliament will be in Edinburgh, but will belong to Scotland, to the Scottish land. The Parliament should be able to reflect the land it represents."[137] Tagliabue tells of the architects' search for an appropriate symbolism for Scottish identity. She discusses the way the building sits in the land: "We wanted something really Scottish to be part of the building ... earth is a really Scottish thing and an amphitheatre is about parliament … it is about the movement of earth."[138] Miralles and Tagliabue spent some time travelling around Scotland in search of Scottish identity: "We looked at national identity. How did we dare look at Scotland? It's not just castles, it's other things, like boats constructed in towns and then going away. So the debating chamber is this wooden thing, like a boat. It is Scottish, so people are making decisions inside a boat."[139] There is no tradition of Scottish identity, real or invented, that employs this symbolism. In addition to the use of the abstracted imagery of boats under construction, the building's facades have an irregular pattern of a repeated abstract shape. This is a very distinctive and regular feature, but its meaning was not at first identified by the architects and locals gave it their own, mildly humorous, names: anvil, hammer and hairdryer. It has subsequently been revealed that the shape was Miralles highly abstracted profile of Henry Raeburn's eighteenth-century painting, *The Skating Minister*.

The opening of the building was marred by a three-year programme overrun and a massive over-spend from an original (and quite unrealistic) budget of £50 million to a final cost of £430 million. The building received six international architectural awards but was voted amongst the twelve most disliked buildings in Britain in a popular television vote in 2005.[140] While for many in Scotland the building symbolises the new independence of the nation regardless of its appearance, the Scottish National Tourist Organisation invites visitors to "admire the eco-design" but describes its appearance cautiously as "arguably stylish design and controversial architecture" (figure E).

In common with many buildings which promote the symbolic identity of the locality or community, the Scottish Parliament has been a largely private matter for the intuition of the architect. Identity is expressed with abstracted or naturalistic metaphor or analogy. In much the same way, Alejandro Zaera-Polo describes Foreign Office Architects' choice of abstracted lacework imagery for the John Lewis Store in Leicester, England, as an attempt to "synthesise identity." These abstractions are rarely direct allusions to past buildings. An explicit assertion of newness and originality is a consistent concern. Sheila O'Donnell prefaced her remarks about what people want (above) with the statement that "We want to relate to the context but not look like buildings of the past."[141] Zaera-Polo states that "Every building we do is not like what is already there but the technologies and possibilities of today make a new identity."[142] Ken Yeang believes that "avoiding pastiche" is critical and that you must "reinterpret in a modern way."[143] Alison Brooks believes that "the authentic is genuine and original and if you do this anywhere in the world you will give identity."[144] Jurgen Mayer tells us that "forward-looking innovation should be the driving force for identity in the future."[145]

Reflexive Modernism, as the inheritor of the avant-garde principles of Modernism, maintains a suspicious distance from public opinion. The British architect Piers Gough believes that, "great art and architecture of the world has always been produced against the norm and that forwarding the art of architecture is the point of having architects," adding that "architecture is a public art but it's far too important to be left to the public."[145] The leader of the British architectural establishment, Lord Rogers (Richard Rogers), maintains that "architecture ... has to be judged by those who are qualified to judge it."[146] The Czech architect, Eva Jiřičná, feels that "it's in the nature of people to be conservative," and that "architects have to fight that."[147] This makes any attempt to relate to the often straightforward identity of communities with the physical appearance of their surroundings difficult.

Some theorists go so far as to promote a positive disconnection from a cultural past to allow universal modernity to become a culturally non-specific receptacle for the identity of those who have been in some way deterritorialised: "*Avant-garde* design schemes—like built heritage in the past—may provide all culturally different social groups and individuals with a 'spatial membership'."[148] It is also asserted, with some credibility, that "residents of neighbourhoods near prominent landmarks ... are more likely to have stronger emotional bonds to where they live."[149] It is, however, questionable that professionally discrete symbolic identity will provide ordinary citizens with any protection from the current threat that globalisation poses to their identity. The French urban designer and academic, Claire Parin, explains the problem: "The mobility of people and the communication of information seem destined to develop without limits, it appears that in whatever cultural context, there is even more demand for material reference points that provide continuity with past times. This suggests that the question of retaining local identity in a globalizing world is central to the design of local space and place. It seems, however, to be a question that is beyond answering effectively within the practical and symbolic value systems that usually apply in the production of contemporary urban projects."[150]

Contextual Urbanism

Buildings individually or collectively can change the identity of a place, but there can be no greater threat to local identity than the loss of the place itself. Post-war reconstruction in Europe and the growth of the consumer economy in the USA, combined with a rapid expansion of car ownership and a belief in the benefits of development, all had a major impact on the North Atlantic countries in the 1950s and 1960s. The destructive effect of development on familiar villages, towns and cities was felt across society, and transcended any architectural preferences.

Urban expansion and redevelopment was driven less by urban design than the economics of demand driven by increased living standards, the political drive for growth and housing supply, and the technical and bureaucratic servicing of vehicular transport. Combined with urban design theories, promulgated but untested in a more authoritarian pre-war condition, the effect could be devastating. While professionals could be blinded by the optimism of their theoretical background, articulate commentators could see what was happening and protest. It is significant that two of the most important figures in this early identification of loss of identity of

place were journalists: the American Jane Jacobs and the Briton Ian
Nairn. Jacobs had been writing on urban issues on the editorial staff
of the *Architectural Record* since 1952, but gave her first lecture on the
destructive effects of urban development on community life at the
inaugural urban design conference at Harvard University in 1956.
Nairn was a travel journalist who published a special issue of the
British journal the *Architectural Review* in 1955 entitled "Outrage,"
which protested at the loss of identity of places under the spread of
anonymous suburban sprawl, for which he invented the name
"subtopia.[1"51] Nairn published a book on his observations in 1959[152]
and in 1961 Jacobs published possibly the most influential book of
the twentieth century on urban design, *The Death and Life of Great
American Cities*,[153] which linked the breakdown of social life with the
destruction of the places where people lived.

A number of other influential publications came out at about this
time. Kevin Lynch brought out *The Image of the City*[154] in 1960, which
describes how key built elements contribute to the popular
perception of the city. In Britain, Gordon Cullen, an architect and
journalist who had been on the editorial staff of the *Architectural
Review*, took up Ian Nairn's protest and turned it into an urban design
methodology in his 1961 book *Townscape*.[155] Townscape became an
urban design movement in its own right centred on the uniqueness
and scale of places. Christopher Alexander and Serge Chermayeff
published *Community and Privacy: Toward a New Architecture of
Humanism*[156] in 1963, which proposed a more human-based
organisation of public, semi-public and private space in urban
design.

By the 1980s the same economic, political and technical forces as
those of the 1960s continued to drive urban development, and the
ideas of these thinkers had only a limited impact on the urban
condition. Jane Jacobs and Christopher Alexander continued to
publish regularly and develop their ideas. Gordon Cullen entered
into practice in 1983 and was commissioned for urban studies of
Docklands in London, Edinburgh, Glasgow and Oslo. In the 1980s

the Krier brothers from Luxembourg, Rob and Léon, began to have an impact on urban design theory and practice.

Rob Krier, the elder of the brothers by eight years, began teaching in Stuttgart in 1973, becoming professor of architecture at the Vienna University of Technology in 1976, and setting up his own practice in the same year. He practiced as a sculptor, architect and urban designer. He published his first book, *Stadtraum* [*Urban Space*],[157] in 1975. His book analyses historic cities and their spatial arrangement, provides a critique of how Modernist planning has ignored the lessons of history, and provides a methodology for contextual urban design. He has continued to publish architectural and urban theory, and has undertaken a number of urban and architectural projects, principally in Germany and Holland.

Léon Krier went to work with the postmodernist architect James Stirling in Britain in 1968, and remained in England for twenty years. He left Stirling's office after three years and taught at the Architectural Association and the Royal College of Art in London. He became one of a number of architects and theorists writing for the journal *Architectural Design* (*AD*), which, under the ownership of Andreas Papadakis, was a major exponent of Postmodernism and classicism in the 1980s. Leon Krier's theories and drawings were published in a special edition of *AD* in 1984.[158] He regularly contributed other articles. These theoretical works attacked modernist planning, the domination of cars and the zoning of cities and promoted a return to a dense, mixed-use and hierarchical traditional historic urban structure. They were illustrated with stylised line drawings illustrating buildings and cities, and supporting polemical points in a cartoon style.

Léon Krier's theories had been studied by the Miami husband-and-wife architects, Andres Duany and Elizabeth Plater-Zyberk, who in 1980 had been asked by a developer, Robert Davis, to plan an inherited tract of land beside the sea in Florida. Advised by Krier, the architects toured historic Florida towns and prepared a master plan and design codes for a new holiday town, Seaside, in 1982 (figure 53). The design was based on the traditional timber-built small towns of the region with relatively narrow streets, squares and alleys centred on a public square, with community and civic buildings. When the Duany and Plater-Zyberk plan was complete, Davis sold most of the land to private buyers in individual lots with close control over the design of individual houses set out in design codes. The new town was quite unlike conventional speculative or modernist planning in the area. The master plan received a series of awards in the USA.

Seaside and Léon Krier came to the attention of the Prince of Wales, heir to the UK throne, who had engaged advisers to prepare a publication of his emerging architectural ideas, following a speech in 1984 when he had controversially attacked the British modernist architectural establishment. In 1988, Charles decided to plan a substantial new settlement outside the southern English town of Dorchester on his privately owned land and, keen to put his ideas into practice, brought in Léon Krier as his master planner. The plan for the urban extension, Poundbury, was unveiled a year later and was widely publicised. It continues to be built under Krier's supervision, and puts into practice the principles that Léon Krier and other traditionally orientated designers had been promoting for the last decade (figures 54).

These designs and theories came forward at a critical time. In the 1980s, businesses had already identified the commercial value of historic and traditional places. Gentrification had been a recognisable phenomenon from the 1970s and was generally based on the upgrading of attractive but degraded historic places. By the 1980s, Saskia Sassen had identified that:

what is different from earlier episodes is the scale on which it has taken ... and the extent to which it has created a commercial infrastructure that anyone can buy into, fully or in part. It has engendered an ideology of consumption that is different from that of the mass consumption of the middle classes in the postwar period ... Style, high prices, and an ultraurban context characterize the new ideology and practice of consumption ... it is a sort of new mass consumption of style, more restricted than mass consumption per se because of its cost and its emphasis on design and fashion.[159]

Figure 53. View of Seaside, Florida; master plan Duany Plater-Zyberk & Company; 1981 to present. A new holiday village planned in a traditional local style and controlled by building codes that began the American New Urbanist movement.

Figure 54. View of Centre, Poundbury, Dorset, England; master plan by Leon Krier; ca 2000. The Prince of Wales's extension to the English town of Dorchester is a large-scale exemplar for contextual urbanism. Building design is controlled by codes to produce a literal interpretation of traditional architecture from the region and beyond.

Figure 55. View of Vauban district, Freiburg, Germany; Forum Vauban; 1999 to present. A new district developed through individual projects with high standards of building sustainability, and controlled by a community forum.

Contextual Urbanism, a new urban design movement based on a response to local context, sustainability and community participation.

Gentrification now went beyond the improvement of residential areas. As the sociologist Bella Dicks points out, "retailers, restaurateurs, stadium managers and traditional cultural institutions all began to realize the role that spectacular cultural display could play in the environments they provided. Making the environment visually varied and stimulating, with plenty of historic and cultural references, was central to the strategy."[160] One of the pioneers was the retail developer, the Rouse Company in the USA, that created "festival marketplaces" in run-down city centres such as in the Faneuil Hall Marketplace in Boston in the late 1970s, or the South Street Seaport in Manhattan in the early 1980s (figure 56). These successful enterprises opened up historic districts and combined restored historic buildings, fashionable retailing and heritage tourism.

The expansion of tourism reinforced the significance of distinctive local places. Julia Nevárez points out that this gave local distinctiveness a commercial value:

The specific features of local identities are among the most important resources available in the competitive marketing of tourism. The realization of the significance of this asset leads to a codification of this cultural inventory, and to its self-conscious promotion as a marketable asset: local landscapes and cultures are precisely what the tourists are prepared to pay to see and experience.[161]

Figure 56. South Street Seaport, Fulton Street, New York; 1983.

The gentrification of run-down historic areas creates up-market fashionable new districts.

Bella Dicks sees this as a catalyst for a wider appreciation of local distinctiveness: "tourism works to cement and promote the idea of places having their 'own' cultural identities. By this logic, the world is divided into numerous 'destinations', all containing their own, particular cultural life-world."[162] It is perhaps no coincidence that Seaside, a town built for tourists, was a pioneer for contextual urbanism.

By the 1990s, the need to re-establish local identity in towns and cities was seen as a necessary response to the homogenising impact of globalisation. Jordi Borja and Manuel Castells believed that "in a

world in which communication is becoming globalized, it is essential
to maintain distinct cultural identities in order to stimulate the sense
of belonging in a day-to-day manner to a specific society. As against
the hegemony of universalist values, the defence and construction of
distinctive identities on a historical and territorial basis is a basic
element of the meaning of society for individuals."[163] Saskia Sassen
saw a new emphasis on localisation in the increasing independence of
cities: "The national as container of social process and power is
cracked. This cracked casing opens up a geography of politics and
civics that links subnational spaces. Cities are foremost in this new
geography. The density of political and civic cultures in large cities
enables the localizing of global civil society in people's lives."[164] In
1992, taking advantage of the coincidence of the Earth Summit in
Rio de Janeiro and the Olympics in Barcelona in the same year, the
two city governments jointly issued the Rio-Barcelona Declaration
on the future of the city which, *inter alia*, stated: "We also favour
cultural differences, every city's own identity, and we believe that
city planning and architecture should emphasize these proper
symbols."[165]

This was the right moment for the formation of an urban design
movement that would promote the creation of distinctive places, use
the symbols of cultural difference, and draw on the existing character
of the locality. The coming together of the theories of the Krier
brothers, the work of Andres Duany and Elizabeth Plater-Zyberk and
their American colleagues, and the high profile of the Prince of
Wales provided the necessary impetus. A series of interrelated
associations emerged in the 1990s and 2000s with overlapping
objectives and some shared membership.

The first organisation formed to promote contextual urbanism
was A Vision of Europe in Bologna in 1992. The name of the group
was a deliberate reference to the title of the Prince of Wales's book,
A Vision of Britain, which had been published amidst great publicity in
1989.[166] The Bologna-based group drew together international
practitioners and theorists that supported traditional principles in
both architecture and urban design at a series of international

conferences and exhibitions. The Prince of Wales sent a recorded video of support for the first conference. The second conference in 1994 was entitled "The Sustainable City," emphasising the significance of urban design and its relationship to sustainability. In 1996 the organisation brought together supporters from Europe, America and Asia to prepare its "Charter of the City of the New Renaissance." In the five-point charter it "emphasises" that "it privileges ... the creation of villages, neighborhoods, cities and even metropolises, marked by new structural and formal qualities that will make them comparable to their historic counterparts," and promises that "as a result, the new urban and rural architecture will no longer be defined by self-referential 'innovative design,' but by the imitation of the constructive, organizational, and estetic [sic] archetypes that are deeply rooted in every local culture."[167] A Vision of Europe was an important assembly point for early practitioners of traditional and contextual design but, while it continues to function, the wider dissemination of its ideas has reduced its influence.

Following a meeting between a Norwegian urbanist organisation, Byens Fornyelse, and British urbanists at the 2000 Vision of Europe conference, a new organisation was formed to create a network of traditional architects and urbanists at a global level. The International Network for Traditional Building Architecture and Urbanism (INTBAU) was formed a year later, and has grown to include eighteen national chapters from all five continents. Its short Charter includes the statements: "Local, regional and national traditions provide the opportunity for communities to retain their individuality with the advance of globalisation. Through tradition we can preserve our sense of identity and counteract social alienation. People must have the freedom to maintain their traditions."[168] This small organisation has 4,000 members worldwide and maintains its objective of promoting traditional design by acting as a global network connecting practitioners and supporters.

In the USA in 1991, the Local Government Commission called on Andres Duany and Elizabeth Plater-Zyberk and five other American urban designers who supported contextual urbanism to develop a set of community principles for land-use planning that they could promote with government officials. The Local Government Commission is a private, non-profit organization from Sacramento, California, that "provides inspiration, technical assistance, and networking to local elected officials and other dedicated community leaders who are working to create healthy, walkable, and resource-efficient communities." The principles, later called the "Ahwahnee Principles for Resource-Efficient Communities," largely concerned sustainability but, in support of these objectives, included mixed use, restricted use of the motor car, public transport and higher density development—all the diametric opposite of the general direction of post-war development in the USA. These included "Regional Principles" stating that: "Materials and methods of construction should be specific to the region, exhibiting continuity of history and culture and compatibility with the climate to encourage the development of local character and community identity."[169]

The group that had been formed to write these principles decided to continue their work and in 1993 created what they called the "New Urbanist" movement. In that year they held their first congress and established their organisation as "The Congress for the New Urbanism" (CNU). In 1996 they drew up their charter which opens with the declaration that they "view that disinvestment in central cities, the spread of placeless sprawl, increasing separation by race and income, environmental deterioration, loss of agricultural lands and wilderness, and the erosion of society's built heritage as one interrelated community-building challenge."[170] Much of the charter sets down in more detail how the same broad principles that had informed the Alwahee Principles could be enacted at differing urban scales. These include, at metropolis, city, and town levels, that "development and redevelopment of towns and cities should respect historical patterns, precedents, and boundaries,"[171] and at the block, the street, and the building level, that "architecture and landscape design should grow from local climate, topography, history, and building practice."[172]

The CNU became a highly organised and proselytising organisation which has grown in influence, drawing in traditional architects, environmental activists, retail and highway consultants, and many others. Its Congress attendance, which tours different cities in the USA annually, has grown from 100 to more than 1,000. It has promoted a form of highly structured public participation process, known in the USA as a "charrette" (from a last-minute design studio in the French Beaux Arts architectural education system used in the USA from the nineteenth century). The CNU has also been active in developing design codes and has developed an elementary biology-based species-distribution analogy for zoning, which sets up a simple grading system of urban-to-rural densities called "the transect." CNU practitioners have been successful at combining the status of the USA in the New Global Era with the messianic mission of the CNU to export their services to other countries. The Chief Executive of the Prince of Wales's Foundation for the Built Environment is a former Chairman of the CNU.

In 1998 the UK Government set up an "Urban Task Force" to "identify causes of urban decline in England and recommend practical solutions to bring people back into our cities, towns and urban neighbourhoods." The task force, and the publication of its conclusions, *Towards an Urban Renaissance*,[173] published a year later, was based on a remarkable assembly of different architectural and urban design interests that could only have been brought together by an invitation from central government. It was chaired by Richard Rogers, the well-established modernist star architect, but also included the then Chief Executive of the Prince of Wales's Foundation, environmentalists, developers and mainstream architects. It even had a forward by Pasqual Maragall, by then the *former* mayor of Barcelona. While it was a wide-reaching report and was careful to avoid upsetting any vested interests, one of its key themes was remarkably close to the objectives of the contextual urbanists: "Urban neighbourhoods should be attractive places to live. This can be achieved by improving the quality of design and movement, creating compact developments, with a mix of uses, better public transport and a density which support local services and fosters a strong sense of community and public safety."[174] Within the extensive text can also be found the statement that: "The future development of urban neighbourhoods must ... be based on an understanding of their historic character."[175] This report enhanced the significance of urban design in Britain and drew government policy close to the principles of contextual urbanism. John Prescott, the British Deputy Prime Minister, who had commissioned the report, spoke at CNU Congresses in 2003 and 2007.

British urban design had a well-established history and an interest in context dating back to the early twentieth century Garden City Movement, and later the work of Gordon Cullen. Public consultation techniques had been pioneered in the 1970s, and contextual urbanism was well-established in practice by the 1980s. In 2006, British urbanists were brought together by the then president of the Royal Institute of British Architects to bring urbanism closer to the architectural profession. This led to the creation of the Academy of Urbanism that was based on a specified number of first one hundred, and then four hundred academicians. The purpose of the academy is to research and disseminate the principles of good urbanism, and it is a broad-based organisation with academicians from a wide range of disciplines, beyond architects and urban designers. These range from local politicians and senior civil servants, real estate and development, to engineering and academia. The principles of the academy are broadly in line with other contextual urbanist organisations, and include mixed use, reduced reliance on motor vehicles, public engagement and density. They also include specifically contextual principles such as, "The identity, diversity and full potential of the community must be supported spiritually, physically and visually," and "The design of spaces and buildings should be influenced by their context and seek to enhance local character and heritage whilst simultaneously responding to current-day needs, changes in society and cultural diversity."[176]

Contextual urbanists were also individually active in continental Europe. French, German, Dutch, Swedish, Norwegian, Greek and

Belgian, as well as Italian, urban designers attended the early Vision of Europe conferences. In 2003 a group of European urbanists gathered in Bruges, called together by German contextual urbanists and some Europeans who had been working with the American New Urbanists, to establish a pan-European contextual urbanist group. Although clearly related to the CNU (Andres Duany was present at the key meetings), the new organisation avoided too close an identification with the CNU, and decided not to refer to "new" urbanism as this had become an American brand, and contextual urbanism in Europe would relate to an urban context that was historically commonplace, rather than new. In November that year the group re-assembled in Stockholm and issued their Stockholm Charter under the name of the Council for European Urbanism (CEU). Its structure and content was similar to that of the CNU but with greater emphasis on urban form and rural conditions. Most particularly, the charter contains a specific section on Architecture and Landscape Architecture that defines its contextual objectives. It is in three parts:

1. Individual buildings must be sensitively linked to their surroundings. This issue transcends questions of style. Urban architecture must respect the history and urban context of its location, be diverse, and be receptive to the new;
2. Architecture and landscape design must grow from local climate, topography, history and building practice and harmonize with and enrich their context;
3. All buildings must provide their inhabitants with a clear sense of location, weather, and time.[177]

In the preparation of all these documents, there was debate about how to describe aesthetic objectives. It was clear to all contextual urbanists that architecture had a significant part to play in the local character of the places they wished to create, and that existing character was, almost inevitably, largely made up of traditional buildings. Many of the founding contextual urbanists were also traditional architects. Either a genuinely held modernist viewpoint or a fear of alienating the modernist majority in the design professions made this a particularly sensitive subject. Léon Krier refused to sign the CNU Charter because of its reticence on architectural issues. While A Vision of Europe and INTBAU are explicit about the relationship between context and traditional style, the insertion of phrases such as "this issue transcends questions of style" in both the CNU[178] and CEU[179] Charters "simultaneously responding to current-day needs, changes in society,"[180] in the Academy of Urbanism Manifesto, and the phrase, "there is a need to embrace innovation" in *Towards an Urban Renaissance*,[181] were all inserted to try to make the stylistic neutrality of these organisations clear.

An underlying suspicion in the architectural establishment about contextual urbanism was exacerbated by the high-profile projects that began to emerge in the late 1990s.

In Berlin, shortly after the unification of East and West Germany, Hans Stimmann, the director of Berlin Senate Administration for Urban Development, or city planner, was charged with the reconstruction and re-unification of the most potent symbol of the failure of the Cold War. Stimmann ignored calls for a competition for a radical new plan. He said that, "Berlin is a museum for every failed city planning attempt since 1945, I wanted to go back to a city structure that I call a European city. I wanted to make the city readable again." He went on to say, "I had a drawer and I opened it up and pulled out the old city plan. I said: 'It worked for 250 years. Why do we need a new competition?'" This brought the plain-speaking Stimmann into conflict with star architects drawn by the unique status of the newly-unified city. Rem Koolhaas walked out of an architectural jury and wrote accusing Stimmann of "a massacre of architectural intelligence."[182] Daniel Libeskind wrote that "It was soon evident that Stimmann was determined to keep us from building anything in Berlin, even a phone booth."[183]

While Seaside in Florida had a mixture of architectural styles, it also had codes and a reputation that tended to favour traditional design. When used as a location for the film, *The Truman Show* in

1998, as a fantasy representation of small-town America, this was seen as *prima facie* evidence by modernists that the new town was little more than an exercise in irrelevant nostalgia. The new settlement at Poundbury, in keeping with the Prince of Wales's views on architecture, largely comprised versions of the local Dorset county vernacular and high-style classical buildings. Having upset the modernist establishment in Britain with his attack on Modernism in 1984, and in his 1989 book, Poundbury was at first treated with little more than disdain. As it started to take shape and as contextual urbanism started to become more acceptable, the profession's attitude changed. This can be summed up by the retirement essay of the editor of the *Architectural Review*, Peter Davey, in 2005: "Visually, results are laughable, though buildings are put together with more care than suburban developments. But in planning terms, Poundbury has much to reflect on."[184]

Although much of the contradiction of everything that characterised American post-war development in New Urbanism was related to the restoration of community life through urban structure, as advocated by Jane Jacobs, the call for increased density, mixed use and public transport was also influenced by the energy conservation benefits of this form of urban design. As energy sustainability entered the social and political mainstream in the 1990s, architecture and urban design followed, and contextual urbanists found themselves at the forefront of sustainable urban design. The New Urbanist Peter Calthorpe published *The Next American Metropolis*[185] in 1993 which linked the loss of community to pollution and congestion. In the years that followed, there was an outpouring of literature on sustainable development, not all from authors associated with any of the contextual urban organisations. Amongst these, the Australian environmental scientist Peter Newman in 1996 published a paper "The Land Use-Transport Connection: An Overview,"[186] which referred to New Urbanism, and in 1998 the American academic, urbanist and environmentalist, Stephen Wheeler, published a paper on "Planning and Sustainable Living," which describes a sustainable city as compact with efficient land use, less use of motor vehicles, better access, efficient use of resources, a good living environment, a sustainable economy, a healthy social life with community participation, and the preservation of local culture.[187] As the on-the-ground benefits of contextual urbanism were revealed and the environmental benefits were recognised, certain aspects of contextual urbanism began to be more widely accepted.

As contextual urbanism entered the mainstream, schemes that do not rely on or even encourage traditional architecture have become more common. The new Västra Hamnen district in Malmö, Sweden, (figure H) the Vauban district in Freiburg, Germany (figure 55), Java Island in Amsterdam and the Stapleton Airport development in Denver, Colorado all conform to the layout, density, mixed use and transport principles of contextual urbanism, but do not exhibit an obvious visual relationship with the architectural character of the locality.

While contextual urbanism is a distinct response to the impetus for localism stimulated by the homogenising effects of globalisation, star architects and many other firms continue to design master plans laid out with wide streets, large single-use blocks and undesignated urban space to give the maximum exposure to iconic, or would-be iconic, buildings. Although these projects are based on fundamentally different design principles, the vocabulary of contextual urbanism is becoming universal. Foster+Partners can describe a gridded master plan of glass-walled buildings as "a paradigm for clean, integrated and sustainable future living and a rare opportunity to create a vibrant mixed-use neighbourhood that builds on the unique urban tradition of the city."[188] OMA describes a master plan for the residential neighbourhood of Waterfront City in Dubai as "employing the vernacular qualities of historic Arab settlements: an intricate and varied composition of shaded buildings and alleyways where privacy is embedded and public interaction inevitable … The dense building clusters, irregular streets, and pedestrian paths connect a patchwork of delights in this town, all of them walkable."[189] In spite of the similarity of language, there would be very little relationship

between the outcome of these plans and those envisaged in the
various charters and manifestos of contextual urbanist organisations.

Traditional Architecture

Traditional architecture, which sets out to respond literally to the
character of local or historic design, was closely associated with the
formation of contextual urbanist theories and organisations. In the
case of A Vision of Europe and INTBAU, they are conterminous.
Traditional architects, who never completely disappeared when
Modernism turned them into outcasts in the 1960s, emerged out of
obscurity with the advent of Postmodernism in the 1970s and 1980s.
They survived the collapse of Postmodernism due to the personal
conviction of practitioners and continued demand for their work.

Moving from a sub-group of a widespread movement to the rump
of a despised and abandoned style in the early 1990s threatened the
professional position of the small number of surviving traditionalists.
Modernists, who saw the new traditionalists as the representative of
all that modernist pioneers had sought to overturn, and concerned at
the boost they had been given by Postmodernism, again sought to
isolate them. Traditionalists created their own associations to protect
their interests. As we have seen, the conferences, exhibitions and
publications of A Vision of Europe acted as a meeting place for
traditionalists, and the lists of participants helped to define
traditionalism as a distinct movement. The Prince of Wales created
his own Institute of Architecture in London in 1993 and this became
a destination for traditional architects, urbanists and others that
shared the Prince's views on architecture and the environment. In
the USA in 1991 the Institute of Classical Architecture was created in
New York, and became a vigorous organisation supported by a
number of successful classical architects practicing in the city and
elsewhere in the USA. It has maintained a sometimes uneasy
relationship with the CNU.

Traditional   architecture   has   a   natural   association   with
architectural heritage. The interest in heritage is not just an attempt

to re-create a fantasy past, but is a distinctive part of the modern condition. This is witnessed by its place in the global growth-industry of tourism. As the Peruvian-American sociologist, César Grana, wrote in 1971: "The destruction of local traditions and the assault upon 'the past' perpetuated by industrialization and world-wide modernization seem to make large numbers of people susceptible to an appetite for relics of pre-industrial life. This appetite is so intense that it accounts in part for one of the major and most characteristically modern industries: tourism."[190] Bella Dicks charts the growth of heritage tourism:

> It was in the 1980s that heritage audiences began to soar. Most countries in the Euro-American axis witnessed a boom: heritage visits in Europe, for example, rose 100 per cent between 1970 and 1991. Visits to heritage attractions in Britain rose from 52 million in 1977 to 68 million in 1991. And most commentators agree that the years since the 1980s have continued to witness a remarkable explosion of popular interest in heritage and the past.[191]

As the architect, academic and journalist Roger K. Lewis wrote in the *Washington Post*: "Many of us love to visit character-laden cities. … Much of what appeals to us about these places is traditional architecture that is locally distinct. We admire historic buildings, neighborhoods and communities shaped by site, climate, history, native culture and locally available materials and construction technology."[192] These "character-laden" places continue to be preserved, improved and enhanced, not just because local people identify with them, but also because they have a commercial value. This is described by the social historian, John Allcock: "Specific features of local identities are among the most important resources available in the competitive marketing of tourism. The realization of the significance of this asset leads to a codification of this cultural inventory, and to its self-conscious promotion as a marketable asset: local landscapes and cultures are precisely what the tourists are prepared to pay to see and experience."[193] Place identity through heritage is much more than nostalgia for a lost past (although it may be that): it is part of the economic and social condition of the New Global Era.

The most easily identifiable category of heritage buildings and, for many centuries, the chosen medium for expressing identity, ancestry and status, is classical architecture. This was the dominant architectural tradition of the North Atlantic countries before the onset of Modernism, and traditional architecture is most frequently associated with the classical tradition. The explicit architectural vocabulary of classical design makes it recognisable to the untrained eye, and makes an unambiguous association between new and historic buildings. As a style that took on different forms over many centuries, and had a wide geographic spread, it has the advantage of being both specific and variable, giving a great deal of flexibility and the opportunity for individual innovation and creativity while remaining explicitly traditional.

As a dominant Western style in the colonial period of the eighteenth and nineteenth centuries, it was widely exported as an expression of cultural dominance or just to create a familiar environment for European colonists. Classicism also survived in Russia well into the 1960s, and was a feature of architecture in countries that fell under Russian influence. As post-colonial resentment fades into a distant memory, some colonial classical buildings have become absorbed into the cultural identity of the former colonies. Business and private travellers from the emerging economies, exposed again to the North Atlantic culture of their former colonisers, recognise the surviving classicism of European and American cities and often seek to emulate it.

Modified versions of classical architecture or traces of classical features frequently appear throughout the world, giving the style an international character. These buildings, outside the North Atlantic home of classicism, are often subject to local interpretation, or are drawn from established regional variations where the colonial powers had previously created a hybrid with local styles.

Figure 57. Souq Waqif, Doha, Qatar; Private Engineering Office, Mohamed Ali Abdullah; restoration complete 2008. The restoration and creative reconstruction of an historic district as a focus for local identity.

Figure 58. Yu Garden Bazaar, Old City, Shanghai, China. A shopping area centred on an historic garden made up of imaginative modern versions of historic architecture.

Heritage buildings, real and reinvented, enhance the identity of places for both inhabitants and visitors.

While all classical buildings are traditional, all traditional buildings are by no means classical. Tradition is a universal social phenomenon by which different and diverse cultures express and identify themselves. Traditions vary considerably historically, and by region or nation. It is possible to make an association with different traditions or to combine traditions (indeed hybrid traditions are historically common, but their mixed origins are often forgotten as they become formalised). It is, therefore, possible for traditional architects to follow specific national or local traditions or to move between traditions, with more or less accuracy and understanding. Many untrained designers include traditional elements freely and decoratively in their buildings. Architects who identify themselves as traditionalists may be self-taught but, conscious of being out of the architectural mainstream, are generally enthusiasts with a scholarly as well as a practical interest in their chosen field.

Traditional architects have been encouraged by the same understanding of the crucial role of passive energy saving that has enhanced the status of contextual urbanism. The use of local materials, the lack of reliance on highly engineered products, and high thermal mass construction are all characteristic of traditional design and provide thermal stability and low embodied energy without the need to compromise user comforts.

The defining characteristic of traditional architecture, and the subject of hostility for any professional trained as a modernist, is a deliberate and unambiguous connection with past architecture. As local identity is seen to stand in opposition to global uniformity, any new buildings that explicitly share the identity of existing buildings will, unavoidably, be seen as a reinforcement of the threatened identity of a place. Mike Featherstone describes how local culture is linked to the pre-existing identity the physical environment:

> Usually, a local culture is perceived as being a particularity which is the opposite of the global. It is often taken to refer to the culture of a relatively small, bounded space in which the individuals who live there engage in daily, face-to-face relationships. Here the emphasis

is upon the taken-for-granted, habitual and repetitive nature of the everyday culture of which individuals have a practical mastery. The common stock of knowledge at hand with respect to the group of people who are the inhabitants and the physical environment (organization of space, buildings, nature, etc.) is assumed to be relatively fixed; that is, it has persisted over time and may incorporate rituals, symbols and ceremonies that link people to a place and a common sense of the past. This sense of belonging, the common sedimented experiences and cultural forms which are associated with a place, is crucial to the concept of a local culture.[194]

These cultural forms, be they buildings, ceremonies or relationships are unlikely to be entirely fixed or literal representations of a common past. Events and lifestyles will change and, while societies may wish to maintain continuity, they will be affected by the same outside forces that they may wish to resist. Tradition is, however, continuity with the past and not historical repetition. As the urban historian Christine Boyer says:

> The name of a city's streets and squares, the gaps in its very plan and physical form, its local monuments and celebrations, remain as traces and ruins of their former selves. They are tokens or hieroglyphs from the past to be literally reread, reanalyzed, and reworked over time. Images that arise from particular historic circumstances come to define our sense of tradition; they literally manage our knowledge of the historic.[195]

To make a connection with these tokens of the past a new building must have a sufficiently clear relationship with that past to be recognised by those with whom the connection is important. To be recognisable, the relationship with past buildings, while it may not be identical, will at least be clearly expressed in decoration or form and this relationship between the past its modern representation will be symbolic. The sociologist Anthony Cohen describes the role of symbolic identity in the resistance to global homogeneity:

> The interrelated processes of industrialization and urbanization, the dominance of the cash economy and mass production, the

centralization of markets, the spread of the mass media and of centrally disseminated information, and the growth of transportation infrastructure and increased mobility all undermine the bases of community boundaries. Each is a multi-pronged assault on social encapsulation, and one which results in an apparent homogenization of social forms. Within any country, the language, family structures, political and educational institutions, economic processes, and religious and recreational practices of communities come to have a certain apparent resemblance to each other. At the very least, they may seem to resemble each other more than they do those of communities in other countries. Such apparent similarity may well lead people to suppose that the old community boundaries have become somehow redundant and anachronistic. Indeed, the vested interests of the national media, national political parties, marketing specialists and so forth may well lead them actively to demean and denigrate sub-national boundaries. But this homogeneity may be merely superficial, a similarity only of surface, a veneer which masks real and significant differences at a deeper level. Indeed, the greater the pressure on communities to modify their structural forms to comply more with those elsewhere, the more are they inclined to reassert their boundaries *symbolically* by imbuing these modified forms with meaning and significance which belies their appearance. In other words, as the *structural* bases of boundary become blurred, so the symbolic bases are strengthened through "flourishes and decorations," "aesthetic frills" and so forth.[196]

It is precisely these symbolic flourishes and decorations in modern traditional architecture that are, on the one hand, sought out by those that wish to retain their local identity and, on the other hand, are regarded with hostility or suspicion by the dominant modernist architectural culture. This hostility is common, but since the 1980s is often expressed simply by unspoken exclusion. In its raw form it can be summarised by the comments of the British critic and convert to Modernism, Jonathan Meades. Free to speak unconstrained by any concern for professional etiquette, writing in *The Times* in 2002 he described traditional architecture as:

make-believe of the most insipid order; it is wholeheartedly half-hearted, no matter how convinced its begetters are of its probity. The very idiom seems to defeat those who embrace it. ... there is an ignominious history of architects who have enfeebled themselves by putting their imagination in abeyance while they played an ancient game and played it weakly.[197]

No traditional architecture has been comprehensively tolerated in schools of architecture in the North Atlantic countries for half a century, with the exception of very few schools in the USA. As emerging economies fell in the line with the North Atlantic system in the early 1990s, any residual traditional architectural education that had survived in the communist countries was quickly abandoned. As a consequence, traditional architects are very few in number, and are often deliberately excluded from major architectural projects when there is any professional involvement in the appointment process, or by commercial clients who will select according to experience and professional reputation. The services of traditional architects do, however, remain in demand in the housing market where individuals can build according to their personal inclination or where houses are sold speculatively to buyers who can select according to preference.

Notwithstanding professional misgivings, traditional architecture is only the most fundamental representative of a widespread assertion of individual or community identity and defence of local character that has taken on a new urgency as it is threatened by the uniformity of global culture. As we have seen, this social and political phenomenon is as much a part of globalisation as consumerism and has many manifestations, from identity politics to targeted local marketing. In mainstream architecture it is represented by various forms of abstraction, that may or may not be recognised by those whose identity it is intended to protect, and it has become a significant new direction in urban design. It is at its most literal in traditional architecture.

*Figure 59. Rue de Laeken, Brussels;
G. Tagliaventi & Ass., Atelier 55, S.
Assassin, B. Dumons, P. Gisclard, N.
Prat, J.P. Garric, V. Negre, J.
Cenicacelaya, I. Saloña, L.
O'Connor, J. Robins, J. Altuna,
M.L. Petit, coordinating architect
Atelier Atlante; completed 1995.
Modernist buildings in an historic
city centre replaced with traditional
architecture designed by a group of
architects.*

*Figure 60. New House, Cooperstown, New York State; Fairfax and Sammons; 2009.
Traditional architecture is well established as the architecture of choice for privately
commissioned houses and houses for sale.*

Figure 61. Shriram Junior High School, Mawana, Uttar Pradesh, India; Deependra Prashad; 2008. Traditional architecture applies to all places and cultures.

Traditional design: the literal representation of local identity or a connection to an admired past. Outside the mainstream, it survives as an established minority in architectural practice.

References

1. Arjun Appadurai. *Modernity at Large: Cultural Dimensions of Globalisation*. Minneapolis: University of Minnesota Press, 1996, 191.
2. David Held, Anthony McGrew, David Goldblatt & Jonathan Perraton. *Global Transformations: Politics, Economics and Culture*. Cambridge: Polity Press, 1999, 336–7.
3. Zygmunt Bauman. *Globalization: The Human Consequences*. Cambridge: Polity Press, 1998, 62.
4. Manuel Castells. *The Power of Identity*. Oxford: Blackwell, 2004, 333.
5. Benedict R. & O'G. Anderson. *Imagined Communities: Reflections On the Origin and Spread of Nationalism*. London: Verso, 1983, Revised Edition 1991, 5.
6. David Hooson, ed. *Geography and National Identity*. Oxford: Blackwell, 1994, 2–3.
7. Marshall McLuhan. *Understanding Media*. New York: Mentor, 1964, 5.
8. Wendell Berry. *The Unsettling of America. Culture and Agriculture*. New York: Avon, 1977, 44.

9. Kwame Anthony Appiah. *Cosmpolitanism: Ethics in a World of Strangers*. New York: Norton, 2007, 98.
10. Simone Weil. *The Need for Roots*. London: Routledge and Kegan Paul, 1952, 41.
11. Edmund Burke. *Reflections on the Revolution in France*, 1790.
12. Zygmunt Bauman. *Identity: Conversations with Benedetto Vecchi / Zygmunt Bauman*. Cambridge: Polity Press, 2004, 46.
13. Marc Augé. *Non-Places: Introduction to an Anthropology of Supermodernity*, London: Verso, 1995, 34–5.
14. National Intelligence Council, USA; *Global Trends 2025: a transformed world,* 2008, xi.
15. J Weatherford. *Savages and Civilization*. New York: Crown, 1994, 236.
16. Alain Touraine. "The New Capitalist Society." In *Identity, Culture and Globalization*, edited by Eliezer Ben-Rafael. Leiden and Boston: Brill, 2002, 74.
17. Roland Robertson. *Globalization: Social Theory and Global Culture*. London: Sage Publications, 1992, 130.
18. Inuit Circumpolar Council, *Charter*, Nuuk, 1980, Preamble.
19. World Council of Indigenous Peoples, *The Declaration of Principles of Indigenous Rights*, Panama, 1984, Principles 4 and 19. The WCIP was disbanded in 1996 "due to internal conflict."
20. General Assembly of the United Nations, *47/135, Declaration on the Rights of Persons Belonging to National, Ethnic, Religious and Linguistic Minorities*, 18 December 1992.
21. Council of Europe, *European Charter for Regional and Minority Languages*. Strasbourg, November 5, 1992, Preamble.
22. European Union, Committee of the Regions, *Mission Statement*. Brussels, April 21, 2009.
23. United Nations General Assembly, World Conference on Human Rights, *Vienna Declaration on Human Rights*. Vienna, 14–25 June 1993, Paragraphs 5 and 19.
24. UNESCO, *Our Creative Diversity: Report of the World Commission on Culture and Development*. Paris July 1996, 15 and 21.
25. UNESCO, *Universal Declaration on Cultural Diversity*. Paris, November 2, 2001, Article 1.
26. Ibid., Article 4.
27. Ibid., Article 5.
28. Ibid., Article 7.

29. Raimondo Strassoldo. "Globalisation and Localism: Theoretical Reflections and Some Evidence." In *Globalisation and Territorial Identities*, edited by Z. Mlinar. Aldershot: Avebury, 1992.

30. Michel Wieviorka. "Some Coming Duties of Sociology." In Eliezer Ben-Rafael, op. cit., 588.

31. Fredrik Barth. "The Analysis of Culture in Complex Societies." *Ethnos*, 54 (3–4): 120–142. 1989: 130.

32. Bauman 2004, op. cit., 30–31.

33. John Gray. *Enlightenment's Wake: Politics and Culture at the Close of the Modern Age*. London: Routledge, 1995, 109.

34. Interview with Arjun Appadura, "Minorities and the Production of Daily Peace." In *Feelings are Always Local*, edited by Joke Brouwer et al. Rotterdam, V2 Publishing/NAi Publishers, 2004, 122–3.

35. W James Booth. "Communities of Memory: On Identity, Memory and Debt." *The American Political Science Review* 93 (2) (1999): 261.

36. P Berger, B Berger & H Kellner. *The Homeless Mind: Modernisation and Consciousness*. New York: Vintage Books, 1974, 82.

37. Anthony P Cohen. *The Symbolic Construction of Community*. London: Routledge, 1985, 46.

38. John B Thompson. "Tradition and Self in a Mediated World." In *Detraditionalisation* Paul Heelas, Scott Lash & Paul Morris. Oxford: Blackwell, 1996, 99.

39. J. A. Scholte. *Globalisation: A Critical Introduction*. Basingstoke: Palgrave Macmillan, 2005, 146–7.

40. H. Tajfel. *Experiments in Intergroup Discrimination*. New York: Scientific American 223, 1970.

41. M. Brewer. "Subordinate Goals Versus Superordinate Identity as Bases of Intergroup Cooperation." In *Social Identity Processes*, edited by B. D. Capozza. London: Sage, 2000, 122–123.

42. Cohen 1985, op. cit., 118.

43. Thompson, op. cit., 91–3.

44. E. Hobsbawm & T. R. Grainger. *The Invention of Tradition*. Cambridge: Cambridge University Press, 1983.

45. J. A. Howard. "Social Psychology of Identities." *Annual Review of Sociology* 26 (2000): 367–8.

46. R. Jenkins. *Social Identity*. London: Routledge , 2004, 142.

47. Salman Rushdie. *Imaginary Homelands*. London: Granta, 1991, 394.

48. J. A. Scholte. *Globalisation: A Critical Introduction*. Basingstoke: Palgrave Macmillan, 253.

49. Manuel Castells. *The Rise of the Network Society*. Oxford: Blackwell. 2000, 69–70.

50. S. Taylor. *Narratives of Identity and Place*. London: Routledge , 2010, 43–4.

51. G. Matthews. *Global Culture/Individual Identity: Searching for Home in the Cultural Supermarket*. London: Routledge, 2000, 192.

52. Anthony D. King. *Spaces of Global Cultures: Architecture Urbanism Identity*. London: Routledge, 2004, 129.

53. S. Anholt. *Places: Identity, Image and Reputation*. Basingstoke: Palgrave Macmillan, 2010, 157.

54. T. F. Gieryn, "A Space for Place in Sociology." *Annual Review of Sociology* 26 (2000): 463–96.

55. Mike Featherstone. "Postnational Flows, Identity Formation and Cultural Space." In Ben-Rafael, op. cit., 482.

56. Mike Featherstone. *Undoing Culture: Globalization, Postmodernism and Identity*. London: Sage, 1995, 103.

57. "*Dochakuka*" originally meant adapting farming technique to one's own local condition in Japanese. Claimed as a source for "glocalization" by Roland Robertson from issues of the Harvard Business Review in the late 1980s, the term appeared in the financial press in Jeremy Main, "How to go Global and Why," New York, *Fortune*, August 28, 1989, 76.

58. Roland Robertson. *Globalization: Social Theory and Global Culture*. London: Sage, 1992, 173–4.

59. *Glocalization: Research Study and Policy Recommendations*. Rome: Glocal Forum, 2003, 11.

60. W. Ruigrok & R. van Tulder. *The Logic of International Restructuring*. London: Routledge, 1995, 188.

61. *Longman Dictionary of Contemporary English*, London, Longmanpearson.

62. Tamotsu Aoki. "Aspects of Globalisation in Contemporary Japan." In *Many Globalizations: Cultural Diversity in the Contemporary World,* edited by Peter L Berger & Samuel P Huntingdon. Oxford: Oxford University Press, 2002, 70–71.

63. Anshu Chatterjee. "Globalisation, Identity, and Television Networks: Community Mediation and Global Responses in Multicultural India." In *The Network Society: A Cross-Cultural Perspective*, edited by Manuel

Castells. Cheltenham UK and Northampton MA: Edward Elgar Publishing, 2004, 415.

64. James Davison Hunter & Joshua Yates. "The World of American Globalisers," in Berger & Huntingdom, op. cit., 342.

65. Yunxiang Yan. "State Power and the Cultural Transition in China." In Berger & Huntingdom, op. cit., 35.

66. Ian Angell. "The Information Revolution and the Death of the Nation State." *Political Notes No 114*. London: Libertarian Alliance, 1995, 1–2.

67. United Nations General Assembly, Resolution 38/161. "Process of preparation of the Environmental Perspective to the Year 2000 and Beyond," established Bruntland Commission.

68. The World Commission on Environment and Development, *Our Common Future*, Oxford University, 1987.

69. "The Chinese Miracle Will End Soon," *Spiegel Online*, July 3, 2005. http://www.spiegel.de/international/spiegel/0,1518,345694,00.html

70. "China Lowers Growth Rate Target in Sustainability Drive." *BBC News*, February 27, 2011.

71. Jonathan Porritt. *Globalism and Regionalism*. London: Black Dog Publishing, 2008, 58.

72. World Health Organisation, *International Consultation on the Health of Indigenous Peoples*. Geneva: November 23, 1999.

73. S.Shrybman. *A Citizen's Guide to the World Trade Organisation*. :Center for Policy Alternatives, 1999, 43.

74. G Chanan et al. *Regeneration and Sustainable Communities*. London: Community Development Foundation, 1999, 16.

75. Alfred H Barr. Preface, Henry-Russell Hitchcock & Philip Johnson. *The International Style*. New York: Norton, (1932) 1995, 35.

76. Lewis Mumford. *The South in Architecture: The Dancy Lectures Alabama College*. 1941, 18.

77. Ibid., 15–16.

78. Liane Lefaivre. "Critical Regionalism, a Facet of Modern Architecture since 1945." In *Critical Regionalism: Architecture and Identity in a Globalized World*, edited by Liane Lefaivre and Alexander Tzonis. Munich, Prestel, 2003, 26.

79. Ibid., 44.

80. Vincent Canizaro. "Introduction." In *Architectural Regionalism: Collected Writings on Place, Identity, Modernity and Tradition*, edited by Vincent Canizaro. New York: Princeton Architectural Press, 2007, 24.

81. Alexander Tzonis. "Introducing an Architecture of the Present. Critical Regionalism and the Design of Identity." In Lefaivre & Tzonis, op. cit., 10.
82. Lefaivre, op. cit., 34.
83. Mumford, op. cit., 18.
84. Karen Vogel Wheeler, Peter Arnell & Ted Bickford, eds. *Michael Graves: Building and Projects, 1966–1981*. New York: Rizzoli, 1982.
85. First published in *The Anti-Aesthetic: Essays on Post-Modern Culture*, edited by Hal Foster. Seattle: Bay Press 1983. This influential essay was reprinted and revised in 1987 as *Ten Points on an Architecture of Regionalism: A Provisional Polemic* and in 1992 as *Critical Regionalism: Modern Architecture and Cultural Identity*.
86. Paul Ricoeur. "Universal Civilization and National Cultures." In *History and Truth*, trans. Charles A Kelbley. Evanston: Northwestern University Press, (1961) 1968, 277.
87. Kenneth Frampton. "Towards a Critical Regionalism: Six Points for an Architecture of Resistance." Foster op. cit.
88. Kenneth Frampton. "Ten Points on an Architecture of Regionalism: A Provisional Polemic," In *Center 3: New Regionalism*. : Center for American Architecture and Design, 1987, 20–7.
89. Frampton 1983, op. cit., 23.
90. Idem. 28–29.
91. John Engelen. "Glenn Murcutt—The Pritzker Prize winning 'Tin Man'." *DeDeCe Blog*, Australia, January 11, 2011. http://www.dedeceblog.com/2011/01/11/glenn-murcutt-the-tin-man (accessed January 2012).
92. http://delhi-architecture.weebly.com/architecture-and-identity.html (accessed January 2012).
93. Lefaivre & Tzonis, op. cit.
94. *US Department of Energy Review*, 2006. UK Green Building Council, *Deutsche Gesellschaft für Nachhaltiges Bauen* and others.
95. UN Department of Economic and Social Affairs, Division for Sustainable Development, *Agenda 21*. Rio de Janeiro: 1992, Principle 4.
96. United Nations Framework Convention on Climate Change, *Kyoto Protocol*. Kyoto, Japan: December 11, 1997.
97. Ibid, Article 2a.
98. Ibid, Article 10bi.

99. Catherine Slessor. *Eco-Tech: Sustainable Architecture and High Technology*. London: Thames and Hudson, 1997, 19.

100. Adam Architecture with Atelier 10. *A Study of the Energy Performance of Two Buildings with Lightweight and Heavyweight Facades*. Winchester: Adam Architecture, April 2008.

101. "Glass buildings are set to become 'pariahs'." *Building Design*, March 5, 2010, 1.

102. Slessor, op. cit., 10.

103. Letters Page, *Architects' Journal*, July 15, 2010.

104. Diane Pham & Jill Fehrenbacher, "1 Bryant Park Tower Gets LEED Platinum Certification!" http://inhabitat.com/photos-worlds-greenest-skyscraper-nycs-one-bryant-park, August 19, 2010.

105. Blair Kamin. "Gehry's 8 Spruce Street isn't Pursuing LEED Certification; Gang's Aqua is." *Chicago Tribune*, February 15, 2011.

106. Mark Lamster. "Castles in the Air." *Scientific American*, September 2011, 63 and 64.

107. Elif Sungur. "David Scott of Arup to Chair Council on Tall Buildings." *Dexigner*, January 20, 2006. http://www.dexigner.com/news/6676

108. Faber Maunsell. *Tall Buildings and Sustainability*. Corporation of London, 2002.

109. Mark Lamster, op. cit., 69.

110. Dominic Bradbury. "The Only Way is Up." *Daily Telegraph Magazine*, November 12, 2011, 56.

111. SOM website, www.som.com (accessed January 2012).

112. G. J. Treloar, R. Fay, B. Ilozor & P.E.D. Love. "An Analysis of the Embodied Energy of Office Buildings by Height." *Facilities Year* 19 (5/6) (2001): 204.

113. *Tall buildings: Report and Proceedings of the House of Commons Transport, Local Government and the Regions Committee*. Sixteenth report of Session, 2001–02. London, UK Stationery Office, September 4, 2002, HC 482-I.

114. Notes by author from RIBA Conference, "Identity," Barcelona, October 25–26, 2008.

115. Notes by author from World Architecture Festival Conference, Barcelona, October 23–24, 2008.

116. Author's interview with Peter Oborn, November 6, 2010.

117. Notes by author taken at Royal Institute of British Architects Seminar, Shrinking World, London, September 22, 2011.

118. L. Oltmanns. Interview in *A + U. Tokyo* 11 (386) (2002): 32.

119. *Introduction to Foreign Office Architects' Lecture at the Pratt Institute*, November 12, 2007.
http://www.core.form-ula.com/2007/11/12/alejandro-zaera-polo-lecture-november-12-at-6pm

120. "David Chipperfield in Conversation with Jonathan Sergison." *Architects' Journal*, October 29, 2009, 50.

121. Juhani Pallasmaa. "As Architecture Veers Towards Aesthetics, it Risks Losing a Sense of Meaning and Compassion." *Architects Journal*, November 19, 2009, 16.

122. Notes taken by author at World Architecture Festival, Barcelona, October 23–24, 2008.

123. Ibid.

124. Pallasmaa, op. cit.

125. Notes by author from RIBA Conference, "Identity," Barcelona, October 25–26, 2008.

126. Ibid.

127. Ibid.

128. Ibid.

129. Ibid.

130. Ibid.

131. Ibid.

132. Pratt Institute, op. cit.

133. Notes taken by author at World Architecture Festival, Barcelona, October 23–24, 2008.

134. "Building for the future." *BBC News*, April 7, 1999.

135. *Building the Scottish Parliament, The Holyrood Project*, Standard Note: SN/PC3357, London, House of Commons, January 12, 2005.

136. Ibid.

137. "Scottish Parliament—Concept." Barcelona, EMBT Architects, December 22, 2006.

138. Notes by author from RIBA Conference, 'Identity', Barcelona, October 25–26, 2008.

139. Ibid.

140. Poll conducted by Channel 4 Television, UK, for "Demolition" programme, December 15, 2005.

142. Notes by author from RIBA Conference, "Identity," Barcelona, October 25–26, 2008.

143. Ibid.

144. Ibid.

145. Piers Gough. "Should Architects try Harder to Please the Public?" *Building Design*, February 19, 2010.

146. Will Hurst. "Cuts Spell Disaster for Design, Rogers Warns." *Building Design*, October 29, 2010.

147. Alan Berman. "Why do Architects Love Stirling's Buildings, While the Public and Users Hate Them?" *Architects Journal* August 8, 2010.

148. Aspa Gospodini. "European Cities and Place-Identity." *Discussion Paper Series, 8 (2)*. Dept of Planning and Regional Development, University of Thessaly, Volos, March 2002, 29–30.

149. Gieryn, op. cit., 481.

150. Claire Parin, C. "Reconceptualising the City. Introduction: New Way to Read Difference." In *Cross-Cultural Urban Design*, edited by C. Bull et al. London: Routledge, 2007, 15–16.

151. Ian Nairn, ed. "Outrage, Special Number." *The Architectural Review* 117 (702) (1955).

152. Ian Nairn. *Outrage: On the Disfigurement of Town and Countryside*. London: Architectural Press, 1959.

153. Jane Jacobs. *The Death and Life of Great American Cities*. New York: Random House, 1993 (1961).

154. Kevin Lynch. *The Image of the City*. Cambridge MA: MIT Press, 1960.

155. Gordon Cullen. *Townscape*. London: The Architectural Press, 1961.

156. Christopher Alexander & Serge Chermayeff. *Community and Privacy: Toward a New Architecture of Humanism*. New York: Doubleday, 1963.

157. Rob Krier. *Stadtraum in Theorie und Praxis. An Beispielen der Innenstadt Stuttgarts*, Solingen, Umbau-Verlag, 1975. First published in English in 1979 as *Urban Space*.

158. Demetri Porphyios, guest editor. *Leon Krier: Houses Palaces Cities*, London, *Architectural Design, Academy Editions* 54 (7/8) (1984).

159. Charles Jencks. *Iconic Building: The Power of Enigma*. London: Frances Lincoln, 2005, 323.

160. Bella Dicks. *Culture on Display: The Production of Contemporary Visibility*. Maidenhead: Open University Press, 2003, 70.

161. John B. Allcock. "International Law and the Former Yugoslavia." In *Globalization and Identity*, edited by Alan Carling. London: IB Tauris, 165–6.

162. King, op. cit., 27–8.

163. Jordi Borja & Manuel Castells. *Local and Global, Management of Cities in the Information Age*. London: Earthscan, 1997, 3–4.
164. Martin Wolf. *Why Globalization Works*. Newhaven: Yale UP, 2005, 193–4.
165. Borja & Castells, op. cit. Rio-Barcelona Declaration, Point 4, 227–30.
166. The Prince of Wales. *A Vision of Britain*. London: Doubleday, 1989.
167. A Vision of Europe, *Charter of the City of the New Renaissance*, 1996. www.avoe.org/charter.html (accessed January 2012).
168. International Network for Traditional Building Architecture and Urbanism, *Charter*, 2001, www.intbau.org (accessed January 2012).
169. Peter Calthorpe, Michael Corbett, Andres Duany, Elizabeth Moule, Elizabeth Plater-Zyberk & Stefanos Polyzoides. *Ahwahnee Principles for Resource-Efficient Communities*, Sacramento CAL, Local Government Commission, 1991.
170. The Congress for the New Urbanism, *Charter of the New Urbanism*, ratified 1996, www.cnu.org/charter (accessed January 2012).
171. Ibid. The Region: Metropolis, City, and Town, paragraph 6.
172. Ibid. The Block, the Street, and the Building, paragraph 24.
173. *Towards an Urban Renaissance,* London, Her Majesty's Stationary Office, distributed by E and FN Spon, 1999.
174. Ibid., *Executive Summary*, 5.
175. *Towards an Urban Renaissance*, op. cit., 42.
176. Academy of Urbanism, *Manifesto*, 2006, Principles 3 and 11. www.academyofurbanism.org.uk/images/aou_manifesto (accessed January 2012).
177. Council for European Urbanism, *Charter of Stockholm*, 6th November 2003. www.ceunet.org/charter.html (accessed January 2012).
178. The Congress for the New Urbanism, op. cit., paragraph 20.
179. Council for European Urbanism, op. cit. paragraph VI.31.
180. Academy of Urbanism, op. cit., Principle 11.
181. Towards an Urban Renaissance, op. cit., Achieving Design Excellence, 41.
182. Andreas Tzortzis, "The Planner Who Saved Berlin—Or Did He Fail?" New York, *International Herald Tribune*, September 29, 2006, 22.
183. Nathaniel Popper. "Master Architect Reclaims His Status as an Underdog." *Jewish Daily*, October 8, 2004.
184. Peter Davey. "The Death of High Modernism." *The Architectural Review,* March 2005, 51.

185. Peter Calthorpe. *The Next American Metropolis*. New York: Princeton Architectural Press, 1993.

186. Peter Newman. "The Land Use-Transport Connection: An Overview." *Land Use Policy* 13 (1) (1996): 1–22.

187. Stephen Wheeler. *Planning Sustainable and Livable Cities*. London: Routledge, 1998.

188. Foster + Partners website, www.fosterandpartners.com (accessed January 2012).

189. OMA website, www.oma.eu (accessed January 2012).

190. César Grana. *Fact and Symbol*. Oxford: Oxford University Press, 1971, 98.

191. Dicks, op. cit., 120.

192. Roger K Lewis. "Will Forces of Globalization Overwhelm Traditional Local Architecture." *Washington Post*, November 2, 2002.

193. John B. Allcock. "International Law and the Former Yugoslavia." In Carling op. cit., 165–6.

194. Mike Featherstone, 1995, op. cit., 92.

195. M. Christine Boyer. *The City of Collective Memory: Its Historical Imagery and Architectural Entertainments*. Cambridge MA: MIT Press, 1996, 72.

196. Cohen, 1985, op. cit., 44.

197. Jonathan Meades. "We Don't Write Music Like Haydn, or Paint Like Gainsborough—So Why all These Dismal Pastiches of Georgian Architecture." *The Times*, May 11, 2002, 24.

CONCLUSION:

THE END OF THE ERA, WHAT NOW?

The Present and the Future

The New Global Era may have ended in 2008 (or it may just be entering into a new stage) but, one way or the other, it is certain that events since that date and that continue at the time of writing will permanently transform the global social, political and economic condition. Writing in mid-2012, we do not know the outcome of the major events that are unfolding with alarming speed. Predictions under these circumstances are perilous; the only thing we can know about the future is that it is unknown. Events such as the "Arab Spring," that is transforming the south-Mediterranean Arab nations, began in Tunisia in December 2010 and took the world by surprise. It has not yet played out, and other major uncertainties stalk the world stage, in particular the transformation of the common European currency and its political ramifications. As with all such series of events, the impact is widely felt and, before any kind of normality returns, they may yet de-stabilise other nations or create economic conditions that have not yet been anticipated.

In all this, architects and urban designers are passive observers. Projects are being completed that were conceived before 2008 and in due course, when economies recover, those who commission buildings will be responding to new and as yet unknown conditions. Architects and urban designers will also unavoidably respond to these conditions but, in the short to medium term, will most likely do so in accordance with ideas formed in the previous decades.

It is, however, the fundamental premise of this book that if we are to understand architecture and urban design we must first look at the social, political and economic conditions that will inevitably drive them. As architecture and urban design are slow to change, to see if there is anything in the current condition that is likely to influence the future direction of architecture, we should look at what is happening in the wider theatre of events. The chances of misinterpretation are high and, if this book is ever republished, this chapter will have to be re-written.

As some of the changes that are taking place will probably alter the geographic balance of power, new cultural conditions will emerge from outside the previously dominant North Atlantic nations. As culture always follows power, albeit in a variable time frame, it would also be valuable to look at the ways that cultures deal with imported influence and turn it around to something of their own—the process called indigenisation.

The 2008 Bank Crash and End of North Atlantic Supremacy

The banking collapse of 2007 to 2008 revealed serious fault lines in the global financial system. Underlying problems were built in by the free-market fundamentalism that had driven the 1980s boom. At that time, the liberalisation of financial markets led to a combination of previously separated retail, broking and insurance banking. Combined funds released larger sums for trading, and made possible complex investments that brought together retail loans and debt-default insurance. This fuelled a financial trading culture which, as the legendary sign above the trading floor in the (now defunct) New York investment bank Bear Stearns said, was based only on the principle of "let's make nothing but money." Added to this, the entry of new emerging economies into the financial markets at the start of the New Global Era in the early 1990s increased available capital and trading opportunities.

Free global trade gave improved access to the consumer markets of the North Atlantic countries and Japan. The low labour costs of the new entrants created opportunities for economic expansion based on manufacture, services or raw materials for export. The income raised by these exports created large cash surpluses held in US dollars. These capital reserves needed to make a return while protecting the funds against potential political instability at home, and they were used for income-generating loans. The most willing borrowers were the developed economies, which could fund their political and consumer demands with cheap money. Their consumers, in turn, would support the export markets of the same emerging economies that had lent them the money in the first place. This set up an economic Faustian pact between lending-exporters and borrowing-importers. As the emerging economies grew for the next fifteen years they pumped more capital and goods into the indebted countries leading to the impression that the old cyclical seven-year economic pattern had ended. The prosperity of the New Global Era was put down to the permanent benefits of globalisation and called by economists "The Great Moderation."

Economic growth and easy borrowing encouraged investors to take advantage of the profits available from a rising property market, setting in train a boom in real-estate prices. In the United States this was exacerbated by a political objective to open up home loans to lower income families. The rush to sell mortgages launched large numbers of unsecured loans onto the market which were then put together with other investments and debt-default insurance to create, what bankers' statisticians believed, were risk-free investment packages. The political advantage of increasing public services and state employment and the low cost of borrowing also encouraged countries to increase their national debt from an average of two hundred per cent in 1995 to three hundred per cent in 2008[1] (chart 6).

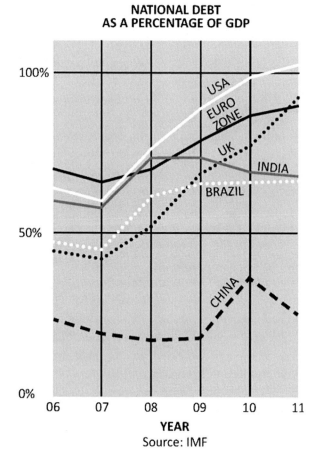

**NATIONAL DEBT
AS A PERCENTAGE OF GDP**

Source: IMF

Chart 6. National Debt as a Percentage of GDP 2006–2011

By 2007, however, the tide turned and the economic benefits of
government loans began to slow down as borrowing was used to inflate
the unproductive public sector, and the cost of each dollar borrowed
started to depress rather than stimulate growth.[2] In the same year
defaults in low-value unsecured mortgages led to a collapse in the
United States housing market. This revealed the fragility of the
mortgage-based investment packages, by now traded around the

international money markets. There was a dramatic collapse of confidence leading to a run on banks. The banks could not repay their capital depositors as their funds had been used for loans which, secured by insurance guarantees, had been rolled over into further loans and then insured and used again, often many times over. The global banking system crashed on September 15, 2008 when America's fourth-largest investment bank, Lehman Brothers, filed for bankruptcy.

The crash, often called the "sub-prime credit crunch" after the failed sub-prime mortgages that had set off the collapse of confidence, affected the entire global economy. It was at its worst in the North Atlantic countries which experienced the most severe depression for seventy-five years. In the fourth quarter the value of all the goods and services (Gross Domestic Product or GDP) fell by 1.6 per cent in the United States and 1.4 per cent in the European Union countries (chart 7).

When the world's twenty leading nations gathered in London in April 2009 at the Group of 20 (G20) summit to see how to resolve the growing global financial crisis, a fundamental change in the balance of world power was revealed. As Robert Hormats, Vice-Chairman of the bankers Goldman Sachs said: "It's the passing of an era, the US is becoming less dominant while other nations are gaining influence."[3] Nobel Laureate economist Joseph Stiglitz said "This is … a reversal of the ideology of the 1990s, and at a very official level, a rejection of the ideas pushed by the U.S. and others."[4] The economist Anatole Kaletsky believes that we are entering new financial era as significant as the Reagan/Thatcher revolution of the 80s and has named it "Capitalism 4" in his 2011 book, *Capitalism 4.0: The Birth of New Economy*.[5]

Variations in the impact of the crisis had shown the strength of the Indian and Chinese economies—while experiencing a small downturn, both had avoided recession. The fast-growing Indian economy was driven more by internal growth than exports. China had amassed US $2 trillion in foreign exchange reserves and was going to be the largest potential lender to the International Monetary Fund, which would be the instrument for the rescue of failing economies.

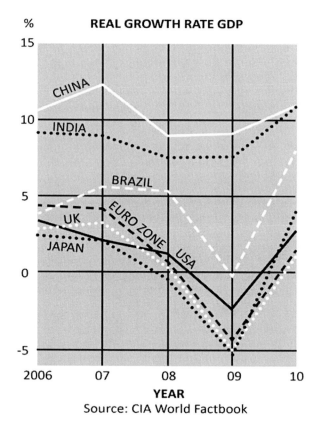

Chart 7. Comparative Real National Growth Rate GDP 2006–2010

The state-owned paper, the *China Daily*, made it clear that "the country will have a bigger say in the global financial system."[6] The governor of the People's Bank of China had little sympathy for the North Atlantic *laissez-faire* system that had led to the crisis, saying that the Chinese financial system had, "prompt decisive and effective policy measures demonstrating its superior system," and suggested a new international reserve currency, managed by the International Monetary Fund, to replace the US dollar.[7]

The new reserve currency was not adopted but China and the United States were major contributors to a huge allocation of US $1.1 trillion as, in the words of the G20 Final Communique, "support to restore credit, growth and jobs in the world economy." This would be "a global plan for recovery on an unprecedented scale" as it was recognised that "We face the greatest challenge to the world economy in modern times … A global crisis requires a global solution."[8] Even this sum was not enough to save the weaker European economies which, two years later, were unable to service their grossly inflated national debt, setting in train a political crisis in the European Union. At the next G20 summit in Cannes in November 2011 the possible collapse of the Euro threatened to drive the world economy into a second recession. The United States was preoccupied with its own political deadlock over national debt and was only able to comment from the sidelines. China, by now with a US $3.2 trillion foreign currency reserve, took centre stage but was not prepared to bail out the faltering Euro. The Xinhua News Agency, an informal mouthpiece for the government, declared on October 30 that "China can neither take the role of saviour to the Europeans, nor provide a 'cure' for the European malaise."[9]

These events signalled the beginning of the end of American dominance of the world economy, cemented at the Bretton Woods Agreement in 1944, taking its North Atlantic allies down with it. Although China, as the dominant member of the group of emerging economies has not supplanted the USA as the primary world power, and the US dollar remains the world reserve currency, 2008 clearly marks the end of an era.

Power Moves East

The status of the US dollar as the global reserve currency is not secure. A reserve currency is only one which is chosen for international trade based on the security of its issuing nation, according to the size of its economy and foreign assets and, since the collapse of the Bretton Woods agreement in 1971, the US dollar has no formal position. China is now the second largest world economy and holds the largest reserve of foreign assets. The IMF predict that the Chinese economy will overtake the United States economy in five years.[1] The Chinese yuan is constrained by exchange controls, but liberalisation has begun. Residents can export capital to fund enterprises such as the takeover of foreign companies. Although it has been much more difficult for foreigners to buy goods with the yuan, in the last few years companies such as McDonalds and Caterpillar have issued yuan bonds, and the Chinese government has sold twenty billion yuan of government debt. If the yuan becomes the reserve currency, or even an equal reserve currency, it will enjoy what Valery Giscard d'Estaing called in 1965 the "exorbitant privilege" (once only vested in the US dollar) of the ability to print money to balance trade deficits and freedom from the uncertainties of exchange rate fluctuations.

Commercial expansion in foreign economies has expanded Chinese influence abroad. Four of the world's ten largest banks are now Chinese, up from none in 2004. A non-judgemental foreign policy has eased Chinese trade in Africa, and it is the continent's largest trading partner—often using infrastructure works to gain political influence—and buys more than a third of Africa's oil. It is now the largest trading partner for Australia, India and Brazil. In 2010 Chinese buyers were responsible for one tenth of all global deals, including high-profile company purchases such as Volvo cars, the Australian food group Manassen, and a thirty-five year lease of the Greek port of Piraeus. Chinese firms are stalking the world markets for take-over opportunities.

As major Chinese companies are often state owned—eighty per cent of the stock market listed firms are state controlled—this aggressive expansion has led to some nervousness abroad. The US government blocked a bid from a Chinese telecommunications firm to invest in a new national wireless network and the Icelandic government prevented a Chinese company from purchasing 300 square kilometres of land. Security concerns behind these interventions have not been reassured by a more assertive foreign policy, a quadrupling of military spending since 2000 and regular reports of Chinese originated cyber attacks on North Atlantic defence networks. As the American political scientist David Shambaugh wrote in the *Washington Quarterly*, "2009–2010 will be remembered as the years in which China became difficult for the world to deal with."[11]

The longer-term view is mixed. As the world economy slows down, export income is diminishing and Chinese policy is for the stimulation of home demand for its own products. While its GDP is seventy per cent of the United States and growing, its GDP per capita is only sixteen per cent of the United States. There is room for a continued increase in personal prosperity (the unspoken post-Tiananmen Square stability pact), which, with the growth of the largest middle class in the world, is creating a vibrant consumer market. Increased wealth has, however, raised expectations, while labour is starting to cost more, and an increase in strikes is an indication that workers are demanding higher standards. As the up-and-coming generation becomes accustomed to, rather than grateful for, improved living standards, demands for more political freedom may occur. Add to this the longer term impact of the one-child policy—a peak in population by 2023, double the numbers of over-sixties by 2030 and a decline in the working-age population—and the expansion and competitiveness of China is likely to decline. The political consequences of this are unknown.

Coming up behind China, but with quite different social, political and economic conditions, is India. Although India's GDP is less than half that of China, when the developmental stages are compared it is on the same upward trajectory and its rate of growth is expected to outgrow that of China in the next three years.[12] India's economy is predicted to be the third-largest in the world by 2030. As the world's largest democracy, India's dramatic expansion can be dated to the government's liberalisation of the economy as one of the key events in origins of the New Global Era but otherwise, unlike China, business is not state controlled. A complex governmental and federal political system has hampered any improvement in the country's poor infrastructure, and the corporate regulatory system is shaky and often corrupt. With a long uninterrupted history of private enterprise, however, it supports leading global industries such as the IT service provider Infosys and the world's largest aluminium mills. Its huge family-run conglomerates and entrepreneurs have been embedded in the world business community for decades, and it has the benefit of a globally dispersed community of non-resident Indians (NRIs) dating from both the British Empire and more recent migration, principally to the United States. Indian companies have widespread international interests that include the world's largest steel firm, a car industry that owns two iconic British brands (Jaguar and Land Rover), a major brewing conglomerate, and one of Africa's expanding mobile phone companies. With a fast-expanding middle class, the working-age population is set to increase by 126 million in the next ten years (far ahead of any of its economic competitors), and with a relatively low level of GDP per capita, there are considerable opportunities for growth. Without any signs of geo-political ambitions beyond border disputes and a political system capable of absorbing change, there seems to be little reason to doubt the future global role of India.

While China is now firmly established as a global power and India is catching up fast, other countries have high growth rates. Brazil has a growing consumer economy and workforce and abundant raw materials. In 2009, growth in the Indonesian economy led the American investment bank Morgan Stanley to suggest adding the country to a list of the four major developing economies summarised by the acronym BRICs (Brazil, Russia, India and China—invented by Jim O'Neill of Goldman Sachs in 2001), to form a new acronym, BRICIs. It is noticeable, however, in all current assessments of the future of the world economy that the North Atlantic countries that had dominated the global economy for at least two centuries and the New Global Era for fifteen years are shown in relative decline. The twenty major nations at the London G20 summit in 2009 made it clear that: "The only sure foundation for sustainable globalisation and rising prosperity for all is an open world economy based on market principles, effective regulation, and strong global institutions."[13] A globalized world economy is unlikely to be dismantled but the historic North Atlantic domination of that economic and political system began to fade in that same year and this will have profound social and cultural consequences (chart 8).

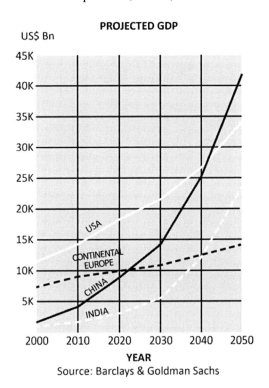

Chart 8. *Comparative Projected National GDP to 2050*

Changing Global Priorities

As the nation state world political structure is based on the nineteenth century European system, and was institutionalised by the creation of the United Nations; as the global financial system was established on a North Atlantic model with the establishment of the World Bank and the International Monetary Fund after the Second World War; and as the global regulatory system was based on Anglo-Saxon legal principles (British lawyers have privileged access to international practice), if there is a next global era it will for some time have a superficial resemblance to the declining New Global Era. They may be hard to detect, but changes of some sort will occur.

Rapidly ageing European nations not only face economic challenges in supporting their dependent pensioners, but extensions to the working age and employment protection disadvantage younger workers entering the workplace. This will benefit the more open and youthful emerging economies as talented individuals will, as they have always done, travel to the places where their abilities find the most receptive outlets. This will not only boost the knowledge economies of the destination countries directly but will stimulate local talent.

To gain the high levels of education required for emerging-economy entrepreneurs, scientists and business executives, English-speaking further (and even secondary) educational institutions are in high demand. Some of these universities have taken the logical step and created outposts to where there is unsatisfied supply. Middle Eastern states have brought in American Universities to create what is called in Doha, Qatar, "Education City," where there are branches of six American universities, as well as one from France and one from Britain. In 2008 there were seven outposts of American universities in China. In a drive to expand further education in India the *Foreign Educational Institution Bill* was introduced in 2010 to facilitate and control the entry of foreign universities. A leading British independent school, Wellington College, is building an architectural and institutional replica institution in Tianjin, near Beijing. While North Atlantic educational exports may seem to represent a straightforward cultural export, with their idiosyncrasies preserved as curiosities, by locating the institutions outside their country of origin they will not only have to adapt to local conditions but will stimulate national universities to raise their standards.

As corporations and industries are taken over, and as local service or supply industries trade with these organisations, commercial transactions have to adapt to the business culture of the new owners. With the growth of the power and influence of emerging-economy businesses the need to adapt to the host country will diminish, and new business practices will become more widely accepted. The importance of family and personal connections is already opening up trading opportunities to non-resident Indians with their country of origin, which is denied to foreigners. Chinese professionals are being given employment opportunities in North Atlantic practices and companies to facilitate trade communication with China. Business travel and hospitality, up to now dominated by the needs of the North Atlantic executive, is adapting to the demands of Chinese travellers. By 2011 China had twice as many internet users as the USA, and to gain from global developments in internet use it may be more profitable to accommodate to the Chinese than the American market.

The internet, as the primary global communication medium, can be seen as a key indicator of current trends. It remains in principle the open worldwide system envisaged by its free society, largely American, pioneers, represented by *Wired* magazine, launched in 1993. The free movement of communication was not, however, conducive to the social and political controls of the Chinese state and, at the same time as encouraging the commercial benefits of internet use, filtering software was developed and national controls were introduced. These are now employed by up to fifteen countries. Middle Eastern countries filter content for religious as well as political control, and even liberal democracies are policing internet use for pornography, crime or potential antisocial behaviour. The Domain Name System, designed in the Latin alphabet, is breaking up as more Chinese, Cyrillic and Arabic users come on line and wish to communicate in their own script (much more readily facilitated digitally than with movable typeface). The growth of internet users towards saturation level in some developed countries has enabled networking sites to establish numerous discrete social, religious, interest and political networks, reinforcing the collective identities of the participants, often at an international level. On the other hand, the IP number address system is now used to restrict cross-border access to protect commercial interests, leading to a growth of closed or semi-open user platforms. Data analysis, developed to target advertising, is leading to the increased personalisation of user sites. The social and political internet analyst Evgeny Morozov predicts that "instead of the internet, we may well start talking of a billion 'internets'."[14]

This spread of global systems from the universal to the particular is mirrored in the dichotomy of homogenisation and localisation, discussed at length in Parts III and IV. As internet development indicates, however, while the universal nature of global communication remains fundamental, there remain opportunities for an enhanced expression of regional, national, local and even personal identity.

The 2008 crash had the immediate effect of raising the need for even more universal political control of the global economy. A key part of the 2009 G20 Communique was the need "to build a stronger, more globally consistent, supervisory and regulatory framework." At the same time, memories of the Great Depression and the role of American protectionism have subsequently led all economists to understand that, as the Communique says, "to promote global trade and investment" it was necessary to "reject protectionism."[15] This recognises the tendency that, as voting is local and finance is global, the popular response to economic hardship will often be to protect national economies from international contamination. On September 6, 2011, Dilma Rousseff, president of Brazil, provided a textbook statement promoting this phenomenon: "In the case of the current international crisis our principal weapon is to expand and defend our internal market."[16] There is further evidence from the USA (historically prone to isolationism) in the Senate's *Currency Exchange Rate Oversight Reform Act* of 2011 which proposed that the United States could judge a currency to be "fundamentally misaligned" and take restrictive action on its imports.

The target was clearly China. As the Swiss currency has been driven up in value by the failures in the surrounding Euro, Switzerland is seeking measures to protect the Swiss franc from free-market pressures.[17]

While these measures may be moderated by finance ministers who understand the dire consequences of trade wars, the popular mood may find its outlet elsewhere. Much as localisation has become the other side of cultural homogenisation, increased uniformity in the management of the global economy combined with an enhanced feeling of helplessness, particularly in the North Atlantic countries as their self-confidence declines, is likely to stimulate an enhanced desire for the security of local identity.

Evidence is to be found at a national level.

China shows signs of moving from its 2008 Olympic slogan "one world, one dream" to a more inward looking cultural outlook. It pressured its allies to boycott the 2010 Nobel Peace Prize when the rest of that "one world" chose a Chinese human rights lawyer for an award. But in a significant break from the Communist Party's ambivalent attitude to Confucius, and for the first time since the revolution, Beijing held large scale celebrations in 2011 to honour his 2,561st birthday to celebrate, as the official website china.org declared, "the great Chinese scholar and social philosopher, whose thoughts and teachings have profoundly influenced Chinese, Korean, Vietnamese, and Japanese thoughts and life."[18]

The apparently spontaneous emergence of the populist and politically fundamentalist right-wing Tea Party movement in the USA has been largely inward looking. While it is less a political movement than a party and has no clear manifesto, let alone a articulated foreign policy, its supporters are, according to Walter Russell Mead in the New York Times, "united in their dislike for liberal internationalism—the attempt to conduct international relations through multilateral institutions under an ever-tightening web of international laws and treaties."[19] Even a Republican Party presidential contender was criticised for speaking French.[20]

In Europe, where the European Union is a microcosm of the stresses of globalisation, the threatened collapse of the Euro presents such an economic catastrophe that most countries in the Union have accepted a major surrender of economic sovereignty. This must be contrasted with the growth of anti-internationalist movements. In Holland the anti-immigration Freedom Party won fifteen per cent of the national vote and has entered the ruling coalition. A similar Danish People's Party has been part of a minority government since 2001. In Finland, the anti-European Union True Finns party came third in the 2011 election and combines left wing economic policy with cultural activities which, as it states in their election manifesto, "promote the Finnish identity." In Scotland the left wing Scottish Nationalist Party is more international in outlook, but has come to power on a wave of nationalism that is likely to win the country some level of independence from the United Kingdom.

At a more local level there are similar small-scale indicators. In Britain the homogenisation of accent that was anticipated from exposure to national media has been arrested as regional accents are consolidating. The forensic linguist Dominic Watt sees this as a sign that "people want to protect their identity," and although people dress the same and have the same interests and their cities look the same, "what still makes these places separate and distinct is the dialect and accent."[21] In Italy, a number of cities have taken steps to ban foreign food outlets in order to, as the mayor of Forte de Marmo said, following a unanimous vote in the town council, "protect the genius loci, what's typical of the real place."[22] In 2009, the German foreign minister, concerned that global English was corrupting German, launched the campaign to protect the German language, "*Deutsch: sprache der ideen*" [German, the language of ideas].[23] Mark Malloch Brown, former director of the United Nations Development Programme, sums up the continuing attraction of localisation: "Today the power over economic management, security and countless other areas has been swallowed up … Meanwhile, valuing what is local—be it indigenous cultural events, local organic food or a shared communal history—fits in with our growing instincts as citizens and consumers."[24]

These social, political and economic forces will have an impact on architecture and urban design. An increase in demand for overtly local or traditional design would be expected, but the small size of this sector, the continuing hostility of the profession and the fact it has an established market would make it hard to assess. Some new conditions are, however, evident now: a crisis in city expansion in the developing world and a reassessment of iconic architecture.

Urban Crisis in the Emerging Economies

The most organised urban design theory at the end of the twentieth century, the various versions of contextual urbanism, was born out of dissatisfaction with the post Second World War North Atlantic urban condition. In its most influential form, New Urbanism, it has taken this version of American culture around the world. The urban condition in the world is, however, changing at a pace that will outstrip these small-scale developments and methodologies.

The McKinsey Global Institute, in its recent publication, *Urban World: Mapping the Economic Power of Cities*, describes the emerging urban condition:

> Economic power is shifting eastwards. Today, 22 of the 25 largest cities ranked by GDP are developed economies, but this situation will change radically in the next 15 years with the rise of Asian cities, particularly those in China. By 2025, nine of the world's top 25 cities ranked by GDP will be located in Asia, up from two in 2007, according to our analysis. During this period, our research suggests that three cities in North America and four in Western Europe will drop off this ranking.[25]

The current condition is reported in the Knight Frank and Citi Private Bank World Cities Survey of 2009, directed to the real estate market. Based on a combined measure of economic activity, political power, knowledge and influence, and quality of life, the top ten world cities have been put in descending order, all but two in North America and Europe[26] (chart 9). The McKinsey analysis of the projected top ten by GDP has some similarities, but three Chinese cities come into the listing. When cities are ranked by projected GDP growth, however, the picture is transformed and moves entirely to China (chart 10). When the ranking is set by the anticipated increase in middle-class wealth, a measure of success beyond size, (calibrated by the numbers of families with an annual income about US $20,000 a year on present day prices), a more subtle but similar picture emerges with five Chinese cities, two Indian cities, one South American city, and one surprise entry in the Middle East. The only city in the old developed world—albeit in Asia—is Tokyo (chart 11).

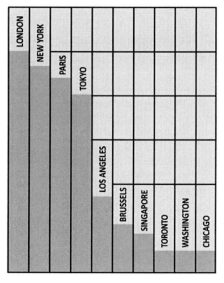

KNIGHT FRANK WORLD CITIES SURVEY 2009

Assessment based on economic activity; political power; knowledge & influence and quality of life

CITY

Chart 9. World Cities Survey 2009

**PROJECTED TOP 10 CITIES BY GDP PER
CAPITA AND GDP GROWTH BY 2025**

RANK	GDP PER CAPITA 2025	GDP GROWTH 2007-2025
1	New York	Shanghai
2	Tokyo	Beijing
3	Shanghai	New York
4	London	Tianjin
5	Beijing	Chongqing
6	Los Angeles	Shenzhen
7	Paris	Guangzhou
8	Chicago	Nanjing
9	Rhine-Ruhr	Hangzhou
10	Shenzhen	Chengdu

Source: McKinsey Global Institute

Chart 10. Projected Top Ten Cities by 2025

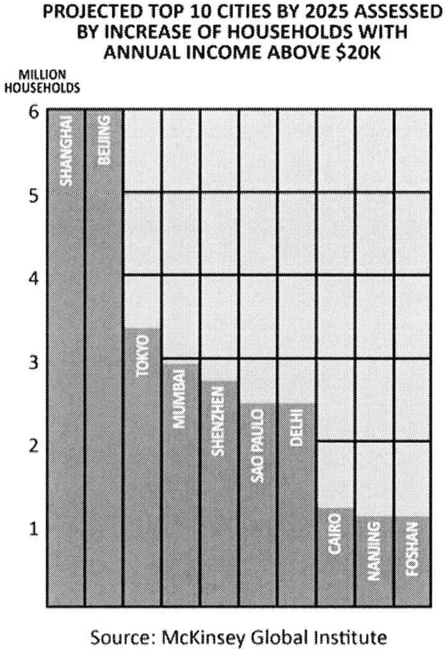

**PROJECTED TOP 10 CITIES BY 2025 ASSESSED
BY INCREASE OF HOUSEHOLDS WITH
ANNUAL INCOME ABOVE $20K**

Source: McKinsey Global Institute

Chart 11. Projected Top Ten Cities for Middle Class Growth by 2025

While the headline megacities tell one story, at another level a recent report by the Boston Consulting Group estimates that by 2030 there will more than 1,000 cities in emerging markets with populations over half a million.[27] According to the United Nations, by 2050 the world population is expected to be more than nine billion, with the urban population exceeding six billion. In other words, two in three people born in the next thirty years will live in cities. This indicates a critical human situation far beyond a simple increase in wealth.

In 2012 it was reported that the urban population of China now exceeds its rural population. This has put additional pressure on an already rapid programme of city expansion.[28] Other countries face similar pressures but lack organisation and forward planning. Doug Saunders, author of the 2010 prize-winning analysis of cities in emerging economies, *Arrival City*, describes the new conditions created by this massive shift to urban living:

> We are at a halfway point in the history's largest population shift, as Asian, Middle Eastern and South American countries move from rural, subsistence-based economies to more sustainable nations based on commercial farming and large urban populations. As a result of this shift, which is creating five million new city dwellers in the developing world each month, there are now thousands of transitional urban neighbourhoods, which have one foot in the originating village and one in the established city's economy. These "arrival cities" … are driven by the ambitions of their rural-born founders.[29]

What Saunders calls optimistically "arrival cities" are the slums, shanty-towns, *gandi basti* [dirty localities] or *jhopadpattis* [strip of huts] and *favelas*. Robert Neuwrith lived in squatter communities around the world while researching his influential 2004 book, *Shadow Cities: A Billion Squatters, a New Urban World*.[30] He says that one in seven of the global population now lives in shanty towns, and these dense settlements are all in the emerging economies. They are the only place that poor internal migrants can find to live, are almost always illegal, on expropriated land, and without any of the normal urban services—piped water, sewage disposal or electricity. Fearful that the illegal status of these settlements will become permanent if city administrations recognise them, they are sometimes forcibly cleared (usually returning on the same site or elsewhere almost immediately) or simply ignored. New Delhi bulldozed its *Yamana Pushta* slums in 2004, but declared the displaced inhabitants ineligible for re-housing: within a month its residents started re-building in the same area.[31] Nairobi's shanty town of Kibera, home to about one fifth of its population, is shown as a forest on official maps.

The inhabitants of these slums are forced by deprivation to create their own economies—the size of their populations and the enterprise of their traders have created a significant economy beyond regulation and taxation. It is estimated by the OECD that 1.8 billion people—or sixty per cent of the world's working population—will earn their living in this "informal economy."[32] According to a Harvard Business School study, Mumbai's famous slum, Dharavi, has an established textile industry selling to the global market through approximately five thousand informal businesses and earning US $600 million a year.[33] The growing mobile phone industry in Nigeria makes most of its income through street vendors selling phone-recharge cards from casual stalls under umbrellas—"umbrella people." Akinwale Goodluck, corporate services executive for MTN, Africa's leading telecommunications provider, says: "The umbrella market is a very, very important market now. No serious operator can afford to ignore the umbrella people."[34]

Squatter communities and informal street markets have developed their own institutional structures. Mumbai slum dwellers run shared savings schemes. In favelas there are mutual construction societies or *muritores*. In Kenya women from shanty towns pool their money to pay one another the accumulated sum once a week as a business development fund. Robert Neuwirth believes that "these massive do-it-yourself street markets and self-built neighbourhoods are a vision of the urban future."[35]

Community life in these settlements is often not so benign. Ignored by the authorities, and outside the rule of law, slums can fall under the control of criminal gangs. The Jardim Angela favela in São Paolo, with an estimated population of a quarter of a million, formerly had a murder rate of 123 per 10,000—a violent-death rate higher than most war zones—and was run by rival drugs gangs. In order to bring this centre of criminal activity under control, the city authorities changed their attitude and identified them as "transitional neighbourhoods whose move from rural poverty into urban societies had been blocked" by their exclusion from civil life. Starting with the provision of a day and evening school, and a community-based police force, public transport was provided to employment areas and the land, originally expropriated illegally, was given to the slum dwellers. Between one fifth and one third of the inhabitants became home owners and, confident in the security of ownership, replaced their makeshift shacks with brick and stucco dwellings. Between 1999 and 2005 the murder rate fell by about seventy-three per cent.[36] As Jardim Angela entered into the civil society of São Paulo it retained in permanent form the urban structure of its illegal favela.

The scale and pace of city expansion in the emerging economies, from the forests of tower blocks of the new Chinese cities to the *jhopadpattis* of India, is creating new urban conditions faster than any theory can catch up with events. As North Atlantic contextual urbanists export their consultation procedures and create small-scale master plans, new urban contexts are being created either by fast-moving state-sponsored expansion or large-scale illegal expropriation. Contextual urbanists are practicing in deprived areas such as the West Indies and are promoting their services in the huge evolutionary test bed of the emerging Eastern economies, but their work, commendable though it may be, will be never be more than a boutique activity in an emerging urban condition of superstore dimensions.

The speculative fiction author William Gibson describes a diverging urban world where he sees that the North Atlantic countries:

run the risk of Disneylanding themselves, of building themselves too permanently into a given day's vision of what they should be. ... Meanwhile, though, some of the world's largest human settlements are now ... places that have by-passed the ways in which Europeans and North-Americans have assumed cities necessarily need to grow: Rio, Mumbai, Nairobi, Istanbul, Mexico City ... vast squatter conurbs, semi-neo-Medieval in their structure and conditions. The future will emerge from such cities as surely as it will emerge from the Disneylanded capitals of an Old World that now includes North America.[37]

Figure 62. Favela, Caxias do Sul, Brazil.

Slums, the fastest growing urban type.

Iconic Architecture Reassessed

As the North Atlantic countries struggle to reduce their national debt and service their interest, taxation is increased, state expenditure reduced, banks become risk-averse and consumers cut back on expenditure. In a time of austerity, it becomes not just hard to justify expensive and ostentatious construction projects, but they also become unfashionable. An obvious target for accusations of profligacy is the iconic building phenomenon that symbolised the confidence of the Great Moderation. The idea that an iconic building would deliver unique benefits to the economy as well as the status of its commissioning city only dates back to the completion of the Guggenheim Museum in Bilbao in 1997 and so, at the time of the crash, the phenomenon had only been in full flow for eleven years. As a major building can readily take up to ten years from inception to completion, many buildings were only just completed at the time the economic tide turned. A number of buildings that were commissioned in the first flush of enthusiasm for the Bilbao effect are now being assessed in a less sympathetic environment. Zaha Hadid's MAXXI in Rome, for example, won in competition in 1999, but only opened at the end of 2009. Peter Eisenman's City of Culture of Galicia Archive and Library in Santiago di Compostela in Spain, which also won in competition in 1999, is still under construction. A plan for an iconic waterfront building in the northern English port of Liverpool was first put forward in 2001 but, after controversy and the scrapping of a winning design, a new Museum of Liverpool was commissioned from the Danish architects 3XN and completed in 2011 (figure 64).

All these buildings have been the subject of controversy. Hadid's MAXXI was delayed by funding problems and cost €150 million. It has had relatively low visitor numbers of between 250–500,000 and led the editor of one professional journal to declare: "I can't think that I have ever encountered an art gallery that addresses its nominal function with such seeming cynicism."[38] Eisenman's City of Culture of Galicia has escalated in cost from €108 million to €400 million. It has been described by a member of the original selection jury as "an expensive mistake. Probably one of the largest in the history of architecture."[39] The original architects of the Museum of Liverpool, 3XN, were sacked from the project "over cost-control issues" and the £72 million design was modified to control expenditure (figure 63). Another architectural critic thought it rare for "a 'flagship building' to be so spectacularly botched, so comprehensively fouled up and so completely at odds with its context as the Museum of Liverpool."[40]

Perhaps the most iconic of the icons, and the most tortured design process, has been Ground Zero in Manhattan, New York City, rebuilding on the site of the Twin Towers terrorist attack, the most psychologically damaging event in the United States since its Civil War. After two architectural competitions and the emotive participation of the public, Daniel Libeskind won from a field of stellar competitors with a spiralling asymmetric design with gardens in the sky to be called the "Freedom Tower"—1776 feet high to represent the foundation year of the United States. Little remains of this design as the leaseholder of the site quickly sidelined Libeskind, bringing in a more commercial architect for a more commercial scheme, while keeping a nominal role for the competition winner (figure 64). Now a conventional tapering tower in reflecting glass has been prosaically renamed "1 WTC." The New York Port Authority, in the meantime, embarked on another iconic project on the site, a new transport hub by the Spanish star architect Santiago Calatrava. The cost of the spectacular bird-like design has gone from US $2.2 billion in 2003 to US $3.44 billion in 2011,[41] leading the Port Authority to raise its road tolls amidst public protest.[42]

Spiralling costs have become a feature of iconic buildings: their deliberately complex forms are hard to construct and, as the designs set out to be unprecedented, comparative costing is impossible, and budgets are often coloured by enthusiasm and optimism. At the same time, the well-recorded benefits to the economy of the City of Bilbao have proved to be hard to reproduce. A number of projects have failed to live up to expectations.

Frank Gehry's Experience Music Project for the City of Seattle never reached its anticipated visitor numbers, curators left, staff were cut, and part of it was let to a science-fiction museum.[43] The Bellvue Art Museum in Washington was designed by Steven Holl to be a "bold glass, aluminium and textured concrete structure … crafted to support the Museum's mission of providing opportunities not just to see art, but to explore and make it as well."[44] The museum failed after three years and had to be shut down, "foiled by a combination of a tough economy, white-elephant architecture and a failure to find an audience"[45] (it was later re-opened after a major fundraising campaign). In Britain, the architect Will Alsop was appointed in the late 1990s to design an ambitious arts building in the declining British industrial town of West Bromwich. It was called, ambitiously, "The Public," and the culture minister at the time said: "It chimes exactly with the way the arts in the twenty-first century are going. It will act as a trailblazer for regeneration in the area and will place West Bromwich at the forefront of this country's brilliant cultural scene."[46] The project was funded by central and local government, but nonetheless went bankrupt in 2006 and was rescued by more state funds to reach a final total of £65 million. After it opened in 2010 sections had to be sublet for commercial use, and it still survives only with the contribution of public funds and may close in 2012.[47]

Although projects such as Herzog and de Meuron's fifty-storey Triangle Tower in Paris are still coming forward, others such as Santiago Calatrava's residential tower in New York and Kohn Pedersen Fox's Pinnacle Tower in London have been delayed or cancelled. In North Atlantic countries the days of iconic buildings are probably over. Image consultants, such as Simon Anholt, will advise cities that want to commission "big, glamorous buildings" that, "if it's done for its own sake and there's no long-term strategy behind it, it will add nothing to the city's overall image at all."[48] Observers of the Bilbao effect tended to concentrate on the dramatic building without noticing that the infrastructure and historic fabric of the city were a part of the wider economic strategy.

For all the failures, there have been successes. The thriving "7 Star" Burj al Arab hotel in Dubai (figure 65), by the less-well-known architect Tom Wright of the professional conglomerate WS Atkins, is still a more powerful image of the Gulf State than its featureless world's-tallest-building. 30 Mary Axe in London or "The Gherkin" by Norman Foster is a prime business address and has been adopted as one of the silhouette images of the city. The architectural profession still admire their star architects—Zaha Hadid was given the Royal Institute of British Architects' highest award two years running.

Figure 63. Museum of Liverpool, Liverpool, England; 3XN; 2011. A design chosen to be an icon for the City of Liverpool compromised by political, financial and managerial problems.

Figure 64. (left) 1WTC, New York; Skidmore, Owings and Merrill; completion programmed 2013. Daniel Libeskind's competition-winning icon replaced with a commercial glass-walled office block.
Figure 65. (right) Burj al Arab, Dubai; Tom Wright, WS Atkins; 1999. Some buildings designed to be iconic have become iconic.

Iconic architecture is being reassessed as the financial record and commercial success of buildings are being revealed.

The record of overspending and failure is, however, now so much a part of the story of iconic buildings that it would be politically very unlikely for any city or government in the North Atlantic economies to embark on such a project in the near future. As the critic Hugh Pearman said of a recently completed building by Zaha Hadid in Glasgow, Scotland, a "pre-crash cultural building on the Clyde, first designed in 2004, does have the whiff of another era about it."[49] Even star architects are starting to tire of the culture. At the end of 2011 Rem Koolhaas said: "We have become a little bit worried about the constant pressure to outperform and to outrage and make more and more exceptional buildings."[50]

The picture is different outside the indebted nations. Regional political events can, nonetheless, have an effect. The colony of iconic buildings by star architects planned on the Saadiyat Island in Abu Dhabi has been continually delayed leading to rumours of fall-out from the Arab Spring.[51] In the emerging economies, where the political situation is stable, however, the debt crisis has only been an economic rebound from the reduced consumption of the developed nations. Here there are no financial or moral pressures to abstain from seeking status with high-value buildings by star architects. As Zaha Hadid said, when confronted with the impact of the financial crisis in 2009, "I think that it's too simplistic to say that there'll be no more exuberant architecture."[52] It may be that the development of iconic architecture will transfer to the emerging economies and change them in a way quite different from their origins in the North Atlantic countries.

Modernist artistic culture, which lies at the heart of iconic architecture, has been successfully promoted by North Atlantic countries as a part of what was presented as a modern economic system. Modernism is now traditional in Europe and the Americas, but it has been exported to countries outside its place of origin. As a recently introduced foreign style it is not so deeply engrained in the emerging economies. Much as the economic system is now being remodelled rather than recast by the newly dominant countries, so North Atlantic Modernism and iconic architecture are likely to be modified to suit newly confident cultures. This process is called "indigenization," and is a well-known phenomenon that has existed from the earliest of times when different cultures came into contact with one another.

Indigenization and Hybridized Returns

As the physical symbols of North Atlantic culture have spread around the world, travellers find the familiar and assume that superficial similarity delivers similarities of culture. They might be reassured by the familiarity, or dismayed by the loss. Local people seeing the physical symbols of their identity transformed may feel that something precious has gone or might be excited by the novelty. But while each observer will see the same physical objects, they will be doing so from a different cultural perspective. Loss of a symbol of identity to a traveller is not at all the same as a sense of loss to a member of the community to which the symbol belongs. The sociologist Anthony Cohen explains the persistence of culture that survives the physical similarity of objects:

> … we should not be deceived by their *apparent* similarities into supposing that they are *actually* alike, nor even that they are becoming less different. The residents of Wandsworth, Winnipeg and the Western Isles may all spend much time watching the television—indeed, watching the same television programmes—may use the same terminology to address their parents, may affiliate to the same religious denominations, may observe the same calendar and the same life-cycle ceremonies, and may apparently be dominated by the same economic imperatives. But none of these apparent convergences of life-style entitles us to suppose that the cultural boundaries which separate them are now redundant and anachronistic.[53]

Imperialists, be they territorial or cultural, have for centuries believed that the imposition or acceptance of their institutions or the physical appearance they have brought to subject people has delivered some part of their home culture for the benefit of its recipients.

The urban historian Jyoti Hosagrahar describes how this affected British colonial attitudes to India: "First, it was assumed that environments shaped societies and people and that people who lived in similar environments shared a similar culture. Second, architecture derived from 'scientific reason' and the principles of 'rational design' must be universally valid regardless of culture and politics."[54]

Colonialism seen as a form of cultural superimposition—through introduction or infiltration—is called "diffusionism." The geographer James Blaut explains: "Diffusionism at a world scale usually considers Europe or the west to be the permanent centre of invention and innovation." After the Second World War, there was "the creation and scientific validation of a modern form of the diffusionist model, a body of ideas that had to persuade the now-sovereign Third World states that economic and social advancement consisted of acquiring so-called modernizing traits from the developed capitalist countries." Cultural diffusionism assumes that the greater efficiency or rationality of North Atlantic traits will lead to the displacement of less progressive traits in emerging economies.[55] Such a view seems to be supported by the global adoption of the free-market, consumerism and North Atlantic products. This is, however, as Arjun Appadurai explains, an illusion:

> At the level of popular culture, what might at first sight appear to be processes of homogenization in fact display hybrid characteristics. No cultural message, no aesthetic artefact, no symbol passes through time and space into a cultural vacuum. The cultural context of production and transmission must always in the end encounter an already existing frame of reference in the eyes of the consumer or receiver. The latter involves a process of great complexity—simple notions of homogenization, ideological hegemony or imperialism fail to register properly the nature of these encounters and the interplay, interaction and cultural creativity they produce.[56]

The diffusionist model survives in some North Atlantic attitudes to emerging economies. Nonetheless, as Blaut says, although "diffusionism makes it appear to be so," the "spatial inequality" at its foundation "is not something normal, natural, inevitable, and moral."[57]

The great French historian, Fernand Braudel, put this complex relationship between cultures, or civilizations, into a wider perspective in 1963 in his important book *A History of Civilizations*:

> By accepting it, the world is not taking on Western civilization lock, stock and barrel: far from it. The history of civilizations, in fact, is the history of continual mutual borrowings over many centuries, despite which each civilization has kept its own original character. It must be admitted, however, that now is the first time when one decisive aspect of a particular civilization has been adopted willingly by all the civilizations in the world, and the first time when the speed of modern communications has so much assisted its rapid and effective distribution. That simply means that what we call "industrial civilization" is in the process of joining the collective civilization of the world ...
>
> Still, even supposing that all the world's civilizations sooner or later adopt similar technology, and thereby partly similar ways of life, we shall nevertheless for a long time yet face what are really very different civilizations. For a long time yet, the word civilization will continue to be used in both singular and plural.[58]

This mutual borrowing of culture is a consistent and widely observed phenomenon. It has always been a characteristic of language. English in particular has, and continues to be, a receptor of multiple influences and in its modified form in India and the Caribbean has taken on recognisable but distinct variants. This adaptive process has been described by a number of sociologists. Peter Burns refers to this as "acculturation," and defines it as "the process by which a borrowing of one or some elements of culture takes place as a result of a contact of any duration between two different societies."[59] Mike Featherstone discusses how, "hybridization and creolization emerge in which the meanings of externally originating goods, information and images are reworked, syncretized and blended with existing cultural traditions and forms of life."[60] Appadurai identifies this as "indigenization," in terms that are most appropriate for the condition under discussion here: "at least as rapidly as forces from various metropolises are brought into new societies they tend to become indigenized in one or another way: this is true of music and housing styles as much as it is true of science and terrorism, spectacles and constitutions."[61]

The art and cultural historian Anthony King describes the different processes behind indigenization:

> When ideas, objects, institutions, images, practices, performances are transplanted to other places, other cultures, they both bear the marks of history as well as undergo a process of cultural translation and hybridization. This tends to happen in any or all of three ways.
> Most simply, for material phenomena, they generally change their form, their social use, or function. Second, even though arriving in similar forms (whether material technology or images) they are invested with different cultural, social or ideological meanings. And finally, the different meanings with which material objects, ideas or images are invested, themselves depend on the highly varied *local* social, physical, spatial and also historical environments into which they are introduced and the equally varied local conditions under which they develop [emphasis in original].[62]

Japan has been particularly notable for the cultural translation of North Atlantic ideas and institutions since the forced opening of its ports by American warships in 1853. In the nineteenth century, Japan turned itself into a hybrid of national, European and American political and military institutions. Today, long after their abandonment in Germany, Japanese schoolboys wear a version of a nineteenth-century Prussian military school uniform, and schoolgirls wear a version of British sailors' neckwear popular at British private schools in the early twentieth century.

African Indigenous Churches, also called African Initiated Churches and African Independent Churches but all sharing the same acronym,

AIC, are a fusion of Protestantism and African traditional religion. AICs are one of the more rapidly growing Christian groups and have spread beyond Africa with emigrant communities.

The adaptation of foreign cuisine is common: Chow mein is a Chinese dish created for the American palate; Chinese food is popular in India but has been adapted to suit Indian preferences; Chicken Tikka Masala is an Indian recipe invented for British tastes and, after a survey claimed it was the most popular menu choice in Britain, the British Foreign Secretary called it "a true British national dish."[63]

Indigenization can be more than the adaptation of foreign influence, synthesized forms can become independent phenomena adopted by the synthesizing community as part of their identity. This is described by Anthony Cohen:

> … alien forms were not merely imported across cultural boundaries. In the act of importation, they were transformed by syncretism—by a process in which new and old were synthesized into an idiom more consonant with indigenous culture. But as anthropologists themselves began to recognize the multivocality of symbolism, and the problematic relationship between form and meaning, they also made it apparent that the transformation went beyond a mere marriage of idioms. Communities might import structural forms across their boundaries but, having done so, they often infuse them with their own meanings and use them to serve their own symbolic purposes … different societies, and different communities within the same society, may manifest apparently similar forms—whether these be in religion, kinship, work, politics, economy, recreation or whatever—but this is not to suggest that they have become culturally homogeneous. For these forms become new vehicles for the expression of indigenous meanings. Of particular interest to us is the irony that they may well become media for the reassertion and symbolic expression of the community's boundaries.[64]

Figure 66. Rajbari, North Calcutta, India; mid-nineteenth century.

Figure 67. Lakeside villa, Huangzhou, China; early twentieth century.

Historic indigenized European classical architecture in East Asia

The architectural commentator Chris Abel, in detecting a change in attitude in Malaysia towards colonial attempts to adapt Malaysian architecture, sees "a new willingness to regard these buildings, for all their quirks, as belonging to the national heritage … owed to a growing sense of regional self-confidence, as well as the capacity of building forms to take on new meanings."[65] He records a similar condition in Singapore: "Never a Chinese city in the sense that a city on mainland China could be so described, but developed in the typical dualistic pattern of a colonial city, with a European half and a 'native' half; the latter—already virtually a separate Chinatown—populated by overseas Chinese who migrated to the Malay Peninsula to seek fortune in Stamford Raffles' new trading post." In the post-colonial period it is now "viewed by proud Singaporeans as an Asian city, not so much because it looks like one, but because it was created by Asians, as opposed to the historic rumps which were originally built, or otherwise controlled, by their erstwhile colonial rulers."[66]

Most discussion of this hybridization or indigenization is based on the principle that a dominant or desirable import is indigenized by one culture from another as a one-way process. Bhangra pop music offers a different global model. A synthesis of traditional Punjabi music and western popular music, bhangra pop was created by British bands from Punjabi immigrant communities and became popular in their countries of origin. This has now become a global musical phenomenon, and has been influenced by hip hop and other popular music genres. It is an example of foreign hybridization returning to affect the place of origin. In the history of cultural exchange and indigenization there are other examples of sequential outward and returning cultural phenomena or "hybridized returns."

The Jewish diaspora established by far the largest community in Central and Eastern Europe, the Ashkenazi. At some time in the fourteenth century, a coming of age ceremony for boys, the Bar Mitzvah, was developed in this community. This was a largely small-scale family affair.[67] During the nineteenth century, improved travel, open immigration, and continued persecution and social exclusion in Europe brought large numbers of Jews to the Americas, particularly the United States. Between 1840 and 1900 the Jewish population in the Americas had increased tenfold to five and a half million.[68] In the USA in the twentieth century, the Bar Mitzvah became an extravagant ceremony and in 1922 the first public Bat Mitzvah, a similar coming-of-age ceremony for girls, was held in New York. While orthodox groups did not accept that females could lead communal religious services, the lavish American celebration of the Bar Mitzah and the Bat Mitzvah spread back to Jewish communities in Europe and the newly established state of Israel.

The celebration of Halloween, the eve of All Saints' Day (or All Hallows), was part of the ritual calendar in Catholic Europe. As it was popularly believed that this was the last day the souls of the dead could avenge the living, there was a tradition of dressing in disguise. In the early seventeenth century, Protestant reformers in England discouraged the practice as being Roman Catholic, and a different ceremony involving the ritual burning of Guy Fawkes, a Catholic insurrectionist, took its place, which continues to this day. Halloween survived in Ireland, as a predominantly Catholic country, and in Scotland where the Calvinist church took a more tolerant position. Irish and Scottish immigrants to the United States took their celebration of Halloween with them, including established traditions such as lighting candles in hollowed out turnips, ducking for apples and "guising"—where disguised children went from door to door to perform some congenial task and receive small gifts. In the United States at some time in the early twentieth century guising became "trick or treat" and the turnip was replaced with the pumpkin. A commercialised version of the American Halloween was reintroduced to England in the 1980s and is now treated as an indigenous ceremony.

Hybridised returns are also found in ancient and recent architectural history. Classical architecture originated in Greece and was based on the two tribal architectural types or Orders: Doric for the Dorians and Ionic for the Ionians. As Roman power eclipsed Greek power in the Mediterranean, the status of Greek culture led to its appropriation by the Roman elite. The Romans adapted a minority variant of the Ionic Order by adding a more elaborate capital and created an independent architectural Order, the Corinthian. By the second century BCE Roman power had extended into the east Mediterranean. As part of an alliance with the Seleucids (the remnant of Alexander's Empire), the future king Antiochus IV was taken as an honoured hostage to Rome. Infused with Roman culture and careful of Roman power, in 175 BCE a year after his ascendancy to the throne, he began to complete the construction of a long-planned and colossal Temple of Olympian Zeus in the centre of Athens. He engaged a Roman architect, Decimus Cossutius, and the architecture was changed to the Corinthian Order. In 146 BCE Rome finally absorbed Greece into its Empire and the Corinthian Order (including the final completion of the Temple of Olympian Zeus) permanently joined the two Greek Orders in their place of origin (figure 68).

Modernist architecture had its origins in predominantly left-wing social reformers and visionaries in central Europe. As right-wing regimes in Europe outlawed their politics and banned their work, major exponents fled to the United States. Although the early European modernists had been admired by some architects in the United States, their ideas for social reform were not thought to be appropriate for America. Modernism was successfully developed to suit the commercial market in the United States. It was returned in this form to Europe after the Second World War, alongside American political and economic ascendancy. The tension between surviving ambitions for social reform and commercial success still affect modernist thinking in Europe.

333333

Figure 68. Temple of Olympian Zeus, Athens; Decimus Cossutius; begun 175 BCE. Greek classical architecture was adopted by Rome, where a new type or Order was invented and taken back to Greece.

Figure 69. Telefunken-Hochhaus, Berlin; Paul Schwebes and Hans Schoszberger; 1960. Modernism lost its socialist ideals when its German founders fled to the USA, adapted to capitalism and reintroduced modernism to Germany after the Second World War.

Hybridised returns, architecture exported from its place of origin and re-imported in a modified form.

The Next Modernism?

As power moves to the east it is inevitable that culture will, at some time and in some way, follow. The economic and political power of the North Atlantic countries has been an instrument in the export of their culture, and with it their dominant architectural type. As North Atlantic power under the umbrella of the United States is, at the very least, diminished, what has been exported will come under new influences. China in particular has had a policy both of engaging leading foreign architects and also maintaining economic and political independence. If there is to be any new global cultural influence we may look to China to find the first signs.

The creator of post-Mao China, Deng Xiaoping, on his tour of the south in 1992 shortly after his retirement said "We should be bolder than before in conducting reform and opening to the outside and have the courage to experiment."[69] The Harvard social anthropologist, Yunxiang Yan puts this into a wider perspective:

> … the localization of foreign culture and the indigenous approach toward imported culture are key to understanding the current process of cultural globalization in China, as the majority of Chinese have taken an active and positive approach toward the imported foreign culture. This is officially reflected in the 1990s slogan, *Zhongguo zouxiang shijie, shijie zouxiang Zhongguo* (China to the world, and the world to China), which contains a twofold message. At one level, the emphasis is on the two-way, equivalent process in which China is actively reaching out to the world while the world is reaching out to China. At a deeper level, the slogan indicates movement toward a foreign culture, as revealed in the verb *zouxiang*, which means "walking/marching toward."
>
> At the societal level, many intellectuals, business elites, and professionals have positively appropriated cultural values and cultural products from the West, as described above. For them, ownership of Western culture is neither immutable nor nontransferable; on the contrary, they feel a sense of entitlement in

claiming the localized foreign culture as their own, or as part of the emerging global culture in which they too play a role.[70]

Chinese appropriation of western or North Atlantic culture has included high-profile architectural projects. At first, in the 1980s and 1990s there were concerns that the pace and style of development would affect Chinese identity. In Beijing development was controlled by the "Capital Planning Guidance Committee" which was to "defend the old capital's traditional flavour." The result was a series of temple pavilions on top of otherwise standard modernist buildings. In the 1980s and early 1990s, however, expatriate Chinese architects from the USA, such as I. M. Pei and Clement Chen, along with a number of other American and European architects, were responsible for an increasing number of new buildings.[71] These buildings convinced the authorities that there were distinct advantages in commissioning high-profile foreign architects for major projects. Beijing and Shanghai set the pace. Xuefie Ren describes the motives:

> Face-lifting urban mega projects of all types have mushroomed in Beijing and Shanghai … Museums, opera houses, national libraries, and new business districts are proposed and constructed at blistering speeds. The central and municipal governments intend to use these flagship projects to create a symbolic global city image and promote Beijing and Shanghai for investment and tourism in the international marketplace. In order to achieve this goal, it is considered necessary to make these mega projects look modern, high-tech, futuristic and non-Chinese, so that they can demonstrate the country's urbanization and modernization progress and impress investors. Therefore, many of these "Grand Projects" have been commissioned to [sic] famous international architects.[72]

This was not without opposition in China but by the early twenty-first century, most of what the Chinese call "mega-structures," with "huge scale, high cost, far-reaching influence and unique image," have been designed by foreign architects and Chinese-foreign joint ventures. Charlie Qiuli Xue et al. put this into its cultural context.

"Although these mega structures arrived in China with the rapid development of the economy, they stem from the interaction of globalisation and local awareness."[73] Or as Xuefei Ren puts it: "Chinese architecture is caught between … global aspirations and the search for their own original design language."[74]

While China became a major source of high profile work for North Atlantic architects, it was inevitable that Chinese architects would begin to adopt a similar and competitive profile. Architects such as Ma Qingyun, Yung Ho Chang, Pu Miao, Zhang Lei and Ma Yansong have all become well-known, and have all attended American or European universities for part of their professional education. Zhang Lei, who trained in Switzerland, says that he "feels his architecture is neither Chinese nor foreign."[75] Ma Yansong, who worked with Rem Koolhaas and Zaha Hadid, has named his firm MAD, a witty name that only works in English. The influence of these architects is now spreading outside China. In Britain, the American-trained Shanghai architects Neri and Hu have won a major competition in London amid claims that they undercut the winners on design.[76] The tide of North Atlantic supremacy in Chinese architectural commissions seems to be turning. Lance Taylor of the quantity surveyors Rider Levett Bucknall, which employs 1,250 staff in nineteen Chinese offices, has issued a warning to foreign architects that home-grown design capability might be "a bigger threat to [foreign] architecture that a slow-down in the Chinese market."[77]

There has been a thoroughgoing export of North Atlantic Modernism to China, from the employment of North Atlantic architects to the North Atlantic education of Chinese architects. As the economy enters a new stage, it may be that Chinese architecture will also enter a new period. What form this will take we cannot be sure, and the results of this process may be hard to detect. As the cultural analyst Maureen Turim explains: "We know culture is being produced for global consumption, but we don't know what the world makes of what it receives and we cannot assume inherent meanings, whatever we might take those to mean. Culture is marked by a kind of polyvalence of meaning, a kind of multiplicity that is highly contextual and even internally confused. Knowing the site and means of production and the manner of distribution will not necessarily reveal how the texts of culture are consumed."[78]

We can at least be sure that, as with all cultural phenomena, nothing will stand still. If Chinese political influence increases, if Chinese investment becomes more significant in the North Atlantic economies and if Chinese architects start to take a more dominant role in the development of Modernism, it is likely that Modernism will develop another hybridised return—this time to the North Atlantic economies from whence it came. It may already have started to do so.

References

1. "Repent at Leisure: Special Report on Debt." *The Economist*, June 26, 2010, 3.
2. Leigh Skene & Greg Opie. *Trends, Cycles and Revolutions: The Rhyme of History in the Reason of Markets*. London: Lombard Street Research, May 2011.
3. Rich Miller & Simon Kennedy. "G-20 Shapes New World Order with Lesser Role for U.S. Markets." New York: *Bloomberg*, April 2, 2009.
4. Ibid.
5. Anatole Kaletsky. *Capitalism 4.0: The Birth of New Economy*. New York: Public Affairs, 2010.
6. "China raises financial status at G20." *China Daily*, April 4, 2009.
7. "China and G20: China Takes Centre Stage." *The Economist*, March 31, 2009.
8. G20, London Summit—Leaders' Statement, April 2, 2009, paragraphs 2 and 5. http://www.governo.it/backoffice/allegati/42952-5305.pdf
9. "What's Schadenfreude in Chinese?" *The Economist*, August 20, 2011, 50.
10. "China Overtakes Japan as World's Second-Biggest Economy." *BBC News*, February 14, 2011; "Foreign-Exchange Reserves Reached US $ 3.2 Trillion in September 2011." *Chinability.com*; Alex Newman. "IMF: Chinese Economy to Surpass U.S. By 2016." *The New American,* April 26, 2011.

11. David Shambaugh. "Coping with a Conflicted China." *The Washington Quarterly*, Winter 2011, 7–27.

12. Chetan Ahya & Tanvee Gupta. *India and China: New Tigers of Asia, PartIII, Special Economic Analysis*. New York: Morgan Stanley, 2010.

13. G20 London summit, op. cit, paragraph 3.

14. Evgeny Morozov. "Two Decades of the Web: A Utopia No Longer." *Prospect*, July 2011, 56–58.

15. G20 London summit, op. cit, paragraph 4.

16. Joe Leahy. "Brazil Levies Imports of Chinese Steel Tubes." *Financial Times*, September 7, 2011.

17. Robert Brookes. "Strong Swiss Franc Gives Switzerland the Jitters." *swissinfo.ch*, January 11, 2011.

18. "Confucius' Birthday," china.org.cn (accessed February 2012).

19. Walter Russell Mead. "The Tea Party and U.S. Foreign Policy." New York, *New York Times*, February 21, 2011.

20. Celeste Katz. "Gingrich: Mon Dieu! Romney Speaks French." *New York Daily Post*, January 13, 2012.

21. Dominic Tobin & Jonathan Leake. "It's Baffling Up North As Accents Tighten Hold." *The Sunday Times*, January 3, 2010.

22. Fabio Tonacci. "I ristoranti etnici fuori dai centri storici. Prima era una crociata dei leghisti, ora anche delle giunte progressiste. Che si difendono: favoriamo il made in Italy." Rome, *la Repubblica*, October 20, 2011.

23. "Campaign Kicks off German Language Revival." *The Local*, *Germany*, February 5, 2009.

24. Mark Malloch Brown. "What's Left?" *Prospect*, September 2011, 12.

25. *Urban World: Mapping the Economic Power of Cities*. San Francisco, Seoul, London, The McKinsey Global Institute, March 2011.

26. *Knight Frank Wealth Report 2009, World Cities Report*. London, Knight Frank and Citi Private Bank, 2009.

27. *Winning in Emerging Market Cities*. Boston Consulting Group, September 2010, 5.

28. Peter Simpson. "China's Urban Population Exceeds Rural For First Time Ever." *The Daily Telegraph*, January 17, 2012.

29. Doug Saunders. "Boom or Bust?" *RSA Journal*, Spring 2011.

30. Robert Neuwrith. *Shadow Cities: A Billion Squatters, A New Urban World*. London, Routledge, 2004.

31. "DDA Conducts Demolition Drive at Yamuna Pushta." *Times of India*, July 28, 2004.

32. Johannes P. Jütting & Juan R. de Laiglesia. "Forgotten Workers." Paris, *OECD Observer* 274, October 2009.

33. Lakshmi Iyer, John D. Macomber, Namrata Arora, Dharavi. *Developing Asia's Largest Slum*. Boston, Harvard Business School Premier Case Collection, July 21, 2009.

34. Robert Neuwrith. "Global Bazaar." *Scientific American*, September 2011, 44.

35. Ibid.

36. Saunders, op. cit., 20–21.

37. William Gibson. "Life in the Meta City." *Scientific American* (2011): 75.

38. Ellis Woodman. "Roman Horror Day." *Building Design*, November, 20 2009.

39. "Eight Years Late and Millions Over Budget." *The Art Newspaper* 222, March 2011.

40. Oliver Wainwright. "Liverpool's Scuttled Flagship." *Building Design*, August 12, 2011.

41. Michael M. Grynbaum. "Trade Center Transit Hub's Cost Now Over $3.4 Billion." *New York Times*, February 24, 2011.

42. Josh Margolin. "PA plays $2B hide and sneak at WTC." *New York Post*, August 12, 2011.

43. "Experience Music Project Still Struggling Five Years Later." *USA Today*, March 22, 2005.

44. Bellevue Art Museum Press Release, 2000.

45. Regina Hackett. "Adieu to Bellevue Art Museum." *Seattle Post-Intelligencer*, September 24, 2003.

46. "West Bromwich's Public Gallery Opens To The Public At Last." *Culture 24*, London, The Arts Council UK, June 27, 2008.

47. David Rogers. "Closing The Public is an Option, Admits Council." *Building Design*, January 6, 2012.

48. Simon Anholt. *Places: Identity, Image and Reputation*. Basingstoke: Palgrave Macmillan, 2010, 74–5.

49. Hugh Pearman. "Zaha on Clyde: And the New Wave of British Regional Museums." *The Sunday Times*, June 26, 2011.

50. Oliver Wainwright. "Stealth Wealth." *Building Design*, December 9, 2011.

51. "Abu Dhabi Postpones Saadiyat Island Openings." *Daily Star*, November 1, 2011.

52. Tom Dyckhoff. "Zaha Hadid Defies Recession With Ground-Breaking Architecture." *The Times*, May 16, 2009.

53. Anthony P Cohen. *The Symbolic Construction of Community*. London: Routledge, 1985, 76.

54. Jyoti Hosagrahar. *Indigenous Modernities: Negotiating Architecture and Urbanism*. London, New York: Routledge, 2005, 163–4.

55. J.M. Blaut. "Diffusionism: A Uniformitarian Critique." *Annals of the Association of American Geographers* 77 (1) (1987): 31 and 33.

56. David Held, Anthony McGrew, David Goldblatt & Jonathan Perraton. *Global Transformations: Politics, Economics and Culture*. Cambridge: Polity Press, 1999, 374.

57. Blaut op. cit., 43.

58. F. Braudel. *A History of Civilizations*, trans. R. Mayne. London: Allen Lane and Penguin Press, 1994, 8.

59. P. M. Burns. *An Introduction to Tourism and Anthropology*. London: Routledge, 1999, 104.

60. Mike Featherstone. *Undoing Culture: Globalization, Postmodernism and Identity*. London: Sage, 1995, 116–7.

61. Arjun Appadurai. *Modernity at Large: Cultural Dimensions of Globalisation*. Minneapolis MN: University of Minnesota Press, 1996, 32.

62. Anthony D King. *Spaces of Global Cultures: Architecture Urbanism Identity*, 2004, London, Routledge, 125.

63. "Chicken Tikka Masala: Spice and Easy Does It." *BBC News*, April 290, 2001.

64. Cohen, op. cit., 37.

65. "Regional Transformations." In *Architecture and Identity: Responses to Cultural and Technological Change*, 2nd edn. Oxford, Architectural Press, (1997) 2000, 168.

66. Chris Abel. "Localization versus Globalization," In *Architecture and Identity: Responses to Cultural and Technological Change*, edited Chris Abel. Oxford: Architectural Press, (1997) 2000, 191–2.

67. Hayyim Schauss. *The Jewish Festivals*. New York: Schoken Books, 1938; Bernard J Bamberger. *The Story of Judaism*. New York: Schocken Books, 1970.

68. Jacob Lestschinsky. *Tfutzot Yisrael ahar haMilhamah*. Tel Aviv, 1958; *American Jewish Year Book*, 1968 and 1984.

69. "Excerpts from Talks Given in Wuchang, Shenzhen, Zhuhai and Shanghai, January 18–February 21, 1992." Beijing, *People's Daily* (English).

70. Yunxiang Yan. "State Power and the Cultural Transition in China." In *Many Globalizations: Cultural Diversity in the Contemporary World*, edited by Peter L Berger & Samuel P Huntingdon. Oxford: Oxford University Press, 2002, 34.

71. Charlie Qiuli Xue, Zhigang Wang and Brian Mitchenere. "In Search of Identity: The Development Process of the National Grand Theatre in Beijing, China." *The Journal of Architecture* 15 (4) 2010.

72. Xuefei Ren. "The Chinese Debate about 'Grand Projects' and International Architects." *Perspectives*, Overseas Young Chinese Forum 7 (4) (2006): 189.

73. Charlie Quili Xue, op. cit., 532.

74. Xuefei Ren, op. cit., 191.

75. "Zhang Lei." *People's Architecture*: "a not-for-profit cultural and educational organization that seeks to strengthen the relationship between China and the United States", New York.

76. Elizabeth Hopkirk. "Chinese Practice Scoops Bow Street Hotel Scheme." *Building Design*, June 3, 2011, 1.

77. Merlin Fulcher. "Property Wobble in China Spooks Architects." *Architects' Journal*, December 12, 2011.

78. Maureen Turim. "Specificity and Culture." In *Culture, Globalization and the World System*, edited by Anthony D King. Basingstoke: Palgrave, 1991, 146.

INDEX